KNOWING
JESUS

THE ESSENTIAL TEEN
365 DEVOTIONAL

PUBLISHING GROUP
Nashville, Tennessee

AUTHOR OF CREATION

Read over Genesis 1 in its entirety in your Bible. As you read, take note of what this chapter teaches you about God the Father, Son, and Holy Spirit. Jot down a few notes in your journal.

Take note of Genesis 1:26, where God said, "Let Us make man in Our image." How does this statement support your understanding of a triune God? Explain.

The plural pronouns *Us* and *Our* in this passage hint that God exists in perfect relationship and agreement as the Father, Son, and Holy Spirit. Believers have termed this the Trinity.

Now, read John 1:1–5.

> In the beginning was the Word, and the Word was with God, and the Word was God. He was with God in the beginning. All things were created through Him, and apart from Him not one thing was created that has been created.—John 1:1–3

ASK YOURSELF:

- What does this passage teach about Jesus before His earthly ministry?

- Why is it important that believers understand that Jesus wasn't just present at creation, but that He took an active role in it?

RESPOND

- Take a moment to dwell on the eternal nature of Christ. Thank God that there has never been a moment when He didn't exist or wasn't in control.

- Ponder these thoughts: All things are created through Christ. Everything that has been created came to be because of Him. How does this change the way you view creation or the world's resources? How does it change your attitude toward other people? Jot down three ways this will change the way you live today.

RULER OF CREATION

In your Bible, read Colossians 1:15–20.

> For everything was created by Him, in heaven and on earth, the visible and the invisible, whether thrones or dominions or rulers or authorities—all things have been created through Him and for Him. He is before all things, and by Him all things hold together.—Colossians 1:16–17

The term *firstborn* in verse 15 has nothing to do with the human birth of Christ, nor does it mean that He was created. Instead, Paul used this term to help us understand that Jesus holds first place above creation. He is the One who sustains and rules as Creator God.

DIG DEEPER WITH THESE QUESTIONS:

- What are some of the specific examples Paul gave in this passage that describe Christ's authoritative role in creation? List a few.
- What does it mean to say that all things have been created through Christ and for Him? Explain in your own words.
- What word or phrase would you use to describe Paul's view of Jesus and His importance in today's verses? Why?
- Do you have a high view of Jesus' importance? Why or why not?

RESPOND

- Colossians 1:15–20 is a poem or hymn expressing Jesus' supremacy. Using these verses as a guide, write your own hymn of praise in your journal.
- These verses attest that Jesus is supreme over all things. Are you allowing Him to be the supreme Ruler of your life? If not, what changes will you make this week to do so?
- Ponder this: every law of the universe discovered by human beings is merely a glimpse into the power and ability of our Creator. How will you allow science and nature to point you to the Creator today?

AUTHOR OF SALVATION

Read Hebrews 1:1–3 in your Bible. As you read, look for words or phrases that help you understand how God has revealed His character and plan in Jesus.

> In these last days, He has spoken to us by His Son. God has appointed Him heir of all things and made the universe through Him. The Son is the radiance of God's glory and the exact expression of His nature, sustaining all things by His powerful word. After making purification for sins, He sat down at the right hand of the Majesty on high.—Hebrews 1:2–3

PONDER THESE QUESTIONS:

- How do these verses establish that Jesus didn't just show up in the New Testament? Why is it important that He has always existed? Explain.

- In Jesus, we have the clearest picture of God the Father. Everything Jesus did or said during His earthly ministry points to the Father. What God has said and done in and through Jesus is definitive, His final word. How do these verses help you to understand that truth?

- Study Hebrews 1:3 more closely. While this passage establishes Jesus' authority and power, it also points to the reason He came to live among us. What was that reason, according to verse 3?

- How did Jesus make purification for sin? Explain it in your own words.

RESPOND

Hebrews 1:1–3 helps us to see that Jesus is so much more than a wise teacher or a good man. Jesus is God's Son, His final word, and the only One through whom salvation is possible. He is the eternally existent Son of God who makes forgiveness of our sins possible. Who do you say Jesus is?

ONE LORD OF ALL

A lot of things in our lives are good and important, but they should never overshadow the most important Person in our lives: Jesus. Read 1 Corinthians 8:4–9 in your Bible to find out why Jesus is so important.

> Yet for us there is one God, the Father. All things are from Him, and we exist for Him. And there is one Lord, Jesus Christ. All things are through Him, and we exist through Him.—1 Corinthians 8:6

The Corinthian Christians had argued that eating food sacrificed to pagan idols was okay for them because they knew that there is only one true God. Paul agreed with that statement, but quickly clarified that believers must live in a way that does not cause others to stumble in their faith. Now, focus on verses 5–6.

DIG DEEPER:

- Think about what you've learned about Jesus in this week's devotions. How does this passage build on that theme?

- Underline the words or phrases in verses 5–6 that teach you something about Jesus, His character, His authority, or His role. What do these verses teach you about Christ? Explain.

- Does your life present evidence that you hold Jesus above all other things? Why or why not?

RESPOND

Jesus is the Giver of life and the Creator of all there is. Therefore, nothing in our lives is more important than Him.

- Evaluate your life. Consider how you spend your money and your time, plus the things you talk or think about most. What do these reveal about what's most important in your life? If the Holy Spirit reveals that you've made anyone or anything more important than Jesus, confess it today.

- Take a look at the things you do or say. Is there anything you're doing that could cause those who are weak in their faith to stumble or doubt Jesus' power? Ask God's forgiveness, then outline steps you will take to live in a way that honors God and helps others see Jesus' authority in your life.

- For further study, read Ephesians 4:1–7. Read these verses over a few times and ask God to show you how to walk worthy of your calling as His child.

CHILDREN OF GOD

Read John 1:10–13 several times, at least once aloud.

> He was in the world, and the world was created through Him, yet the world did not recognize Him.—John 1:10

> But to all who did receive Him, He gave them the right to be children of God, to those who believe in His name.—John 1:12

THOUGHTFULLY ANSWER THESE QUESTIONS:

- Verse 10 states that even though Jesus created the world, the world did not recognize Him. What evidence do you see of this blindness in today's culture?

- Read verse 13. In light of your deeper understanding of what it means to believe in Jesus' name, how does someone become a child of God? Journal in your own words.

RESPOND

Jesus, the Creator of all there is, has made a way for us to know Him, to become children of God. Because of who He is and what He has done, Jesus has the right to rule over all of creation—including our lives.

- Is Jesus the supreme Ruler of your life? He has made a way for us to have a relationship with God, but we must respond in faith.

- Even as Christians, we sometimes try to hold back parts of our lives from Jesus' control. Look at your life. Are you acknowledging that He is the Ruler of your life in every area? Confess anything the Holy Spirit reveals.

WORTHY OF TRUST

Think about the most amazing natural wonder you've ever seen—from a magnificent mountain to the vastness of the ocean. How did it call your attention to the Creator? Sketch that scene or journal a few thoughts.

Now, read Isaiah 40:28–31 in your Bible.

> Do you not know? Have you not heard? Yahweh is the everlasting God, the Creator of the whole earth. He never grows faint or weary; there is no limit to His understanding.—Isaiah 40:28

ASK YOURSELF:

- How does the fact that the triune God created the whole earth support the idea that there is no limit to His understanding? That He is powerful and worthy of your trust? Explain.

- In what ways do these truths bring you peace when you seek wisdom from God?

Now, read John 1:3.

ASK YOURSELF:

- Does focusing on Jesus as the Creator of all things give you confidence in His ability to provide strength in spite of your weakness? Why or why not?

- Nothing is created except that which God creates. How might believing this help someone to trust God with the details of his or her life?

RESPOND

- Ponder this thought: As a Christian, you serve a God who is powerful enough to create the entire universe. That means that He is powerful enough to equip you for His service, strengthen you, and empower you. Respond in your journal.

- What is something you know God has called you to do, but you haven't followed through with? What steps will you take to do so this week, confident in His power to guide and help you? Record two action points in your journal.

- Who in your life is going through a difficult time and needs to be reminded that God is trustworthy and faithful? How will you share your hope with that person?

- For further encouragement to trust God, read Romans 11:33–34. While God never needs to seek counsel, He always desires to provide it to those who seek Him.

WORTHY OF WORSHIP

Read Psalm 33:1–22 in your Bible. As you read, underline all the different ways the psalmist called the people to worship God.

Let the whole earth tremble before the Lord; let all the inhabitants of the world stand in awe of Him. For He spoke, and it came into being; He commanded, and it came into existence.—Psalm 33:8–9

ASK YOURSELF:

- Focus on verses 8–9. Why did the psalmist say God was worthy of praise? Journal in your own words.

- The psalmist called the people to praise God as the Creator who created the world with His command. Read verse 18. What aspects of creation remind you to fear (meaning to be in awe of or have reverence for) the Lord? Why?

- What aspects of creation remind you of God's faithful love? Explain your answer.

- Look over the passage once more, noting the things you underlined as you read. What are some active ways the psalmist called the people to praise the Lord? List a few.

- Which of the ones you listed are part of your worship? Why?

RESPOND

God didn't create the world so that we would worship what He had made. He created the world so that we would be in awe of Him and worship Him alone. Creation is meant to point to the Creator and designed to bring glory to God the Father, Son, and Spirit.

- How do you see creation bringing glory to God? What aspects of creation call you to worship Him?

- What steps will you take this week to share with others how God's creation brings glory to Him? List a few in your journal.

8

VERY GOOD

Read Genesis 1:1–31 in your Bible. As you learned last week, creation didn't happen independently of Jesus. As a member of the Trinity, Jesus was active and involved in creation. Read these verses with that in mind.

God saw all that He had made, and it was very good.—Genesis 1:31

Reread verses 1–31 carefully, then list what God created on each day:

Day 1 _____

Day 2 _____

Day 3 _____

Day 4 _____

Day 5 _____

Day 6 _____

THINK THROUGH THESE QUESTIONS:

- Highlight the places in Genesis 1 where God said His creation was good or very good. How many times did He say this?

- In Scripture, repetition is often used to indicate importance. Knowing that, what does the repetition of the phrase "it was good" teach you about creation? Explain.

- Why is it important for us to realize that God considers His creation good?

- Does your opinion about creation's goodness match God's? Why or why not?

RESPOND

Everything God created was useful, full of purpose, and created to bring joy. In a word, it was good. Our triune God created a world in perfect harmony—with no chaos or anything in rebellion with its Creator. While our world is fallen today, we can still see glimpses of that goodness. Praise God for the specific ways you see His goodness in creation. Record your praise in your journal.

FOR YOUR ENJOYMENT

Read Genesis 2:4–14 in your Bible. As you read, pay attention to all of the ways God lavishly met humanity's needs.

ASK YOURSELF:

- Why is it important that God abundantly provided for all of Adam and Eve's physical needs through His creation? Journal your answer.

Food, water, companionship, beauty, purpose—God met all of humanity's needs in His creation. He created the ideal setting for humanity to know Him and be fully known.

Now, read 1 Timothy 4:4 in your Bible. Underline what it teaches you about creation.

For everything created by God is good.—1 Timothy 4:4

RESPOND

- What did these passages teach you about creation? Journal in your own words.

- Today, make an effort to notice ways God's creation meets your needs or brings you enjoyment. Praise God for His detailed provision for you. Journal your praises.

FOR HIS GLORY

Consider the list below, thinking about people you know. What would they say their purpose in life is? Circle all that apply.

To live, then die

To make money

To honor God

To make family proud

To be important

To help others

To work hard

To become famous

Thankfully, God's Word is very clear about our purpose. Read Romans 11:34–36 in your Bible. Underline what it reveals about purpose.

> For from Him and through Him and to Him are all things. To Him be the glory forever. Amen.—Romans 11:36

THINK THROUGH THESE QUESTIONS:

- What does it mean to say that everything comes from God and exists by His power? Explain.
- According to this passage, for what does God intend everything? What does that mean for your life?
- Reread verses 34–35. When have you assumed you knew God's thoughts or even that you knew better than Him?
- How did you discover you were wrong? What did you learn from that experience?

RESPOND

- Personalize Romans 11:36, replacing the word *everything* with your name. Pray this verse back to God as affirmation that you were created to bring Him glory.
- If you were created to bring glory to God, then all parts of your life should be united in that purpose. What parts of your life are not lining up with God's intention for you? What steps will you take today to change that? Write two steps in your journal.

NO EXCUSE

In yesterday's devotion, you focused on your purpose. Today, we'll delve into Scripture to discover the purpose of creation. Read Romans 1:18–23 in your Bible with that in mind.

> For His invisible attributes, that is, His eternal power and divine nature, have been clearly seen since the creation of the world, being understood through what He has made. As a result, people are without excuse.—Romans 1:20

Paul's argument in this passage is that those who reject God will face His wrath because He has already provided sufficient evidence of His existence and power.

ASK YOURSELF:

- According to these verses, how has God proven His existence? Explain.
- What does that teach you about the purpose of creation? Journal in your own words.
- How has creation made our triune God's eternal power and divine nature apparent to you? Explain.
- Why do you think we so often miss the evidence of God in creation?

RESPOND

Creation provides so much evidence of God that those who reject the Creator will face the eternal responsibility of that choice: God's wrath. God has revealed Himself to us through His work, His Word, and, most clearly, through His Son. Jesus is the only way of salvation God has provided and rejecting Him means facing God's wrath. Place your faith in Jesus today!

- As believers, we sometimes allow sin into our lives, which disrupts our relationship with God and takes our focus off of Him, His work, and His goodness. Examine this downward spiral in Romans 11:21–22. Where do you see that spiral in your life? What steps will you take today to turn your focus back to Christ? Record two steps in your journal.
- In today's passage, Paul wrote that the people had exchanged the truth of God for a lie. Ask the Holy Spirit to reveal any lies you are allowing to rule your life. Pray that God would point you to the truth in His Word.

HELPLESS

It's clear from this week's devotions that everything—including you—was created to bring God glory. But when we see the depth of our sinfulness, it's easy for us to wonder how God could ever use us for His glory. We are a people in need of salvation from our sin. But how? Read Isaiah 43:5–13 to learn more.

"I, I am Yahweh, and there is no other Savior but Me."—Isaiah 43:11

In verses 6–7, God promises an ultimate, final restoration to those who truly believe and are called by His name. This is not a promise that all people will experience, but only God's sons and daughters, those with whom He has a personal relationship.

Now, focus on verses 10–13 and thoughtfully answer the questions that follow:

- In this passage, God revealed aspects of His nature. He is Creator, Savior, the only God. Why are each of these facets of His character important? Explain.

- Consider verse 12. Underline all of the action words in this verse, then circle the word that indicates who is doing the action. According to this verse, who makes salvation possible?

- When did you first realize that salvation isn't about being good, doing good works, or your own merit, but rather about trusting what God has already done through Jesus? Jot down a few thoughts.

RESPOND

God is the One who saves, and we are helpless to save ourselves. We don't have to work or strive for salvation, but we do have to respond and receive it in faith. We were created to bring God glory, but we cannot fulfill that purpose if we do not have a relationship with Him through Jesus.

- Because God is the Savior, He has made a way for us to be saved and experience the ultimate restoration discussed in this passage. If you have never placed your faith for salvation in Jesus' life, death, and resurrection, don't let the opportunity pass you by today.

- If you have already received God's gift of forgiveness and salvation, praise and thank Him for doing for you what you could never do for yourself.

MARK OF THE CREATOR

Creation testifies of the Creator. As Christians, the goodness of God's creation should inspire our praise and worship. Read Psalm 19:1–14 in your Bible to see how David's contemplation of God's creation gave way to worship.

> The heavens declare the glory of God, and the sky proclaims the work of His hands.
> —Psalm 19:1

DIG DEEPER WITH THESE QUESTIONS:

- Ponder verses 1–6. What word pictures did David use to stress that creation points to God, our powerful Creator? Explain.

- What word picture or metaphor would you have used? Why?

- Consider verses 7–11. David realized that God's glory isn't only revealed in the beauty of His creation, but also in His Word. What statements did David make about God's law (instruction, precepts, or commandments)? What do these statements teach you about the value of God's instructions?

- Do you value God's instructions? Why or why not?

RESPOND

- Write your own psalm of praise to God, following David's method of first recognizing the goodness of God through His creation, then responding in worship. Journal your psalm.

- As an extra challenge, memorize Psalm 19:1. Pray the verse back to God as your worshipful response each time you get a glimpse of God's excellency in creation.

- For further study of how God's creation declares His glory and inspires us to worship Him, read Psalm 8:1 and Psalm 50:6.

RESPONSIBLE RULERS

In this week's devotions, you've learned a lot about our Three-in-One Creator and His creation. Answer these questions:

- What is the purpose of God's creation?

- How does God feel about His creation?

- What's your responsibility to the earth God created? Explain.

Now, read Genesis 1:28–31 in your Bible, then answer the questions that follow.

God blessed them, and God said to them, "Be fruitful, multiply, fill the earth, and sub-due it. Rule the fish of the sea, the birds of the sky, and every creature that crawls on the earth."—Genesis 1:28

ASK YOURSELF:

- According to this passage, what is humanity's role in creation? Explain it in your own words.

- What is significant about humanity being placed as rulers over His creation?

- The word *rule* in verse 28 does not imply exploitation or treating the earth and the resources God has provided flippantly. This is a call to care and nurture the natural resources God has provided. Knowing this, what are some ways Christians can be good stewards of God's creation? List a few in your journal.

RESPOND

- Your stewardship of God's creation reflects your relationship with Him. Evaluate your life and attitude toward the resources God has provided. What does this reveal about your relationship with God? Confess any sinful attitudes the Holy Spirit reveals.

- Look over the list of stewardship ideas you created earlier. Circle three you'll put into action in your life this week.

- For further study about the importance of God's creation, read Romans 8:18–23.

IN HIS LIKENESS

Read Genesis 1:26–27 in your Bible.

- Underline every instance of the words *image* and *likeness*.

- Draw a triangle around every use of God's name.

- Sketch a square around every reference to humanity.

- What do these symbols tell you about the emphasis of this passage?

So God created man in His own image; He created him in the image of God; He created them male and female.—Genesis 1:27

While we can't derive the entire concept of the Trinity from the use of plural pronouns, we can surmise that this usage reflects the plurality of the Godhead, stressing the involvement of the Father, Son, and Spirit in creation.

These verses state that men and women are made in God's image. This means that humanity reflects God in some manner, including our ability to reason and to exercise authority over creation.

ASK YOURSELF:

- Why is it important that God created humanity in His image? What does it help you to understand about the kind of relationship God created us to have with Him?

- Read 2 Corinthians 4:4 and Hebrews 1:3 in your Bible. We reflect God's image, but Jesus is the image of God and the exact expression of His nature. What does that tell you about Jesus' importance?

RESPOND

- Children inherit the "likeness" of their parents: physical attributes, personality traits, even similar talents or skills. Think about what you know about character. How do you see His likeness in you? Record your response in your journal.

- God created us to know Him. Because of our sin, the intimate relationship He desires to have with us is impossible without Jesus' sacrifice.

WITH PURPOSE

It might surprise you to know that when God created Adam and placed him in the garden, Adam didn't just lounge around. Instead, God gave him a job to do. Read Genesis 2:7–15 in your Bible to find out what it was. Underline it when you read it.

> The LORD God took the man and placed him in the garden of Eden to work it and watch over it.—Genesis 2:15

THOUGHTFULLY ANSWER THESE QUESTIONS:

- What does the fact that God gave Adam a job tell you about God's design for work in our lives? Explain.

- Review what you've learned so far about your purpose. God created humanity for His glory, to have a relationship with Him, and to live a purposeful, meaningful life that included work. Does this fit with society's view of humanity's purpose? Why or why not?

In a fallen, sinful world, it's easy to think that our lives have no meaning. As Christians, it's tempting to consider this life as something we just have to get through until we get to spend eternity with Jesus. But God's intent for our lives, shown in today's passage, and in Jesus' words in Matthew 6:33 tell us otherwise.

Read Matthew 6:33 in your Bible.

ASK YOURSELF:

- What did Jesus have to say about the purpose of our lives? Journal in your own words.

RESPOND

Nothing that God created is meaningless. As believers, our lives should be focused on growing in our relationship with Him and building His kingdom on earth.

- Think about your family, school, community, teams, clubs, and your group of friends. Where has God placed you? How can you live focused on His purpose in those circumstances? List your ideas in your journal. Circle two you'll put into practice this week.

- Are there situations in your life that feel pointless or you wonder how God could ever use them for His glory? Be honest with God about those circumstances today. Ask Him to open your eyes to how He is at work.

NEW KIND OF RELATIONSHIP

Read Genesis 2:18–25 in your Bible. At this point in the creation account, God said that something wasn't good for the first time. Look for it as you read.

> Then the Lord God said, "It is not good for the man to be alone. I will make a helper as his complement."—Genesis 2:18

THOUGHTFULLY ANSWER THESE QUESTIONS:

- What did God say wasn't good? What does this teach you about the need for fellowship in our lives? Explain.

- God has created us for relationship—with Him and with others. How did God act to fulfill that need in Adam's life in today's Scripture passage?

- According to God's own words in verse 18, we were not created to live in isolation. Community is God's creation and also a reflection of His character, since He is a triune God. How has God acted to fulfill the need for community in your life? Explain.

RESPOND

- Evaluate your life. Are you trying to live in isolation, fueled by a false belief that you don't need relationships or a desire to protect yourself from getting hurt? Admit this to God. Ask Him to open your eyes to deep friendships that will bring you closer to Him.

- Look at the list you created earlier. Praise God for the family members and friends He has placed in your life. Pray for Christian family members and friends, thanking God for how they help you grow in your relationship with Him. Pray that God will soften the hearts of those who aren't Christians.

- For further study of what it means to live in Christian community, read Matthew 18:20, Galatians 6:2, and 1 Thessalonians 4:18 and 5:14.

DESIGNED FOR THIS

God created us to know Him, enjoy Him, and bring glory to Him. But because our sin separates us from Him, God made a way for us to have a personal relationship with Him. Read John 17:1–3 in your Bible, then flip over to 1 John 5:11–12 and read it carefully. As you read both passages, circle every instance of the word *life*. Underline each reference to *Son* or *Jesus*.

> This is eternal life: that they may know You, the only true God, and the One You have sent—Jesus Christ.—John 17:3

> And this is the testimony: God has given us eternal life, and this life is in His Son. The one who has the Son has life. The one who doesn't have the Son of God does not have life.—1 John 5:11–12

ASK YOURSELF:

- Consider the words you circled and underlined in both passages. Based on your findings, how we can have a relationship with God? Explain it in your own words.

- The word translated "know" in John 17:3 implies a continuing personal experience with God. What is the difference between knowing about God and actually having a relationship with Him?

- According to 1 John 5:11–12, God desires a relationship with us that will last throughout all eternity. In light of these verses, how do we know that we have eternal life? Explain.

RESPOND

Scripture is clear that from the beginning God created us to know Him, enjoy Him, and bring glory to Him. But humanity chose sin, which separated us from God and made that kind of intimate relationship impossible. But He made a way for that relationship to be restored through the life, death, and resurrection of His Son, Jesus.

- Do you have a personal relationship with Jesus Christ? Based on what? If the Holy Spirit urges you to respond, don't delay!

- Being a Christian doesn't mean that you will never sin again. You will, and it will disrupt your relationship with God. When the Holy Spirit convicts you of that sin, remember the gospel and repent, trusting what Jesus has already done for you to make you right with God.

DEEP WITHIN

It's one thing to know that God created humanity with purpose and another to believe that He created you on purpose and with purpose. Regardless of how you feel, you are not a mistake. Read Psalm 139:13–16 in your Bible.

> For it was You who created my inward parts; You knit me together in my mother's womb. . . . Your eyes saw me when I was formless; all my days were written in Your book and planned before a single one of them began.—Psalm 139:13, 16

THINK THROUGH THESE QUESTIONS:

- What words or phrases in these verses point to God's purpose and design for your life? Underline them, then explain why you chose them.

- If God has created you with purpose and ordained the days of your life, should you consider your life meaningless? Should it be characterized by aimless decisions? Why or why not?

- How would trusting that God has a plan and purpose for your life reorder or refocus your life? Explain.

RESPOND

- Write Psalm 139:13,16 in your journal, replacing every "me," "my," or "I" with your name. Pray the verses back to God, thanking Him for His sovereignty over every part of your life.

- You may be in the middle of circumstances or a cycle of sin that make it difficult for you to believe God could ever have a plan for your life. That's okay. Ask God to help you trust Him, even when you feel like you can't. Confess any sin that is disrupting your relationship with God and turn away from it. Pray Psalm 130:13, 16 as a way of actively placing your life in God's hands.

- Knowing God has a plan for your life doesn't mean you'll always know what the next step is. Ask Him for wisdom in the areas of your life that seem confusing and pray that He will guide you through His Word and Spirit.

HONORING THE DESIGN

You are an image bearer of God, but so are all people. Think about that statement as you read James 2:1–12 in your Bible.

> If you keep the royal law prescribed in the Scripture, Love your neighbor as yourself, you are doing well. But if you show favoritism, you commit sin and are convicted by the law as transgressors. . . . Speak and act as those who will be judged by the law of freedom.—James 2:8–9, 12

ASK YOURSELF:

- If every person bears the image of God, how should we treat other people?

- James points out the damages of favoring the rich over the poor. What other types of favoritism do you see in our world? In your church? In your own life?

- The "law of freedom" in verse 12 is a reference to the gospel. James instructed Christians to live as people who would be judged on Jesus' merit rather than their own. How should the knowledge of the great grace God has shown to you in Jesus change the way you live, particularly how you treat others? Explain.

RESPOND

- Evaluate your own heart and life. Is there prejudice? Favoritism? Are there certain people or people groups you overlook or ignore because they're not important enough? If the Holy Spirit reveals any of these things, confess and repent of those attitudes.

- Did you identify prejudice or favoritism in your church, family, or community? How can you live as an example and honor all people as image bearers of Christ in those situations? What steps will you take this week to invite others to join you? Record two in your journal.

- For further study, read Mark 12:28–34. Imagine a world where everyone was able to keep Jesus' commandment to love our neighbors as ourselves. What would that world look and sound like? What would change? Record your thoughts in your journal.

TRUE FELLOWSHIP

This week you've learned that you were made in God's image and created for a relationship with Him. You've also realized that God has hard-wired you for relationship with other people. With that in mind, read Hebrews 10:19–25 in your Bible. Focus on verses 24–25.

> And let us be concerned about one another in order to promote love and good works, not staying away from our worship meetings, as some habitually do, but encouraging each other, and all the more as you see the day drawing near.
> —Hebrews 10:24–25

- What does this passage have to do with what you've learned this week? Explain it in your own words.

- Dig a little deeper. What do these verses say that Jesus has done for us?

- List three actions that the writer of Hebrews says we should do because of what Jesus has done:

  1. Let us _____

  2. Let us _____

  3. Let us _____

As a Christian, you are not called to a lone-ranger faith. You were made for relationship and need the fellowship of other believers. We are not only to be concerned with our own journeys of faith, but also have a responsibility to other believers. We must regularly meet with other Christians to encourage one another and spur each other on in love and godliness.

RESPOND

- What are some practical ways that you can be mindful of others or love and encourage fellow Christians? In your journal, write down four actions that you will take this week in order to live out these verses.

- Who in your church family needs encouragement? Who needs to be reminded of our need to pursue godliness? Who simply needs to know that he or she isn't alone in the journey of faith? What steps will you take to live out Hebrews 10:24–25 in the lives of those people this week? Jot down two ideas in your journal.

- For further study of the church and Jesus' love for it, read 1 Corinthians 12:12–31, Ephesians 1:20–23, and Ephesians 5:25–33.

CHOOSING SIN, REJECTING GOD

When was the last time you chose to disobey an authority, like a parent or teacher? Why did you do it?

Now, think about some possible reasons why Adam and Eve chose to disobey God. Jot down a few thoughts in your journal.

Read Genesis 3:1–7 in your Bible, then consider the questions that follow.

"No! You will not die," the serpent said to the woman. "In fact, God knows that when you eat it your eyes will be opened and you will be like God, knowing good and evil."—Genesis 3:4–5

ASK YOURSELF:

- What are some ways we try to change or redefine God's commands like Eve did? Explain.

- Look at what the serpent said about God's command in verses 4 and 5. What did he imply? Journal in your own words.

- The serpent contradicted God's command and questioned His goodness and provision. When Adam and Eve acted on that temptation, they were declaring that what God had provided wasn't good enough and rejecting His authority over their lives. How is sin a rejection of Jesus' Lordship? Explain.

RESPOND

We sin when we believe that the way God has provided isn't good enough or that we know better than Him and He has no authority over our lives. Both of these ideas are deceptive and dangerous.

- Think about recent sin in your life. How did your sinful choices reflect a rejection of Jesus' Lordship or the belief that God's way wasn't good enough? Record your thoughts in your journal.

- Ask the Holy Spirit to examine your heart and life and reveal any ways you are rejecting God's authority over your life. Confess and repent from anything He reveals.

- For further study about humanity's tendency to reject God's authority, read Ecclesiastes 7:29.

HEARING GOD, HIDING SIN

The creation account shows us that God created us to have a unique relationship with Him that no other created being can enjoy. But when sin entered the world, it destroyed the intimacy of that relationship. Read Genesis 3:8–13 in your Bible to learn more.

> Then the man and his wife heard the sound of the LORD God walking in the garden at the time of the evening breeze, and they hid themselves from the LORD God among the trees of the garden. So the LORD God called out to the man and said to him, "Where are you?" And he said, "I heard You in the garden and I was afraid because I was naked, so I hid."—Genesis 3:8–10

ANSWER THESE QUESTIONS:
- What did Adam and Eve do when they heard God coming? Why?
- The imagery of God "walking" in the garden with Adam and Eve describes the kind of fellowship they had previously enjoyed. How had sin changed that fellowship? Explain.
- In what ways do people "hide" from God today when they know He is speaking to them? Explain.

RESPOND
- In your journal, list any sin you've been trying to hide or ignore.
- As you look over the list, how do those things affect your relationship with God? Is it worth it? Why or why not? Confess these sins so that your fellowship with God can be restored.
- For further study of sin and how it has affected humanity's relationship with God, read Isaiah 59:2.

PAINFUL CONSEQUENCES, REVEALING NEED

Read Genesis 3:14–19, underlining in your Bible every consequence God named for Adam and Eve's sin.

> "I will put hostility between you and the woman, and between your seed and her seed. He will strike your head, and you will strike his heel."—Genesis 3:15

DIG DEEPER WITH THESE QUESTIONS:

- How have you personally experienced the effects of the curses outlined in today's passage? Explain.

- What hope for the remedy of sin is given in verse 15? How does this hope point to Jesus?

- God created humanity knowing we would need a Savior. How do these verses point to Jesus' eternal nature? To the eternal nature of God's plan of redemption? Explain.

RESPOND

- On a scale of 1 to 10, how much do you recognize your need for Jesus on a daily basis? Explain your answer.

- It is easy to focus on the consequences of sin outlined in this passage, but in verse 15, God was already pointing to the remedy for sin, Jesus, and our deep need for Him. Set aside time today to focus solely on Jesus, His character, and what He has done to save you. Thank God that before the foundation of the world, He was making a way for you to be saved.

- For further study of how Jesus fulfills the prophecy in Genesis 3:15, read Hebrews 2:14, 1 John 3:8, and Romans 16:20.

DESTRUCTIVE SIN, TARNISHING EVERYTHING

Read Genesis 4:1–16 in your Bible. Note the chain of events that describe Cain's downfall into sin.

> Cain said to his brother Abel, "Let's go out to the field." And while they were in the field, Cain attacked his brother Abel and killed him.—Genesis 4:8

THINK THROUGH THESE QUESTIONS:

- How does Cain's life exemplify the destructive nature of sin? Explain.

- Do you ever think of your own sinfulness as destructive? Why or why not?

- How did sin destroy God's original intent for relationships? Explain.

RESPOND

- In your journal, list temptations to sin you are facing right now. Don't hold anything back. When you've completed your list, write *God is better* over it. Pray that God would open your eyes to His better plans and ways.

- When sin entered the world, it corrupted God's original intent for relationships. Have you allowed sin to disrupt or damage relationships in your life? Do you need to forgive someone or ask someone for forgiveness? Pray about the relationships that come to mind, then be faithful to follow through with the actions the Holy Spirit leads you to take.

- For further study of the destructiveness of sin, read and meditate on Romans 6:23.

THROUGH ONE,
AFFECTING ALL

Think about the time you first became aware that you needed God's grace. How long did it take you to accept His grace? What hurdles did you have to get past in order to do so? Journal your thoughts.

Read Romans 3:21–26 and Romans 5:12–17 in your Bible.

> Therefore, just as sin entered the world through one man, and death through sin, in this way death spread to all men, because all sinned. In fact, sin was in the world before the law, but sin is not charged to a person's account when there is no law.
> —Romans 5:12–13

Reflect on these passages, then list the effects of Adam's and Jesus' lives in your journal.

ASK YOURSELF:

- What do these passages teach you about how Adam's sin has affected you? Explain.

- Romans 5 teaches that sin entered the world through Adam and affected all of us. We cannot have the kind of relationship God intended us to have with Him or with others because of the sinfulness we inherited from Adam. But these verses also give us hope for salvation. Through whom does salvation come? How?

RESPOND

Adam's sin had far-reaching consequences. It affected creation and changed humanity's relationship with God. Sin became our inheritance.

- You are a sinner. Your flesh is sinful, and you make sinful choices. But you don't have to stay mired in sin with no hope of salvation. God has already made a way for our salvation through Jesus Christ, His Son.

- As believers, we sometimes think we can manage our sin or overcome it through our own effort. But we can't. If you're trying to overcome the sin in your life in your own strength, stop. Refocus on the gospel and Jesus' finished work. Confess and ask the Holy Spirit to empower you to live for Christ in those areas.

- For further study of how Jesus makes us right with God, read 2 Corinthians 5:21.

BROKEN RELATIONSHIPS, RESTORING SAVIOR

Earlier this week, you learned that sin had affected relationships. Distrust, enmity, prejudice, and shame entered the picture, destroying the unity and companionship God had designed relationships to provide. But in Jesus, even relationships are restored. Read Galatians 3:27–29 in your Bible to learn more.

> There is no Jew or Greek, slave or free, male or female; for you are all one in Christ Jesus.—Galatians 3:28

THINK THROUGH THESE QUESTIONS:
- What sorts of things tend to divide people of different races? People from different church backgrounds? People in different social groups at school? Journal a few thoughts.
- According to these verses, how does being unified with Christ change the way we regard others? How does that fly in the face of prejudice toward others? Explain.
- How has the gospel changed your perspective on the things that tend to cause division in relationships? Be specific.

RESPOND
- Think about the relationships in your life, especially those with other believers. Has racial prejudice, disunity, or mistrust disrupted or damaged any of your relationships? Pray about those specific relationships. Confess any sin the Holy Spirit reveals and ask Him to guide you as you seek restoration.
- Who is one person who is different from you in some way that you need to reach out to with the gospel of Jesus? What steps will you take to do so this week? Record two steps.
- For further study of how Jesus restores relationships, read Colossians 3:11.

GROANING CREATION

Adam and Eve's sin had far-reaching consequences. It created separation between humanity and God and distorted our purpose. It brought disunity and strife into our relationships with others. And Scripture tells us that God's good creation even bears the curse of sin. Read Romans 8:19–25 in your Bible to learn more.

> For the creation was subjected to futility—not willingly, but because of Him who subjected it—in the hope that the creation itself will also be set free from the bondage of corruption into the glorious freedom of God's children.—Romans 8:20–21

ASK YOURSELF:

- Think about the stories you've seen on the news or read about. How do you see evidence of the "groaning of creation" in our world today?

- Look back at Genesis 3:17–18. When Adam and Eve disobeyed, God cursed the ground. Growing a crop would no longer be easy; instead, the ground would produce thorns and thistles. According to Romans 8:19–25, how and when will creation be set free from its bondage? Explain.

- According to Paul, how are we to live in the meantime while we wait for this future glory? (See v. 25.)

- What does it mean to "eagerly wait for it with patience"? What does that look like? Explain it in your own words.

RESPOND

Even God's good creation suffered—and still suffers—under the consequences of sin. But when Jesus returns and sin is ultimately destroyed, creation will be set free.

- As believers, we have a glorious hope in Jesus. But in our fallen world, it's easy to be overwhelmed by the destruction and damage sin continues to cause. What steps will you take this week to focus your heart and mind on God's faithfulness and your hope in Christ, even when it seems like the world is falling apart? Record two ideas in your journal.

- How can you encourage other believers to live in hope and patience as we face our present sufferings? How will you do so this week?

- For further study of creation's restoration, read Revelation 22:1–5.

MASTERPIECE REVEALED

Read Ephesians 2:1–10 in your Bible.

For we are His creation, created in Christ Jesus for good works, which God prepared ahead of time so that we should walk in them.—Ephesians 2:10

In your journal, write any phrase in today's passage that begins with "you."

ASK YOURSELF:

- How did Paul describe the human condition in verse 1? Explain it in your own words.

- Why is it important that we understand that apart from Christ, we're not just bad or messed up, but spiritually dead?

- The word translated "creation" in verse 10 is the Greek word *poiema*, which implies artistic skill or craftsmanship. You were carefully crafted by God for a specific purpose. According to verse 10, what is that purpose? Explain.

- Why is it important to know that God didn't just save us from something, but to something: good works?

RESPOND

God didn't just create you and make a way for you to know Him so that you could aimlessly walk through your life. He created you for good works that He will do in and through you as you follow Him in obedience and faith.

- In your journal, record a prayer of thanks to God for not only bringing you from death to life, but also for giving you an important role in His kingdom.

- Ask God to open your eyes and heart to the good works He has prepared for you. Pray that you would be faithful to respond in obedience when He gives you an opportunity to do kingdom work this week.

- Think about the people in your youth group or church who need a reminder that they are God's masterpieces, created for good works. How will you encourage and remind them of that truth this week?

- For further study about good works, read Matthew 5:16 and James 2:14–17.

PURSUING LIGHT, OPENING EYES

Read Ephesians 5:8–11 and Acts 26:18 in your Bible.

For you were once darkness, but now you are light in the Lord. Walk as children of light.—Ephesians 5:8

"To open their eyes so they may turn from darkness to light and from the power of Satan to God, that by faith in Me they may receive forgiveness of sins and a share among those who are sanctified."—Acts 26:18

HEADING?

- List the commands Paul gave in Ephesians 5:8–11. Explain each command in one sentence, using your own words.

- Acts 26:18 records Jesus' words to Paul and serves as a commission. What did Jesus commission Paul to do?

- How does the gospel bring light into the darkness of someone's life? Explain.

- When have your eyes been opened, turning you from darkness to light? Who or what helped to open your eyes?

RESPOND

- Evaluate your life. Are there any "fruitless works of darkness" in your own life that you need to bring into the light? Confess anything the Holy Spirit reveals, placing your hope once again in what Jesus has already done to set you free from sin.

- Think about the people in your class, your community, your coworkers, friends, or family members. Who in your life is lost in the darkness of sin and needs the light of the gospel? Pray for opportunities to share Jesus with those people this week. Ask God to make you bold to follow through when those opportunities arise.

- We live in a dark world. Besides sharing the gospel, what choices will you make this week to bring light into the darkness? Write two in your journal.

- For further study about the light of Christ, read John 1:5 and 8:12.

A COVERING OF GRACE

Read Genesis 3:14–24 in your Bible. To review, list the consequences of sin for each individual.

Woman

Man

Serpent

> The LORD God made clothing out of skins for Adam and his wife, and He clothed them.—Genesis 3:21

Reread verse 21 and answer the questions that follow:

- Why did God make clothing for Adam and Eve?

- How was this an expression of grace and mercy after all they had done?

- For God to make clothing for Adam and Eve, an animal had to be sacrificed. Blood had to be shed to atone for their sin. How does this act foreshadow the Old Testament sacrificial system? How does it point to Jesus? Explain.

RESPOND

Verse 21 foreshadows the blood sacrifices of the Old Testament that would be required to atone for sin. More than that, it points to Jesus' sacrifice on the cross through which we have the hope of salvation.

- God was the One who made the sacrifice to cover Adam and Eve and deal with the consequences of their sin. He has done the same for us. Meditate on the gospel and the fact that in Jesus, God has done everything necessary to save you. Thank Him for that truth today.

- The consequences outlined in today's passage and the extreme nature of God's actions to restore Adam and Eve illustrate the seriousness of sin. Even as Christians, sin can disrupt our fellowship with God. If the Holy Spirit has revealed sin in your life through this devotion, confess it now.

GOD DELIVERS FROM HARM

Read Genesis 6:11–22 in your Bible. Take note of how these verses describe the corruption of humanity at the time God commanded Noah to build the ark. Underline every form of the words *corrupt* or *wicked*.

> "Understand that I am bringing a flood—floodwaters on the earth to destroy every creature under heaven with the breath of life in it. Everything on earth will die. But I will establish My covenant with you, and you will enter the ark with your sons, your wife, and your sons' wives."—Genesis 6:17–18

ASK YOURSELF:

- Today's passage describes the state of humanity a while after sin had entered the world. Look at the words you underlined in these verses. How had sin affected the world? Explain.

- How was Noah different from the rest of the world? (Hint: Look back at v. 9.)

- How was the ark a gift of grace and mercy to Noah and his family? Explain.

- How does God's rescue of Noah and his family via the ark point to the rescue Jesus provides? Explain.

RESPOND

Just as the ark delivered Noah from death, Jesus delivers us from the penalty we deserve for our sins—death. He is the greatest ark and source of rescue we could ever need.

- Write a few sentences in your journal thanking God for sending Jesus to rescue and deliver you from sin and death. Praise Him for loving you so much.

- The flood reveals the severity of God's wrath against sin. In His righteousness, He cannot let sin go unpunished. Mull over this question: Do you have a casual, flippant attitude toward sin or do you take the seriousness of sin to heart?

- For further study of the seriousness of sin, read John 8:34, Colossians 2:13, and 1 John 1:8–10.

A PROMISE FULFILLED

Read Genesis 12:1–4 in your Bible. In each verse, circle the phrase *I will* every time it appears.

"I will bless those who bless you, I will curse those who treat you with contempt, and all the peoples on earth will be blessed through you."—Genesis 12:3

The phrase *I will* is most often the first part of a promise or covenant. Genesis 12:1–4 is exactly that—a promise from God to the man who would be the father of a great nation. It is through this great nation that God's only Son was born. Jesus came through the lineage of Abram. (See Matthew 1:1–17.)

Look over God's words to Abram in Genesis 12:1–4 one more time. Think through these questions:

- In what ways is Jesus the "blessing" people would eventually experience? Explain.
- How has Jesus been a blessing in your life? Journal a few thoughts.
- Why is it important that God keeps His promises? What does that help you understand about salvation?

RESPOND

Through Abram's lineage, God made salvation available to all people—including you.

- Mull over the scope of God's plan. Redemption through Jesus wasn't a spur-of-the-moment decision or Plan B; it was God's plan from the beginning. Thank Him for the ways He worked across the centuries to make salvation possible. Record your prayer in your journal.

- God is trustworthy and always keeps His promises, as today's devotion illustrates. Thank God for the promises He has kept in your life. Express your desire to trust Him in the areas where it seems difficult to believe He will be faithful.

- For further study, use a concordance to find verses about God's trustworthiness. Find a verse that speaks to you and share it on social media to encourage others to trust that God is faithful.

A SACRIFICE GIVEN

God had promised Abram that he would be the father of a great nation, but it was years before God gave Abram and Sarai a son. Then, after all those years of waiting, God asked Abram to sacrifice his only son. Read Genesis 22:1–18 in your Bible.

Abraham answered, "God Himself will provide the lamb for the burnt offering, my son."—Genesis 22:8

Abraham looked up and saw a ram caught in the thicket by its horns. So Abraham went and took the ram and offered it as a burnt offering in place of his son. And Abraham named that place The Lord Will Provide, so today it is said: "It will be provided on the Lord's mountain."—Genesis 22:13–14

- How does this story point to Jesus and His sacrifice on our behalf? Explain.
- Why is it important that God was the One who provided the ram as a substitute for Isaac? How has He done the same for us in Jesus?

Read John 1:29–34 in your Bible. In this passage, John the Baptist identified Jesus as the Lamb of God. The Jews would have recognized the terminology as referring to a sacrifice that provided atonement for their sins.

- With that in mind, what was John the Baptist declaring about Jesus when he called Him the Lamb of God?
- How does this relate to the story of God asking Abraham to sacrifice Isaac?

RESPOND

- Meditate on this thought today: God provided a ram that died in Isaac's place; Jesus died in your place, for your sin. Record your response in your journal.
- Write out and memorize John 1:29. Let it be a reminder that Jesus is the Lamb of God who willingly sacrificed His life to make a way for your salvation.
- The gospel is the story of how Jesus died in your place so that your sins could be forgiven and you could spend eternity with God. Admit your need for a Savior today and place your faith in what Jesus has already done.

ATONEMENT REQUIRED

God instituted a sacrificial system among His people during the time of Moses. The Old Testament sacrifices were the way God provided people at that time to seek forgiveness and atonement for their sins. The animal would symbolically take the sinner's place, paying the penalty for his or her sin. To learn more about the sacrificial system and its deeper meaning, read Leviticus 1:1–15 in your Bible.

> He is to lay his hand on the head of the burnt offering so it can be accepted on his behalf to make atonement for him.—Leviticus 1:4

ASK YOURSELF:

- Look at verse 4. What did the person offering the sacrifice have to do?

- What did this act symbolize? Explain.

- The action of sinners placing their hands on the sacrifice symbolized the transfer of their sin to the animal. The animal would take the punishment its owner deserved. How does this practice point to Jesus? Explain.

Jesus Christ became the ultimate sacrifice for our sin. When He died on the cross, He took on the sins of all who would believe in Him—past, present, and future. In that moment, He became the one perfect, sacrificial offering that could atone for the sins of all of humanity. He became sin for us so that we could become the righteousness of God in Him (2 Corinthians 5:21).

RESPOND

- If you've never surrendered your life to God by receiving His gift of salvation through Jesus, find a couple of trustworthy adults such as a parent, student pastor, or pastor and ask them to share their testimony with you.

- As a believer, meditate on the reality of what Jesus has done for you. Consider how you feel about His sacrifice and His incredible love for you. Are you amazed? Thankful? Humbled? Whatever your emotions, express them to God. Journal a prayer, write a poem, sing a worship song that expresses your thankfulness, or talk with someone else about the great thing Jesus has done.

- For further study of atonement, read Romans 5:1–2, Hebrews 12:1–2, 1 Peter 2:21–25, and 1 John 2:2.

SAVE THE WORLD

Today, you'll study Joseph, Abraham's great-grandson. Joseph is a Savior figure in the Old Testament. Sold into slavery by his brothers, Joseph was purchased by a man name Potiphar and rose to a position of authority in Potiphar's house before Potiphar's wife accused him of assaulting her. Joseph was thrown into prison where he remained for years, seemingly forgotten, even though Scripture tells us that the Lord was with him. Finally, after interpreting Pharaoh's dream, Joseph became one of the most important people in Egypt. Read Genesis 41:53–57 in your Bible.

> Every nation came to Joseph in Egypt to buy grain, for the famine was severe in every land.—Genesis 41:57

Now, read Genesis 47:25.

ASK YOURSELF:

- How was Joseph a Savior figure in the verses you read today? How did he provide physical salvation for the people during this time of famine? Explain.

- Reread Genesis 41:57. Scripture says people came from every nation and every land to experience the physical salvation Joseph offered. What does that teach you about the spiritual salvation Jesus offers?

Joseph lived in a time when people were dying from their physical hunger and thirst. He knew what they needed, and he was faithful to provide it. We live in a time when people are spiritually hungry and thirsty. They know that there is a deep need in their lives, but they don't know how to fill it. So, they grasp at everything the world says will fill that void: relationships, power, money, stuff, knowledge, and fame. As a Christian, you know what they need: Jesus. Will you be faithful to share the good news of salvation with a world that is spiritually dead and thirsting for redemption?

RESPOND

Think about the people closest to you—your family, friends, classmates, and people in your community. Who in your life is hungering and thirsting for the salvation only Jesus can provide? Pray for an opportunity to share your hope with those people this week.

A BLESSING FOR ETERNITY

Read Genesis 49:1–28 in your Bible, then focus on verses 9–12. Circle any phrases that tell you something about Jesus.

> The scepter will not depart from Judah or the staff from between his feet until He whose right it is comes and the obedience of the peoples belongs to Him.
> —Genesis 49:10

Thoughtfully answer these questions:

- What does Jacob's blessing to his son Judah reveal about Jesus? Explain.

- Jacob's blessing declared that from Judah's lineage would come the King of kings who would reign forever. When you consider this promise of the Messiah—along with all the other ways God pointed to Jesus that you have learned about this week—what is your response? Journal a few thoughts.

- God has fulfilled His promise to send Jesus, and we can trust that Jesus will one day return to rule and reign forever, as Jacob declared in his blessing. Do you live like you believe God is faithful? Would your friends and acquaintances answer the same way? Why or why not?

RESPOND

- Think about the believers in your life who are facing difficult circumstances right now or may be doubting that God is trustworthy and faithful. What steps will you take today to encourage them with God's Word or promises? To remind them of His character?

- For believers, the certainty of Jesus' second coming is a source of hope and comfort. But to those who don't know Him, it is frightening and points to the reality that they will one day face judgment. Those who reject Jesus now will not experience eternity with Him. Pray that the Holy Spirit would lead you to the people in your life who need to hear the gospel this week.

- For further study of Jesus' second coming, read Matthew 25:31–46, 1 Thessalonians 4:16–17 and 5:2, Titus 2:11–13, and Revelation 19:11–16.

THE MESSIAH

Mull over what you learned in last week's devotions, considering how God was already revealing His plan of salvation through Jesus in Genesis and the Law. Jot down a few of the ways He did that in your journal.

These weren't the only ways God pointed to Jesus in the Old Testament. Through the prophets, God proclaimed that He was sending a Messiah to save His people. Read Isaiah 9:2–7 in your Bible to learn about the Messiah's character and power. Circle any words or phrases that describe Him.

> For a child will be born for us, a son will be given to us, and the government will be on His shoulders. He will be named Wonderful Counselor, Mighty God, Eternal Father, Prince of Peace.—Isaiah 9:6

Underline the prophecy in Isaiah 9:6–7. Journal in your own words.

Turn to Matthew 4:12–17 in your Bible.

- According to these verses, to whom does the Isaiah 9 passage refer? Explain.

- Why is it important to realize that this prophecy can only be completely fulfilled in Jesus?

RESPOND

- Consider the words or phrases you underlined in the Isaiah 9 passage. How has Jesus displayed these characteristics in your life? How has He been your Prince of Peace? Your Counselor? How has He displayed His power or might? Be specific as you record your prayer and praise in your journal.

- Ponder the circumstances you are facing right now. How does the promise of eternal peace, justice, and righteousness He will usher in bring you hope in those circumstances? What actions will you take to express your trust in Him this week?

THE KING IS COMING

Read Zechariah 9:9–12 closely in your Bible, focusing your attention on verses 9 and 10. As you meditate on these verses, write a 1 beside the verse that speaks about the first coming of Jesus and a 2 beside the verse that points to His second coming.

> Rejoice greatly, Daughter Zion! Shout in triumph, Daughter Jerusalem! Look, your King is coming to you; He is righteous and victorious, humble and riding on a donkey, on a colt, the foal of a donkey.—Zechariah 9:9

ANSWER THE QUESTIONS BELOW:

- Reread verse 9, then consider Matthew 21:1–10 and John 12:12–15. According to the New Testament, who fulfilled Zechariah's prophecy about the Messiah? When did He fulfill it?

- Why is it important that Jesus fulfilled this portion of the prophecy during His earthly ministry? Explain.

- Ponder verse 10. What will Jesus do when He returns to earth? How will His second coming be different from His first?

Verse 10 describes Jesus ushering in a time of great peace with His second coming. This peace isn't just general well-being, but rather the end of hostility between humanity and God. It is complete restoration of the relationship with God that our sin destroyed. While that kind of peace will ultimately be revealed only at Christ's return, God is already displaying it in the lives of His children. How have you experienced the peace that only Jesus can give? Explain.

RESPOND

- Take a moment to simply thank Jesus for coming to live among us. Praise Him for remaining faithful to the Father's plan so that prophecy could be fulfilled and you could experience true salvation and peace.

- In Jesus' promise to return, we have the hope of an eternity where sin has been put to death. Think about the temptations you face daily or the sin that so often disrupts your relationship with God. Confess any sin God reveals, but also praise Him for the joy you have that these things will be completely gone.

4 0

THE REDEMPTIVE KING

Read Jeremiah 23:5–8 in your Bible.

> "The days are coming"—this is the Lord's declaration—"when I will raise up a Righteous Branch of David. He will reign wisely as king and administer justice and righteousness in the land."—Jeremiah 23:5

After the exile of the Israelites, the word *Branch* had come to refer to the Jews' expected ideal king. But many of the Israelites' expectations were based on what they knew an earthly king to be—a powerful political Messiah who would deliver them from Rome's rule. Yet, Jesus came to set them free spiritually.

ASK YOURSELF:

- The Jews had misplaced expectations about the Messiah and rejected Jesus when He didn't meet those expectations. What are some misplaced expectations or beliefs people have about Jesus today?

- Sometimes, we place our own expectations, personalities, or thoughts on Jesus and expect Him to behave, think, or act as we would. What does this passage teach you about that idea? Explain.

- Righteousness involves living a life that matches with God's commandments, love, and purposes. Jeremiah proclaimed the Messiah would be Yahweh's true righteousness (v. 6), and He would not fail, as the earthly kings had. Why is it important that Jesus lived a righteous life? What does His righteousness have to do with us? Explain.

RESPOND

Faith in Christ isn't about being good or trying harder. It's about trusting what Jesus has already done and resting in His righteousness.

- Even as a Christian, it's easy to start relying on your own effort or goodness to make you somehow more acceptable to God. Admit to God any ways you are trying to make yourself more worthy or deserving. Ask Him to help you rest in Jesus' righteousness rather than your own.

- For further study about the Messiah and the Branch, read Jeremiah 33:15, Zechariah 3:8 and 6:12, and Isaiah 4:2.

41

THE MESSIAH

Read Isaiah 7:10–17 in your Bible. Underline the name *Immanuel* when you read it.

> Therefore, the Lord Himself will give you a sign: The virgin will conceive, have a son, and name him Immanuel.—Isaiah 7:14

Scholars believe that Isaiah's prophecy had some sort of immediate fulfillment in King Ahaz's time, but was only completely fulfilled by Jesus.

ASK YOURSELF:
- Immanuel means God with us. Knowing this, what would King Ahaz and the people have been reminded of every time they heard the child's name? Why is that important?
- Ahaz faced a decision: trust God or place his hope in Assyria, a pagan but powerful nation. When have you been tempted to try to find your own solution for a problem rather than trusting God to provide?
- Consider Matthew 1:23. How does Jesus ultimately fulfill Isaiah's prophecy? Explain.
- What does the name Immanuel reveal about the kind of relationship God wants to have with us? Explain.

RESPOND
It's nice to know facts about Jesus, but He came so that you could know Him personally, not just information about Him.

- Jesus came as Immanuel in the flesh, making a way for us to have a relationship with God that we never could have through our own effort or merit. Do you know Him personally?
- In what situations in your life do you need a reminder that God knows, cares, and is with you? Write about those situations in your journal, asking God to open your eyes to how He is at work and to help you sense His presence.

HEALING AND PEACE

Read Isaiah 53:2–12 in your Bible. As you read, record your notes.

> But He was pierced because of our transgressions, crushed because of our iniquities; punishment for our peace was on Him, and we are healed by His wounds.
> —Isaiah 53:5

ASK YOURSELF:

- What do these verses teach me about Jesus' purpose in coming?

- What do these verses teach me about what Jesus' suffering accomplished?

- What do these verses have to do with me, personally?

- How did Jesus fulfill the prophecy detailed in Isaiah 53? Explain.

- Reread verse 5. How would you use this verse to explain the meaning of Jesus' death to someone?

- Why did Jesus, who never sinned, have to be the One to die on our behalf? (See verses 10–11 for help.)

RESPOND

Though it was written centuries before Jesus was born, Isaiah 53 details His sacrificial death on our behalf. Jesus took on the consequences of our sin and suffered in our place so that we might be reconciled to God.

- You have been presented the gospel today, and the gospel demands a response. Will you trust the One who died and rose again for your salvation or will you go your own way?

- If you are a Christian, meditate on Isaiah 53 today, thanking Jesus for what He has done to make sure you will never face the consequences of your sin. Using Isaiah 53 as a template, journal your own prayer of praise for what He has done.

- To learn more about how the New Testament interprets this passage, read Matthew 27:38–60, John 1:29, Acts 8:32–34, and 1 Peter 2:22–23.

BE THE LIGHT

Carefully read Isaiah 60:1–22 in your Bible, then examine verses 1–5.

- Circle any words that have to do with light.

- Underline any words that have to do with darkness.

- Draw a square around any words that have to do with eyes.

Arise, shine, for your light has come, and the glory of the Lord shines over you.
—Isaiah 60:1

Look over verses 1–5. What did these verses teach you about the Messiah? About what it means to live for Him? Explain.

Isaiah was pointing to a time in the future when God would restore Jerusalem and people of all nations would praise Him. As Christians, we know that the Messiah has come, and salvation has a name: Jesus. Darkness may cover the earth, but we have the light of Christ, and it is our joy and honor to reflect His light to the world.

- What does it look like to shine His light through your daily life? Be specific.

- How is shining His light as believers a response to the great salvation you've received? Explain.

- How is the light you shine a reflection of God's glory?

RESPOND

Because we know Jesus, our lives should be different. We don't have to be mired in the gloom of this world because we know the Source of light and hope.

- Examine your life. In what ways might you be trying to hide God's light? What steps will you take to let Christ shine in every area of your life this week? Record three ideas.

- Who has been a light for Christ in your life? Who in your life is a good example of reflecting Jesus in every situation he or she faces? Thank God for those people and their influence in your life. Consider personally thanking those people for their faithfulness to live the gospel.

- Who is looking to you to learn what it means to be a Christian? Thank God for the position of influence He has given you and ask Him to help you faithfully reflect His glory even when it isn't easy.

THE KING RETURNS

Read Daniel 7:1–28 in your Bible. In this passage, Daniel was prophesying about an event far in the future. This is a vision of Christ's second coming and His sovereign, eternal reign.

> I continued watching in the night visions, and I saw One like a son of man coming with the clouds of heaven. He approached the Ancient of Days and was escorted before Him. He was given authority to rule, and glory, and a kingdom; so that those of every people, nation, and language should serve Him. His dominion is an everlasting dominion that will not pass away, and His kingdom is one that will not be destroyed.—Daniel 7:13–14

ASK YOURSELF:

- What do these verses help you to understand about Jesus? About His second coming? Explain.

- How does knowing that Jesus will one day return and rule forever help you to live with hope and purpose?

- What are some places people seek hope or purpose other than Jesus? Why do believers sometimes need to be reminded that our hope is in Christ and the certainty that He will do what He has said? Explain.

RESPOND

- Think about the other believers in your life who are walking through difficult situations. How can you help them to refocus on Jesus and the hope they have in Him?

- Identify the people in your life who are seeking hope and purpose in someone or something other than Jesus. How can you help to point them to Christ this week? Pray for God-given opportunities to do so.

- For further study of Jesus' second coming, read Matthew 28:18, Revelation 19, and Revelation 20:4–6.

PAID IN FULL

Words of wisdom and family stories are often passed down to the next generation. List some reasons you think people share stories or advice in your journal.

Now, read Psalm 22:1–31 in your Bible. As you read, highlight the words or phrases that reveal something about Jesus or His sacrifice.

> Their descendants will serve Him; the next generation will be told about the Lord. They will come and tell a people yet to be born about His righteousness—what He has done.—Psalm 22:30–31

THINK THROUGH THESE QUESTIONS:

- Take note of the words or phrases you highlighted. What connections did you see between this passage and Jesus? Explain.

- After reading this passage, what do you think is the important thing Jesus has done that we're supposed to tell others about?

- According to verses 30–31, what are we supposed to do with the good news of Jesus' sacrificial death on the cross? Why is it important to share that news with future generations?

RESPOND

On the cross, Jesus became sin for us and bore God's righteous wrath on our behalf. Jesus endured separation from God so that we would not have to experience that separation for all eternity.

- Think about what Jesus has done for you. Christ bore your sin on the cross, suffered separation from God, and was resurrected so that you could come into relationship with the Father. In your journal, write a prayer of thanksgiving for Christ's atoning work.

- Because Jesus fully satisfied God's righteous demands on the cross, we can live to honor God, something we can't do in our own effort. That's good news that needs to be shared. Who in your life needs to hear it? In your journal, jot down three names the Holy Spirit brings to mind.

- For further study about Jesus' finished work on the cross, read John 19:28–37.

RISEN

Another psalm of David that points to Christ is Psalm 16. Read Psalm 16:1–11 in your Bible. Underline all the ways David expressed confidence in God despite the adversity he faced.

> For You will not abandon me to Sheol; You will not allow Your Faithful One to see decay.—Psalm 16:10

Now, focus on verse 10. David clearly found his protection in God and trusted Him, believing that nothing—not even death—could separate Him from God.

- In verse 10, what other aspects of God's character did David focus on? Why is it essential that God is faithful?

- Read Acts 2:25–31.

- To whom did Peter say David's reference to the "Faithful One" in Psalm 16:10 referred?

- What does it mean to say the Faithful One, Jesus, will not see decay? Explain it in your own words in your journal.

- Why is it important that Christians believe in Jesus' resurrection? Explain.

RESPOND

Think about the power of God—so great that it resurrected Christ from death!

- David was so confident of God's power that even the thought of death could not rob him of his joy. What threatens to rob you of your joy in Christ? Ask God to remind you of His power and presence in your life today.

- Memorize Deuteronomy 31:8 and Hebrews 13:6. Recite them when you doubt that God is powerfully present in your life.

- If Christ has not risen, then our faith is worthless (1 Corinthians 15:17). Meditate on the importance of Jesus' resurrection. Thank God for doing what was necessary to save you.

- For further study of how the New Testament interprets Psalm 16, read Acts 2:8–31 and 13:34–39.

EMBRACING HIM

Read Psalm 2:1–12 in your Bible.

> Serve the LORD with reverential awe and rejoice with trembling. Pay homage to the Son or He will be angry and you will perish in your rebellion, for His anger may ignite at any moment. All those who take refuge in Him are happy.—Psalm 2:11–12

ANSWER THESE QUESTIONS:
- How do verses 1–3 reflect the world's response to Jesus the first time He came? Explain.
- Underline verse 3. How do you see the world today trying to "free" themselves from God's control?

Read Psalm 2:4–9. Despite humanity's revolt against God's rule in their lives, He remains sovereign and His plans are sure. How do these verses display . . .

- God's holiness?
- God's righteous wrath against sin?
- Jesus' authority and eternal reign?
- Jesus coming as God in the flesh?

Finally, reread Psalm 2:10–11. Underline verse 11. What do these verses reveal about the urgency of trusting and following Christ? Explain.

RESPOND
Instead of resisting God, sinners must turn from sin and turn to Christ, the only way of salvation God has provided.

- Those who choose to reject Jesus as their Lord and Savior will face God's wrath against sin. Have you placed your faith in the Savior?
- Sometimes, even as Christians, we try to take control of our lives rather than letting Jesus reign in every area. Ask the Holy Spirit to reveal any ways you are doing so. Confess anything He reveals.
- Thank Jesus for being your refuge and for making a way for you to live with Him forever. Recall the day you placed your faith in Him and celebrate His goodness.

OUR REDEEMER

The Book of Ruth is a story of obedience, sacrifice, and redemption. In many ways, it pictures the work of Christ. Read Ruth 4:1–22 in your Bible. Focus on verses 12–17.

> Then the women said to Naomi, "Praise the LORD, who has not left you without a family redeemer today. May his name become well known in Israel."—Ruth 4:14

ASK YOURSELF:

- Consider the definition of a family redeemer. How did Jesus act as our family redeemer? Explain.

- Look up 1 Corinthians 6:20. What does it mean that we were bought at a price? What does this verse have to do with the idea of Jesus being our Redeemer?

- Think about Boaz's willingness to take action and do what was necessary to redeem Ruth from her distress. Why is it important to recognize that Jesus didn't just inadvertently stumble into a plot that resulted in His death?

RESPOND

He willingly took on our sin and laid down His life so that we could be redeemed from our sin. He paid the price for our sin so that we would never have to.

- Jesus has already paid the price to buy you back from your sin so that you can know Him and spend eternity with Him. Place your faith in the finished work of your Redeemer today!

- Read Ruth 4:18–22 and compare it to the genealogy of Christ in Matthew 1. Ruth and Boaz became important figures in Jesus' earthly lineage. Their faithfulness to God in this situation benefited all generations and left a legacy greater than they could have ever imagined. In what seemingly small ways will you choose to be faithful today, trusting God to build a legacy of faith in your life? Jot down three ideas in your journal.

- For further study of the significance of Jesus' ancestry, read Luke 3:31–32, Romans 1:3, and Revelation 22:16.

REDEEMING HOPE

Read Job 19:25–27 in your Bible. Circle the word *redeemer* every time you read it.

> But I know my living Redeemer, and He will stand on the dust at last. Even after my skin has been destroyed, yet I will see God in my flesh. I will see Him myself; my eyes will look at Him, and not as a stranger. My heart longs within me.—Job 19:25–27

According to these verses, who or what was the source of Job's hope? Which phrases make that source apparent?

Early in Israel's history, the word *redeemer* had been a legal term, referring to the family redeemer concept illustrated in the Book of Ruth. But by the time of the prophets and the writing of the Psalms, the word had taken on theological significance, envisioning Yahweh as Israel's Redeemer.

ASK YOURSELF:

- Knowing this, what was Job declaring in Job 19:25? Explain your answer.

- *Stand on the dust* is a phrase that indicates that Job believed that God would vindicate him in the end. No matter what people said about his life, Job knew God would defend him. Do you have a faith like Job's, trusting God is faithful and true even when circumstances seem to prove otherwise? Why or why not?

- Job's understanding of God's eternal plan of redemption through Jesus was limited, but he undoubtedly understood that the source of his redemption and hope lay only in God. Who or what are you trusting for eternal salvation? Why?

RESPOND

In our world, people put their hope in many things—money, power, relationships, fame. But the only source of true eternal hope is Jesus.

- If you have never trusted Jesus for salvation, let today be the day. Place your faith in the living Redeemer.

- Identify the painful situations in your life that cause you to question God's faithfulness and sovereignty. Ask Him to help you trust Him in those situations, even when you can't see how He is at work.

ROUND OF APPLAUSE

How does it feel when you compliment someone on a great quality they have or a job well done? How do you feel when others compliment you? Journal a few thoughts.

With that in mind, read Psalm 68:1–20 in your Bible.

> May the Lord be praised! Day after day He bears our burdens; God is our salvation. Our God is a God of salvation, and escape from death belongs to the Lord GOD.
> —Psalm 68:19–20

Focus on verses 19–20.

- List the reasons the psalmist was praising God in these verses.

- If you are a believer, you have experienced salvation from sin, so death no longer has any power over you. Why do these things make God worthy of your praise? Explain.

God has done great things through Jesus Christ. He has taken away our burden of sin and made eternal life possible. He has rescued us from the kingdom of darkness and transferred us into the kingdom of His Son (Colossians 1:13). What God has done for us in Jesus isn't just something we believe to become a Christian then get over. The gospel should ignite our praise for the One who made it possible for all eternity.

RESPOND

David praised God for the great things He had done throughout Israel's history and for the joy of salvation that God alone had made possible. Record your own psalm of praise to God, detailing how He has worked in your life in the past and present. Praise Him for the great gift of salvation He has given you in Jesus.

PASS IT ON

Psalm 45 was written as a song of praise to an unnamed king on his wedding day. Moved by the splendor of the occasion, the psalmist sought to express his joy. Read Psalm 45:1–17 in your Bible. Underline verse 17.

> I will cause your name to be remembered for all generations; therefore the peoples will praise you forever and ever.—Psalm 45:17

PONDER THESE QUESTIONS:

- Reread verses 6–7. The writer of Hebrews applied Psalm 45:6–7 directly to Jesus in Hebrews 1:8–9, a passage that stresses Jesus is the focal point of all God has done and, therefore, should be the focal point of the church. How has God revealed everything we need to know about Him in Jesus?

- Why should Jesus be the focal point of the church's worship, theology, and ministry? Explain.

- Return your attention to Psalm 45:17. Originally written about an earthly king, we now know this passage has a deeper messianic meaning. Whose name should we cause to be remembered for all generations?

- What will be the result of Jesus' name being proclaimed throughout generations, according to this passage?

- How would believers truly proclaiming the name of Christ and living like He is the focal point of all they do cause our fallen world to praise Him?

RESPOND

- Evaluate your life. Is Jesus the focal point of your life? If not, repent today.

- Who in your life needs to know about Christ? In what ways can you declare His name this week? Record three ideas in your journal.

- For further study, read Revelation 19:1–10. Learn about when Christ returns and will spend eternity with His redeemed bride, the church.

FORESHADOWING

Today's passages reveal how the person of Christ was foreshadowed in Genesis 14. Abraham was on his way with the plunder from a battle and met Melchizedek, a king and a priest. Read Genesis 14:17–20.

ASK YOURSELF:

- Consider the last sentence of Genesis 14:20. How did Abraham respond to Melchizedek's blessing?

- Tribute is paid from the lesser to the greater authority. With that in mind, what does Abraham giving Melchizedek a tenth of the plunder symbolize?

Now, read Hebrews 7:1–28 in your Bible.

But because He remains forever, He holds His priesthood permanently. Therefore, He is always able to save those who come to God through Him, since He always lives to intercede for them.—Hebrews 7:24–25

ASK YOURSELF:

- The Jews (and the Levitical priests) descended from Abraham, and they thought right standing before God was based on that relationship. But Abraham paid tribute to Melchizedek, recognizing him as superior. How does Jesus' priesthood compare to the Levitical priesthood? Explain.

- According to these verses, what does Jesus offer that the Old Testament priests and sacrifices could not?

- In your own words, explain why Jesus is the ultimate high priest and what that truth means for believers.

RESPOND

Jesus' priesthood is superior to that of the Old Testament priests because His sacrifice is complete and its effects are permanent.

- Jesus became the ultimate High Priest so that our connection with God could be fully restored. Pray and thank Him for making this possible.

- Because He was sinless, Jesus only needed to sacrifice Himself once to cover all our sin, past and present. How will you let this truth change the way you live this week?

THE CONNECTION

Sketch a ladder, then read Genesis 28:10–22 in your Bible.

> And he dreamed: A stairway was set on the ground with its top reaching heaven, and God's angels were going up and down on it.—Genesis 28:12

Jacob was alone and on the run. He was guilty, scared, desperate, and searching for purpose. If you want to know where you fit in this story, know that you and I are just like Jacob. Draw yourself at the bottom of the ladder you sketched earlier. Examine the passage more closely. The word translated "set on the ground" in verse 12 can also mean placed toward the earth. This indicates that the initiative to build a bridge between God and humanity came from God. Think about salvation. How has God made a way for us to have a relationship with Him?

Look at verse 13. Almighty God reigned and ruled from the top of the ladder that night. Today, God is still omnipotent (all powerful), omnipresent (all places), and omniscient (all knowing). Write God at the top of your ladder sketch. Now, for the most remarkable part. Read John 1:51. Early in the Gospel of John, Jesus alluded to Jacob's dream, identifying the One who is the bridge between God and humanity. Underline the name in the verse below.

> Then He said, "I assure you: You will see heaven opened and the angels of God ascending and descending on the Son of Man."—John 1:51

In your sketch, write Jesus' name beside the ladder. He is the Way.

RESPOND
People try many ways to get to God, but the only way we can truly know Him and experience His salvation is through Jesus.

- If you have never placed your faith in Jesus for salvation, don't end your quiet time without considering the gospel.
- Pray and ask God to remind you daily that Jesus is the only way.
- Commit John 14:6 to memory.

GOD DWELLING AMONG US

What do you think of when you hear the word *sanctuary*? Jot down a few ideas.

Perhaps you thought of a specific building, much like the one where you meet to worship God each week. Maybe you thought in broader terms of a place where we encounter God, a safe place, or a holy place.

Read Exodus 25:1–9 in your Bible. Circle the phrase *dwell among them*.

> They are to make a sanctuary for Me so that I may dwell among them.—Exodus 25:8

PONDER THESE QUESTIONS:

- What do these verses reveal about the kind of relationship God wanted to have with His people? Explain.

- In what situations in your life has it been important for you to know that God was present with you? Why?

Now, read Matthew 1:18–25. Underline the name *Immanuel* and its translation.

- How does this verse and the idea of Jesus coming to be God with us connect with the passage you read earlier in Exodus 25? Explain.

- God has always wanted to be present with His people. How did He make that possible for all eternity in Jesus?

RESPOND

Think about some of the people that you know best in this world—they're probably your family, right? Dwelling with someone usually leads to a closer, more intimate relationship.

- In your journal, write a prayer of praise, thanking God that He continues to pursue close contact with you. Thank Him for His Holy Spirit, which dwells inside you today as a believer in Christ.

- In what ways are you seeking to dwell with Christ and get to know your Savior? In your journal, jot down three specific actions you will take this week to invest in your relationship with Him.

OUT OF BONDAGE

Think about the daily life of a slave—always controlled by some other power. *Bondage*, *chains*, *shackles*; all of those words have negative connotations. *Freedom*, on the other hand, carries an incredibly positive connotation. With that in mind, read Exodus 11:1–8 and 12:31–42 in your Bible. Review with the following questions:

- Where were the Israelites at this point in history? What was their social standing? Explain.

- The Hebrew people were living as slaves in Egypt. According to God's words in Exodus 11, who would lead them out of that slavery?

Now, turn to the New Testament and read John 8:31–36.

"A slave does not remain in the household forever, but a son does remain forever. Therefore, if the Son sets you free, you really will be free."—John 8:35–36

- Look at John 8:34. What did Jesus say people were enslaved to?

- Reread John 8:34–36. Who, just as Moses led the Israelites out of slavery in Egypt, did Jesus say would lead those enslaved by sin to freedom? Write the answer in your own words.

RESPOND

Without Christ, we are enslaved to sin. We bow to its desires and commands. It controls our schedules, affects our moods, and keeps us from achieving our purpose of bringing glory to the Father.

- If you're a Christian, ask the Holy Spirit to examine your heart and reveal any sin that has taken root. Resist the urge to ignore or rationalize your sin. Instead, confess it and ask God for forgiveness so your life can once again bring glory to Him.

- Memorize John 8:36. When temptations come your way, remind yourself that sin has no hold over you.

- For further study of this idea, read Romans 6.

NOTHING BUT THE BLOOD

Read Exodus 12:1–28 in your Bible, focusing on verses 12–13. God was going to unleash His wrath upon the people in the form of a plague, but the Israelites could escape the plague if they followed God's command. What was the sign that distinguished them from the Egyptians? Journal in your own words.

The Jews were to sacrifice a lamb and put its blood on the door frames of their houses. The blood would indicate that a sacrifice had been offered on their behalf, while actually placing the blood on their door frames would denote their faith that God's plan was sufficient to save them. With that in mind, read 1 Peter 1:18–21, then compare it to what you learned in Exodus 12.

> For you know that you were redeemed from your empty way of life inherited from the fathers, not with perishable things like silver or gold, but with the precious blood of Christ, like that of a lamb without defect or blemish.—1 Peter 1:18–19

ASK YOURSELF:

- What did the blood accomplish (Exodus 12)?
- What did Jesus' blood accomplish (1 Peter 1)?
- Knowing all of this, how does the Passover point to the redemption God provided through Jesus? Explain.

RESPOND

Jesus became the Passover Lamb for us, covering us with His blood and turning away God's wrath. His sacrifice made a way for our salvation.

- Thank Jesus for willingly laying down His life so that God's wrath toward your sin could be turned away from you.
- First Peter 1:18–19 tells us that Jesus paid a great price, His own blood, to redeem us from our "empty way of life." Evaluate your life. In what ways are you pursuing emptiness rather than things of eternal value? What actions will you take this week to focus your heart and use your time for things of eternal value?

A WAY OUT

Read Numbers 21:4–9 in your Bible. Throughout the Old Testament, a lack of faith characterized the Israelites. Think through these questions:

- How did the Israelites display a lack of faith in God in this passage?

- Rejecting God's provision of food was the same as rejecting His provision of grace. How do people reject God's grace today? Explain.

- What "way out" did God provide for the Israelites? How was the snake a symbol of His grace and deliverance?

Flip over in your Bible to John 3:11–15. In this passage, Jesus referenced the symbol of the bronze snake in the desert as He was talking with Nicodemus about being born again.

> "Just as Moses lifted up the snake in the wilderness, so the Son of Man must be lifted up, so that everyone who believes in Him will have eternal life."—John 3:14–15

The Israelites who looked upon the bronze snake in Moses' day were saved from death because they trusted God and placed their faith in the way of salvation He had graciously provided. Jesus declared that He too would be lifted up and those who placed their faith in Him would escape judgment and experience eternal life.

RESPOND

Just like the bronze snake, Jesus was lifted high on the cross, offering His sinless life to atone for our sin. Those who place their faith in Him will be healed from the brokenness of their sin. Salvation isn't about what you can do, but what Jesus has already done. As Christians, it's sometimes easy to make your life about what you can do to make God love you more or make yourself more deserving of His grace. To do so is to be like the Israelites, looking at what was provided and rejecting it. Rest in what Jesus has done today. Record a prayer of commitment in your journal.

COVERED

The Day of Atonement was an important day for the Israelites. It was a time for the people to come together and confess their sin so it could be atoned for by the high priest. Consider what preparations were necessary as you compare Leviticus 16:1–34 and Hebrews 9:1–10. Record your notes.

Leviticus 16:1–34

- Who or what took on the penalty the people deserved?

- What made atonement for the peoples' sins?

Hebrews 9:1–10

- Who or what took on the penalty the people deserved?

- What made atonement for the peoples' sins?

Now, focus on Hebrews 9:12–15.

> For if the blood of goats and bulls and the ashes of a young cow, sprinkling those who are defiled, sanctify for the purification of the flesh, how much more will the blood of the Messiah, who through the eternal Spirit offered Himself without blemish to God, cleanse our consciences from dead works to serve the living God?—Hebrews 9:13–14

ASK YOURSELF:

- According to these verses, what is Jesus' blood able to do that the blood of the Old Testament sacrifices could not? Explain.

- Consider verse 15. What did Jesus do to liberate people from the sin that holds them hostage?

RESPOND

Jesus' sacrifice has accomplished what the Old Testament sacrifices never could. The sinless Son of God shed His own blood so that our sin could be atoned for and our consciences cleansed. Jesus' sacrifice cleanses our consciences and moves us from a life of sin to eternal life with God. Praise Him for what He has done today!

GUIDING LIGHT

People turn to all sorts of things when looking for guidance. What are some places you've seen people turn to when they needed to know what to do? Journal about all that apply.

friends	prayer
parents	Internet
horoscope	coach/trusted mentor
books	psychic

Now, read Exodus 13:17–22 in your Bible. As you read, look for what guided the Israelites on their journey. Underline it when you find it. Answer these questions:

- Look at the words you underlined in your Bible. Who used these things to guide the Israelites?

- Why is it important that God was the One leading the people? Explain.

- At night, God led the Israelites with a pillar of fire, a bright beacon that would lead them out of the dark. Now, read John 8:12. Underline any imagery that seems familiar from Exodus 13.

Then Jesus spoke to them again: "I am the light of the world. Anyone who follows Me will never walk in the darkness but will have the light of life."—John 8:12

ASK YOURSELF:

- What does this verse have in common with what you read earlier in Exodus 13? Explain.

- What does it mean to say Jesus is the light of the world? If He is light, then what is the darkness?

RESPOND

- Take a moment to prayerfully examine your life. Does your life—your actions, words, thoughts—shine with the light of Christ? Why or why not? Are you allowing darkness to rule in any way? Confess anything the Holy Spirit reveals and ask God to help you make the necessary changes.

- If Jesus is the light of our lives, He is the One who leads us. We align our lives with His purpose and live according to His example, especially in the way we interact with others. Think about your relationships. Have you treated people in ways that reflect more dark-ness than light? Are there any relationships you need His light to shine upon? Commit those relationships to prayer. Ask God for boldness and courage to make the changes you need to make.

FOOD FOR THE SOUL

For centuries, bread has been a staple food because it sustains and satisfies. Think about this idea as you read Exodus 16:1–15 in your Bible.

> When the Israelites saw it, they asked one another, "What is it?" because they didn't know what it was. Moses told them, "It is the bread the LORD has given you to eat."
> —Exodus 16:15

DIG DEEPER WITH THESE QUESTIONS:
- Who provided the manna for the Israelites to eat? What does that reveal about God's character? About His relationship with the people?
- How is God's provision of manna another example of His provision and grace toward them? Explain.

In the wilderness, God met the Israelites' physical need with manna. He graciously provided enough to satisfy them each day. Now, read John 6:35–51 in your Bible. Focus on John 6:32.

> Jesus said to them, "I assure you: Moses didn't give you the bread from heaven, but My Father gives you the real bread from heaven."—John 6:32

ASK YOURSELF:
- What does this passage have to do with manna? Explain.
- According to Jesus, what is the real bread from heaven that God provides?
- How does Jesus meet our deepest spiritual need? Explain.

RESPOND
The bread God provided for the Israelites could only satisfy temporarily, but pointed to the One who satisfies completely.

- Do you look to Jesus for complete fulfillment? He is the only thing that will never leave you spiritually hungry. Examine your life for ways you are trying to find satisfaction other than in Christ. Confess these things today. Ask God for a deeper understanding that Jesus is more than enough.
- Who in your life is trying to build their lives on a foundation that isn't eternal? Maybe he or she is involved in a faith that doesn't center on the gospel or believes that eternal security lies in education, power, or money. What steps will you take this week to share the eternal Bread of Life with him or her?

JESUS BECAME FLESH

The Gospel of John uses a variety of names to describe Jesus. One of the names it uses for Jesus is "the Word." Read John 1:14 below.

> The Word became flesh and took up residence among us. We observed His glory, the glory as the One and Only Son from the Father, full of grace and truth.—John 1:14

Jesus existed before the beginning of time. He is God, the Son. He is full of glory. What does it mean for Him to take up residence among us? Take a moment to journal a few thoughts.

Now, read John 1:1–18 in your Bible. As you read, circle any words or phrases that were used to describe Jesus.

THINK THROUGH THESE QUESTIONS:

- List some of the words that you circled in today's passage.

- What do these words reveal about Jesus, His character, and His purpose? Explain.

- Read verse 18 again. What does it mean to say that Jesus has revealed the Father? How does He do that?

- Look over the words you circled one more time. How do they further illustrate that Jesus reflects the nature of God? Explain.

Because Jesus is God, He was able to reveal God and His character in a way people had never experienced before.

RESPOND

- Meditate on the nature of Jesus: fully human, yet fully God. What difference does it make in your life today that God became flesh? Record your prayerful response in your journal.

- Ponder this thought: *Through Jesus, we received God's clearest message. In Jesus, we see the very heart of God.* Respond in your journal.

- For further study, meditate on John 14:7–11.

LIKE US

Why would Jesus—the Holy Son of God—humble Himself to come live among us? Read Philippians 2:5–11 in your Bible to discover the answer. As you read, circle the phrases that indicate Jesus' divine nature. Draw a box around the WORDS that point to His humanity.

> Make your own attitude that of Christ Jesus, who, existing in the form of God, did not consider equality with God as something to be used for His own advantage. Instead He emptied Himself by assuming the form of a slave, taking on the likeness of men.
> —Philippians 2:5–7

ASK YOURSELF:

- Consider verse 6. What does it mean to say Jesus has equality with God? Journal in your own words.

- Think about Jesus' divinity. What rights, privileges, and glory did He give up to live among us? Explain.

- Why is it important that Jesus was both God and man? Explain.

- Look at verse 8. What was the reason Jesus took on our humanity and came to live among us? Why is that important?

RESPOND

Jesus is God. He has the exact nature of God, yet He became like us so that we can have a relationship with the Father. Jesus emptied Himself to take on the role of a slave. Keep that same attitude yourself. Look for ways you can serve others today. Record two ideas in your journal.

JESUS CONQUERED DEATH

The Bible teaches that death is a consequence of sin (Romans 6:23). But Jesus' incarnation even has an effect on death. Read Hebrews 2:5–18 in your Bible to learn more. Underline what Jesus' death accomplished when you read it.

And free those who were held in slavery all their lives by the fear of death.—Hebrews 2:15

ANSWER THESE QUESTIONS:
- What do these verses help you better understand about Jesus, His divinity, superiority, or the reason He came?
- Reread verses 14–15. In your own words, outline the reasons Jesus came to live among us.
- In His sinless life, sacrificial death, and glorious resurrection, Jesus has defeated sin's power over us and abolished the fear of death. While death still occurs, believers no longer have to live in fear of it. Why? What hope do we have that non-Christians don't? Explain.

Jesus became a man. He suffered and died on the cross. His death paid the penalty of sin, and His resurrection provided a way for eternal life. Those who follow Jesus will still face an earthly death, but will spend eternity with Him.

RESPOND
- Many people list death among their greatest fears. Consider your own thoughts on death. How does the promise of eternal life affect those fears? Be honest with God about your fears as you list them in your journal. To close your prayer and express your trust in Him, write JESUS in large letters on top of the list.
- Scripture teaches that sin and the fear of its consequences can enslave us. Ask the Holy Spirit to reveal any sin you are allowing to have control over you. Boldly confess these sins, seeking forgiveness and placing your trust in what Jesus has already done to set you free.
- For further study of Jesus' power over death, read John 11 and 1 Corinthians 15.

JESUS FREES US FROM SIN

Consider the definition of condemnation in your journal. What words come to mind when you think about the word *condemned*?

The truth is, we're all condemned. We have all broken God's laws, and the law condemns us of our sin. But the story doesn't end there. Read Romans 8:1–11 in your Bible. Underline any form of the word *condemned* when you read it.

> What the law could not do since it was limited by the flesh, God did. He condemned sin in the flesh by sending His own Son in flesh like ours under sin's domain, and as a sin offering, in order that the law's requirement would be accomplished in us who do not walk according to the flesh but according to the Spirit.—Romans 8:3–4

The law reveals the kind of life that pleases God, but it can't empower us to live that way. The law can do nothing about our sin, and we are incapable of living a life that pleases God in our own strength.

ASK YOURSELF:
- Read verses 3 and 4 again. How has God condemned sin? Explain.
- What's the difference between following a bunch of rules to earn God's favor and trusting Jesus to make you pleasing to God?
- Which of those understandings best describes you? Why?

RESPOND
- Even as believers, it's easy for us to make following Christ about a bunch of rules—good things we strive to do in our own strength to earn God's favor. Ask the Holy Spirit to reveal any way you are trying to do that today. Confess these things and choose once again to rest in Jesus' finished work.
- Memorize Romans 8:1. Any time you feel condemned by your sin, speak the verse aloud, remembering what Jesus has done for you.

EMPOWERED FOR RIGHTEOUSNESS

How do people describe you? Jot down a few ideas.

So, what did people say about Jesus? Peter was one of Jesus' closest followers. Read how Peter described Jesus in 1 Peter 2:21–25. Then, focus your attention on verse 24.

> He Himself bore our sins in His body on the tree, so that, having died to sins, we might live for righteousness; you have been healed by His wounds.—1 Peter 2:24

PONDER THESE QUESTIONS:

- Underline the phrase *bore our sins* in verse 24. How would you explain this idea in your own words?

- Jesus took the consequences of our sin upon Himself and died in our place to make atonement for our sin. Because of this, sin no longer has power over those who have a relationship with Jesus. According to verse 24, how should that change the way we live?

- As Christians, sin should no longer define our lives. Righteousness should characterize our lives as believers. Does it characterize your life? Why or why not?

RESPOND

- Think about how well you are reflecting Christ's life of righteousness. If you are known more for your athletic accomplishments, academic achievements, or anything else than for your walk with Christ, pray that Jesus would empower you to live for righteousness.

- Look at your calendar or write down the highlights of your schedule for the rest of this week. Where will you go? Who will you see? What will you do? List ways you will choose to live in righteousness as you go about your daily routine.

TEMPTED

In the incarnation, Jesus was both God and man. How exactly that worked is something our finite minds have trouble comprehending. Knowing Jesus is divine, it's tempting to think that life on earth was somehow easier for Him or that He doesn't really know what it's like to be us. But the fact of His humanity and Scripture tell us otherwise. Read Hebrews 4:14–16 in your Bible.

> For we do not have a high priest who is unable to sympathize with our weaknesses, but One who has been tested in every way as we are, yet without sin. Therefore let us approach the throne of grace with boldness, so that we may receive mercy and find grace to help us at the proper time.—Hebrews 4:15–16

ASK YOURSELF:

- How does this passage acknowledge Jesus' divinity? How does it point to His humanity?

- Why is it important that Jesus faced temptation, just as you do? Explain.

- Jesus faced temptation, yet didn't sin. As a Christian, why is that important? How does this affect the way you respond to temptation? Explain.

- Because Jesus sympathizes with our weakness, we can approach His throne of grace. How do we do that?

RESPOND

Believers have the power to resist temptation and flee from sin in Jesus.

- Identify the recurring temptations in your life. Maybe it relates to lust or pornography; lying to your parents or cheating at school. Maybe it involves failing to stand for Christ in front of your friends. Write a commitment in your journal: When I face _____, I will ask Jesus for the strength to overcome.

- You probably have Christian friends who are currently struggling with temptations. Who needs to be reminded of the power he or she has in Christ to resist? What steps will you take to do so this week? Jot down two steps in your journal.

- For further study of temptation, read Luke 4:1–13 and James 1.

JESUS IS TRUTH

Throughout history, the church has faced a number of false teachings, many centered around Jesus, His role, and His incarnation. Think about the misconceptions about Jesus that people have today. Circle all that apply and list a few of your own in your journal.

Just a teacher	One of many ways to God
Not that important	Wasn't really resurrected
Just a historical figure	Not who He says He is

So, what does the truth of Jesus' incarnation have to do with fighting false teaching? Read 1 John 4:1–6 in your Bible.

> This is how you know the Spirit of God: Every spirit who confesses that Jesus Christ has come in the flesh is from God.—1 John 4:2

What does this verse teach you about how to separate correct teaching from false teaching? Journal in your own words.

Now, read 2 John 1:7.

> Many deceivers have gone out into the world; they do not confess the coming of Jesus Christ in the flesh.—2 John 1:7

ASK YOURSELF:

- What message did John say "deceivers" carry into the world? Explain.

- All week, you've studied Scripture about the incarnation—that Jesus became flesh and lived among us. Why do you think John emphasizes that belief in the incarnation is a way you can know if someone is speaking by the Spirit of God?

- Why would denying the incarnation be detrimental to the gospel?

RESPOND

Listen carefully to the messages you hear about Jesus today. Whether from discussions at school, things you hear on the radio, or messages from a teacher at church, what do they teach about Jesus? Consider: Does this message affirm that Jesus was God in flesh? Or is it some false message?

WHO'S READY?

Scripture tells us that God sent a special prophet, John the Baptist, into the world to prepare His people for the coming Messiah. Learn more about John in Luke 1:2–25, 57–66.

> And he will go before Him in the spirit and power of Elijah, to turn the hearts of fathers to their children, and the disobedient to the understanding of the righteous, to make ready for the Lord a prepared people.—Luke 1:17

CONSIDER THESE QUESTIONS:

- Reread Zechariah's response to the angel in verses 5–25. Was Zechariah ready for the message? How do you know? Explain.

- Were Zechariah and Elizabeth's neighbors and families ready for the truth about John? Why or why not?

- Focus on verse 17. Elijah was one of the most revered Old Testament prophets whose ministry was centered on calling the people back to God and His righteous ways. John would do the same. Why is this important?

RESPOND

- God had a purpose for John, and He has a plan for you, too. Pray that you will grow in relationship with God and walk according to His ways and wisdom and fulfill His purpose for your life.

- Knowing God's purpose for your life is intricately tied to knowing Him. What specific steps will you take this week to grow in relationship with Him? List two of those steps.

- Think about how you came into a relationship with Jesus. How did the Holy Spirit prepare you? Who did God use to bring you close to Him? Record your thoughts in your journal. End in a time of prayer, thanking God for pursuing you.

- For further study of how others responded to God's call, read Genesis 22:11, Exodus 3:4, and 1 Samuel 3:10.

WITHOUT FEAR

What do you think of when you hear the word *rescue*? What images or words come to mind? Sketch or list a few of them.

Now, read Luke 1:67–80 in your Bible. These verses are Zechariah's prophecy after the birth of his son, John the Baptist. Focus on verses 73–75.

> He has given us the privilege, since we have been rescued from our enemies' clutches, to serve Him without fear in holiness and righteousness in His presence all our days.
> —Luke 1:73–75

ASK YOURSELF:

- Underline the word *rescued* in the verses above. What did Jesus rescue us from? Draw a circle around your answer.

- The Jews pictured salvation as rescue from political enemies, but God's salvation is about being free to serve Him without hindrance or fear.

- How does sin create hindrances and fear in serving God? Explain.

- When sin reigns in our lives, we cannot pursue any kind of holiness or righteousness. How do you know this to be true?

- Mull over verses 76–77. Why is it important to understand that God's salvation is centered on the forgiveness of sin? Explain.

RESPOND

Without Jesus, you are a slave to sin. But in Jesus, He has given you the power to not sin! You won't be perfect, but sin doesn't have power over you.

- Evaluate your life. Against what sins do you feel powerless? Have you asked Christ to help? Do so right now.

- Thank Jesus for what He has done to free you from sin and allow you to serve God without hindrance. Record your prayer in your journal.

- When we are mired in sin, we sometimes become afraid of how God will react if we're honest with Him about that sin. He already knows. Be honest, confess your sin, and seek His forgiveness.

WILLING SERVANT

Read Luke 1:26–38 in your Bible. Answer the questions that follow.

> Now listen: You will conceive and give birth to a son, and you will call His name Jesus.—Luke 1:31

ASK YOURSELF:

- What did you observe about Mary and her character in these verses?

- What did you learn about Jesus? Be specific.

- How did Gabriel's words reveal that Jesus is the fulfillment of prophecy? Explain.

Now, focus on Luke 1:38. Underline the word *slave*.

> "I am the Lord's slave," said Mary. "May it be done to me according to your word." —Luke 1:38

Mary's response in verse 38 was a declaration of commitment and submission. She humbled herself before God and was ready to do whatever He asked of her.

RESPOND

Mary's role in God's plan to bring the Messiah into the world wasn't going to be easy. She would never have a "normal" life and risked losing the respect of her family and friends because of her pregnancy. Even so, Mary trusted God's plan and vowed to serve Him.

- Mary's obedience to God risked her relationship with her family and friends and caused her to set aside her plans for her life. If you can honestly do so, write your commitment to obey God, even when you don't understand. If you can't, admit anything that is keeping you from doing so. Ask God to give you willingness to follow wherever He leads.

- Is there something you know God has called you to do, yet you haven't obeyed Him? What steps will you take to obey Him this week? Pray that He would give you the courage and strength to obey Him.

- Memorize Luke 1:38, praying that God will help you respond to Him in the same way.

DO NOT BE AFRAID

What are your plans for today? For this week? For after high school? Circle one of these topics and outline the main points of your plan.

Now, read Matthew 1:18–25 in your Bible. As you read, look for Joseph's plan for how he would respond to Mary's pregnancy. Underline it when you read it.

> So her husband Joseph, being a righteous man, and not wanting to disgrace her publicly, decided to divorce her secretly.—Matthew 1:19

DIG DEEPER WITH THESE QUESTIONS:

- What were the main points of Joseph's plan? What does Joseph's plan reveal about his character? Explain.

- Joseph had a sensible plan to deal with Mary's pregnancy, but God changed all of that. How did His plan differ from Joseph's?

- When have you seen God completely change someone's plans? What did you learn from that experience?

- Do you have trouble being obedient to God when His plan doesn't seem to make sense to you? Why or why not?

RESPOND

Even though Joseph didn't understand what God was doing, he trusted God and actively obeyed Him.

- What is God calling you to do that doesn't make sense? What circumstances in your life seem confusing or senseless? Ask God to help you trust Him and obey Him in those situations, even when His plan is unclear.

- Think about the plans you are already making—for today, this week, for the rest of your life. Lay these plans down before God, asking Him to guide and direct your steps as you seek His wisdom. Record your commitment in your journal using the following format: *Lord, my life is Yours. Guide me in Your wisdom and help me to honor You in all I do.*

GOD'S PLAN

God's preparation for salvation through Jesus didn't begin there. It began before the foundations of the earth. Read Galatians 4:4–7 in your Bible. Pay attention to words or phrases that denote the eternal nature of God's plan to redeem His children.

> When the time came to completion, God sent His Son, born of a woman, born under the law, to redeem those under the law, so that we might receive adoption as sons. . . . So you are no longer a slave but a son, and if a son, then an heir through God.—Galatians 4:4–5, 7

"When the time came to completion" is sometimes translated as the fullness of time. From the beginning, God knew the exact moment Jesus would need to come to live among us.

ASK YOURSELF:

- What does this teach you about God's intentionality and His desire to redeem us? About the importance of Jesus' incarnation?

- Ponder verse 5 and underline the two things Jesus came to do. What did Jesus do to redeem us? Explain in your own words.

- Why is it important to recognize that we can only become God's children through His gift of Jesus, not our own merit or effort?

- What is the difference between a slave and a son? Explain.

RESPOND

From eternity, God's plan was redemption through Jesus—His birth, life, death, and resurrection. Eternal salvation is available, but we must respond to His invitation. God's timing is perfect. He knew the exact moment Jesus needed to come into the world, and He can be trusted with your life. Pray right now over circumstances in your life where you feel like God is silent, too slow, or too fast. Ask Him to help you trust Him and His purposes.

HE IS FAITHFUL

Read Luke 1:39–45 in your Bible. Elizabeth, the mother of John the Baptist, and Mary were related. Soon after Gabriel had informed Mary that she would be the Messiah's mother, Mary went to visit Elizabeth, who was pregnant with John. Reread Elizabeth's response when Mary arrived. How did she respond to Mary and the good news of the child Mary was carrying?

Note the number of times Elizabeth used the word *blessed*. Elizabeth was affirming the great thing God was doing through Mary. Mary's blessedness depended entirely upon the identity and greatness of her child, Jesus. Elizabeth was pointing praise to God, the One who was acting in time and space to make salvation possible. Read Mary's response in Luke 1:46–56.

> And Mary said: My soul proclaims the greatness of the Lord, and my spirit has rejoiced in God my Savior, because He has looked with favor on the humble condition of His slave. Surely, from now on all generations will call me blessed, because the Mighty One has done great things for me, and His name is holy.—Luke 1:46–49

ASK YOURSELF:

- What aspects of God's character did Mary praise in these verses? Explain.

- Look at verses 54–55. Mary declared that God had been faithful to keep His promise of the Savior, the promise He had given to Abraham. How have you seen God's faithfulness in your life? Be specific.

- How does knowing that God is faithful help you to trust Him more?

RESPOND

- Think about how God has been faithful to you in Jesus. How does God's faithfulness inspire your praise? Using Luke 1:46–56 as a model, record your own prayer or song of praise to God in your journal.

- Mary pointed to a time when "all generations" would give praise to God because of the blessing He had given to them in Jesus. Think about your generation—your peers, classmates, and teens around the world. How will you share the blessing God has given us in Jesus with your generation? Pray about this and record any action steps the Holy Spirit reveals.

SPEAKING TRUTH

Over the course of this week, you've studied how God faithfully prepared the world for the promised Messiah. Even so, Jesus came into a world that doubted God's faithfulness, questioned Jesus' identity and purpose, or downright scoffed at His good news of salvation. For a better picture of this, read Acts 13:16–40.

> And we ourselves proclaim to you the good news of the promise that was made to our ancestors. God has fulfilled this for us, their children, by raising up Jesus, as it is written in the second Psalm: You are My Son; today I have become Your Father.—Acts 13:32–33

While all of the rest of this week's devotions occurred before Jesus' birth, this passage happened after His death, resurrection, and ascension. Paul and Barnabas had gone into the synagogue at Antioch to share the good news that Jesus was the Messiah.

ASK YOURSELF:

- How did Paul tie Jesus to these Old Testament events? How did Paul present Jesus as the Messiah?

- Ponder verses 38–39. Paul proclaimed that through Jesus' life, death, and resurrection, God had provided forgiveness of sin and the only way humanity could be set free from sin. Why is this message still vital today?

- Think about the response discussed in verses 40–41. How does the world continue to scoff at the gospel today?

RESPOND

Paul was speaking to a group of people who didn't want to hear the gospel because it was offensive and revealed hard truths about their sin nature.

- Who are the people in your world who have heard the gospel, yet continue to reject Jesus?

- How can you be faithful to the truth of the gospel and share it with them this week? Ask God to give the courage and willingness to share and to provide opportunities to do so.

- When do you feel most threatened because of your faith? Pray about these situations, asking God to help you remain faithful to the gospel.

PROMISED ONE

Read Micah 5:2 in your Bible.

> Bethlehem Ephrathah, you are small among the clans of Judah; One will come from you to be ruler over Israel for Me. His origin is from antiquity, from eternity.—Micah 5:2

What two things does this verse reveal about the promised Messiah?

Micah 5:2 declares that the Messiah will come from Bethlehem, while simultaneously pointing to His eternal nature. While the Jews knew what the prophets had said about the coming Messiah, they had been waiting for His arrival for centuries. Knowing this, read Luke 2:6–7 in your Bible.

> While they were there, the time came for her to give birth. Then she gave birth to her firstborn Son, and she wrapped Him snugly in cloth and laid Him in a feeding trough—because there was no room for them at the lodging place.—Luke 2:6–7

THINK THROUGH THE FOLLOWING QUESTIONS:

- How do these verses reveal that Jesus was the promised Messiah mentioned in Micah 5:2?

- Why is it important that the divine Son of God was laid in a manger? What does that communicate about God's character? About Jesus?

RESPOND

Taken together, Micah 5:2 and Luke 2:1–7 record God's fulfillment of prophecy and attest to Jesus' deity and the eternal nature of God's plan of redemption through Jesus.

- Mull over these thoughts: God planned salvation before the foundation of the earth. Long before I existed, God was making a way for me to know Him and spend eternity with Him. Record your response in your journal.

- Revel in the humility and humanity of Jesus' birth. The Holy One of heaven was laid in a lowly manger. Thank God for a Savior willing to set aside the riches He rightfully deserved so that you might be saved.

GOOD NEWS

Read Luke 2:8–20 in your Bible. Underline the good news in these verses when you read it.

> Today a Savior, who is Messiah the Lord, was born for you in the city of David.
> —Luke 2:11

At this point in history, shepherds were among the least respected members of society. Thought to be dishonest, shepherds were also considered ceremonially unclean according to the law. Therefore, they lived on the outskirts of town and were prohibited from worshiping at the temple.

ASK YOURSELF:

- Knowing how shepherds were regarded, why is it striking that they were the first people to hear the good news of Jesus' birth? Why is that important?

- The shepherds were outcasts, yet God specifically chose to tell them about Jesus first. What does that help you to understand about God? About salvation? Explain.

- Verse 10 proclaims that the good news of the Messiah's birth was for all people. Why is that important to note?

- Consider verse 11. The angel said that the Messiah was born for "you." Why is it crucial that we understand that Jesus invites us to a personal relationship with Him?

RESPOND

Who are the outcasts in your school, community, or world? These are the people you think would be least likely to come to Christ. Ask God to help you love them as He does. Pray specifically for them, by name, this week.

WISE MEN

Read Matthew 2:1–2 in your Bible.

> After Jesus was born in Bethlehem of Judea in the days of King Herod, wise men from the east arrived unexpectedly in Jerusalem, saying, "Where is He who has been born King of the Jews? For we saw His star in the east and have come to worship Him."—Matthew 2:1–2

Sometimes called magi, the wise men were astrologers (people who studied the stars and their movements) who held great influence and power in their culture. They likely knew something about the Old Testament because they knew to be looking for the Messiah. They were also Gentiles. Compare the wise men's reaction to the news of the Messiah's birth with that of Herod and the Jewish religious leaders in today's passage:

Wise men

Herod

The Gentile wise men saw the signs that the Messiah had been born and sought to worship Him. Meanwhile, the Jewish religious leaders and Herod, who should have been looking for the Messiah, apparently missed the star and were disturbed by the suggestion that the Messiah had been born.

ASK YOURSELF:
- What does that teach you about the hearts of the Jewish people and their relationship with God at this point?
- The wise men were the latest in a long line of unlikely Gentiles who sought to worship the Messiah. What does this fact reveal about God's salvation? Explain your answer.

RESPOND
- Which attitude best fits the way you regard Jesus: the wise men's or Herod's? Why?
- If you currently feel more like Herod and the Jewish religious leaders—frightened or resistant to how Jesus is trying to work in your life—be honest with God. Genuinely ask Him to change your heart and help you trust Him to do what He needs to do in your life.
- Because the wise men were Gentiles, the Jews considered them outsiders. Who in your life do you see as an outsider or undeserving of God's grace? Ask God to change your heart toward these people.

TRANSFORMED LIVES

The wise men were educated, likely powerful, and definitely influential. They seemed like they had it all together and had everything going for them. Read Matthew 2:9–12 to learn the rest of the wise men's story.

> Entering the house, they saw the child with Mary His mother, and falling to their knees, they worshiped Him. Then they opened their treasures and presented Him with gifts: gold, frankincense, and myrrh.—Matthew 2:11

The wise men had been searching for signs that the Messiah had come. Reread verse 10. How did the wise men respond when they saw the star?

Now, examine verses 11–12. When you worship something, you recognize its importance or worthiness. You don't accidentally worship.

ASK YOURSELF:

- What does the wise men's willingness to worship Jesus reveal about their understanding of His importance or worthiness? Explain.

- Out of their worship, the wise men were moved to offer Jesus extravagant gifts. When has your worship of Jesus caused you to give Him something that cost you?

RESPOND

The wise men were drawn to Jesus, and they responded with worship. When you truly recognize Jesus for who He is, it brings you to a place of worship and transformation.

- The wise men were drawn to Jesus and responded in worship. Jesus is still calling people to Himself today, inviting us to a new way of life. You must choose how you will respond to His invitation: like the wise men or like Herod. How will you respond today?

- Is your worship all about what you get out of it? Or does it ever involve you giving something—your pride, your fears, your dreams, your time—back to God? If your worship is all about what you get from it, admit this attitude to God and ask Him to change your heart so you can worship Him.

- What steps will you take to share the gospel with them this week? Jot down two names in your journal.

EXPECTATION

Think back to when you had to wait a long time to get something you really wanted, whether it was getting the latest iPhone or a long-held dream be fulfilled. Record a few thoughts in your journal.

Remembering how that felt, read Luke 2:22–32 in your Bible.

> Now, Master, You can dismiss Your slave in peace, as You promised. For my eyes have seen Your salvation. You have prepared it in the presence of all peoples—a light for revelation to the Gentiles and glory to Your people Israel.—Luke 2:29–32

Simeon was a very devout Jewish man who had been waiting in expectation to see the Messiah. Through the work of the Holy Spirit, Simeon knew that God would not let him die until he saw the Promised One. He believed God's promise and had built his life upon it.

ASK YOURSELF:

- Simeon's life was marked by an expectation and trust that God is who He says He is and will do what He has promised. Is yours marked by a similar expectation? Why or why not?

- Consider Simeon's blessing of Jesus in verses 29–32. How would Jesus be a light to the Gentiles and glory to the Jews? Explain it in your own words.

- When he saw Jesus, Simeon knew he had seen the Messiah. More than that, he understood that the salvation God would provide through Jesus was available to all people, Jew or Gentile (v. 32).

RESPOND

Consolation is a word that means comfort or hope. Simeon knew that Jesus was the source of true hope. He is the only One who can give our lives purpose and the only way to be saved.

- Jesus' salvation is available to all people, but we must respond to His invitation. Have you placed your faith in Jesus?

- Think about the difficult circumstances in your life, the situations where you don't understand what God is doing or how He could work in them. Ask God to help you trust Him in those situations.

REJECTED

After blessing Jesus, Simeon spoke directly to Mary. Read his words in Luke 2:33–35.

> Then Simeon blessed them and told His mother Mary: "Indeed, this child is destined to cause the fall and rise of many in Israel and to be a sign that will be opposed—and a sword will pierce your own soul—that the thoughts of many hearts may be revealed."—Luke 2:34–35

PONDER THESE QUESTIONS:

- Imagine Mary standing there in the temple with her newborn Son, listening to Simeon's words. What emotions might she have felt in that moment? Explain.
- Even at this early point in Jesus' earthly life, Simeon was declaring that Jesus and His message would be controversial. How is this still true today? Give examples.
- How can we continue to live for Christ and share the gospel in a world that is still rejecting Him? List a few ideas.

RESPOND

- We live in a world that still actively rejects Jesus and His gospel. Who in your life has heard the gospel many times but continues to reject God's gracious gift? Pray for those people this week, asking God to soften their hearts.
- When you face a lot of rejection, it's tempting to want to water down the gospel so it's less controversial. In your journal, record your commitment to stay true to the gospel no matter what the world thinks.

SHARE THE GOOD NEWS

Think about the older believers in your life, even senior citizens. Who is the best example of what it means to be a godly man or woman? Why? What characteristics does he or she display? Journal a few thoughts.

Now, read Anna's story in Luke 2:36–38. A prophetess, Anna had lived a long life and had spent it in service to God. As you read, underline the actions that display Anna's faithful service to the Lord.

> At that very moment, she came up and began to thank God and to speak about Him to all who were looking forward to the redemption of Jerusalem.—Luke 2:38

THINK THROUGH THE FOLLOWING QUESTIONS:

- Anna's life was marked by her devotion to God. Her faith and trust in Him shaped every part of her life. Could the same be said of you? Why or why not?

- Anna's faithfulness wasn't confined to her actions. When she saw that the Messiah had come, she shared her hope with others. Why is it important that we not only live the gospel, but also talk about it when God gives us opportunities?

RESPOND

- Anna saw the Messiah and couldn't keep the good news to herself. Who in your life needs to hear the gospel? What steps will you take this week to live and speak the gospel into that person's life? Write two in your journal.

- You can choose right now to begin living a life completely devoted to the Lord. What steps will you take to learn more about Him, grow closer to Him, and serve Him? Write a list in your journal.

- Consider godly older Christians whose lives have been well lived for the Lord. Pray about asking one of them to mentor you.

TAKE FLIGHT

Read Matthew 2:13–23 in your Bible.

> So he got up, took the child and His mother during the night, and escaped to Egypt. He stayed there until Herod's death, so that what was spoken by the Lord through the prophet might be fulfilled: Out of Egypt I called My Son.—Matthew 2:14–15

In your journal, write any phrases from the passage where you think Joseph might have wondered what he should do.

ASK YOURSELF:

- What did you learn about Joseph's character in these verses? Explain.

- Once again, Joseph set an example of trusting and obeying God, even when God's plan may have seemed confusing or frightening. Who has been a good example of that kind of trust in your life? Why?

- Reread today's passage, underlining every instance the Bible says something in the story fulfilled prophecy. Why is it important that these events in Jesus' life fulfilled prophecy about the Messiah?

- How do these fulfilled prophecies show that what may seem like a detour in Jesus' story was actually part of God's eternal plan? Explain.

RESPOND

- Ponder the situations you're currently facing that seem like a detour from what you thought your life would be like or what God had planned for you. How will you actively choose to trust and obey Him in those circumstances? List two action points in your journal.

- Jesus' flight into Egypt and the return to Nazareth fulfilled prophecy and further identified Him as the Messiah. This gave His earthly ministry legitimacy. How might your current circumstances or your past testimony serve as preparation for the ministry God has for you in the future? Record your response in your journal.

WITH AUTHORITY

Knowing the definition of authority, what kinds of things were you an authority about at age twelve? What could you talk about with absolute authority? List a few ideas in your journal.

At age twelve, most of us do not have strong understandings of much. The same can't be said of Jesus. Read Luke 2:41–47 in your Bible.

> And all those who heard Him were astounded at His understanding and His answers.
> —Luke 2:47

It was common for rabbis to sit in the temple courts and discuss theology with interested listeners. But it was not common for children to take part in those conversations, much less amaze the crowd with their understanding.

ASK YOURSELF:
- What does this event in Jesus' earthly life teach you about His wisdom? His authority? Explain.

- Why would Jesus have had authority to speak about matters of theological importance, even as a child? Journal in your own words.

- How does this event help you to further understand that Jesus was no ordinary man? Explain.

RESPOND
- Are you astounded by Jesus' wisdom and authority or bored and distracted? In your journal, record a prayer, asking God to give you a deep hunger for His ways.

- Evaluate your life. Are you acknowledging Jesus as the sole authority in your life?

- Even as a Christian, it's easy to try to be the authority in our own lives. Ask God to reveal any ways you are trying to wrestle control from Him. Confess these things today.

PRIORITY ONE

Jesus' experience at the temple revealed more than His wisdom and authority. It also revealed His priority and focus. Read Luke 2:48–52 in your Bible.

> "Why were you searching for Me?" He asked them. "Didn't you know that I had to be in My Father's house?"—Luke 2:49

Mary and Joseph had known Jesus was no ordinary child since before His birth, but Scripture's relative silence about His childhood seems to suggest that it was pretty normal. Now after years of normalcy, Jesus' divine nature broke in again.

THINK THROUGH THESE QUESTIONS:

- Why do you think Mary and Joseph were astonished by Jesus? Explain.

- Mull over Jesus' response to His parents in verse 49. How would you write it in your own words?

- What does verse 49 teach you about Jesus' identity and His understanding of His mission?

RESPOND

Jesus understood that He was God's Son and that His life should be devoted to the things that mattered to God. As believers, Jesus hasn't asked us to make Him one of many priorities in our lives. He is to be our priority. He is the lens through which we view everything and the One who shapes our actions, words, relationships—everything in our lives.

- Evaluate your life. What are you devoted to? What absorbs most of your thoughts or time? Where do you spend most of your money? What is most important to you? Be honest as you list your thoughts in your journal.

- If this examination reveals that something other than God is your primary focus, confess and repent today. Ask God to help you make the necessary changes to center your life on Him.

LAMB OF GOD

Apart from Luke's recounting of Jesus' experience in the temple when He was twelve years old, the Gospels are silent about Jesus' childhood and teen years. The Gospel writers simply pick up with Jesus' life when He was about thirty years old and getting ready to begin His ministry.

Read John 1:29–34 to learn about an important moment in Jesus' life as He was preparing for His public ministry. As you read, underline the names with which John identifies Jesus.

> The next day John saw Jesus coming toward him and said, "Here is the Lamb of God, who takes away the sin of the world! This is the One I told you about: 'After me comes a man who has surpassed me, because He existed before me.'"—John 1:29–30

ANSWER THESE QUESTIONS:
- At Passover, the priests would sacrifice a lamb to atone for the peoples' sin. Knowing this, what was John saying about Jesus when he identified Him as the Lamb of God?

- Reread verse 30. How did John point to Jesus' eternal nature? To His superiority? Explain.

- John also identified Jesus as the Son of God (v. 34), referencing Jesus' eternal nature, but also His ability to reveal the true nature and heart of God in a way the people had never experienced before. How could Jesus—God in the flesh—give the people a clearer understanding of God's character and purposes than God's Old Testament interactions had?

RESPOND

John recognized that Jesus was God in the flesh. He understood that Jesus would be the One who would atone for our sin. If you are a believer, dwell on what Jesus has done for you. Like John, acknowledge His eternal nature and worship Him as He deserves. Thank Him for becoming the Passover Lamb and praise Him for revealing God's heart to you.

TRANSFORMED

Read Matthew 3:1–12 in your Bible. John's message was difficult. He boldly called people to repentance and stressed that those who didn't follow Christ would face eternal judgment.

I baptize you with water for repentance, but the One who is coming after me is more powerful than I. I am not worthy to remove His sandals. He Himself will baptize you with the Holy Spirit and fire. His winnowing shovel is in His hand, and He will clear His threshing floor and gather His wheat into the barn. But the chaff He will burn up with fire that never goes out.—Matthew 3:11–12

THINK THROUGH THESE QUESTIONS:
- After reading these verses, do you think it is possible for someone to be a Christian without anything about their lives or attitudes changing? Why or why not?
- Repentance is more than saying you're sorry. It involves recognizing you have lived in opposition to God, grieving over that, and expressing a desire to live according to God's standard. Why is this important to understand? Explain.

RESPOND
- Everyone has the same choice: follow Jesus or reject Him. If you reject Him, you will face the eternal consequences of our decision. What decision have you made? How do you know?
- If you are a Christian, evaluate your life. How has God transformed not only your actions, but the attitudes and intentions of your heart? Thank Him for the ways He is continuing to transform you to the image of His Son.

EXAMPLE GIVEN

Read Matthew 3:13–17 and Mark 1:9–13 in your Bible. How are they alike? How are they different? Record your notes and findings.

> Then Jesus came from Galilee to John at the Jordan, to be baptized by him.
> —Matthew 3:13

DIG DEEPER WITH THESE QUESTIONS:
- Look at Matthew 3:14. Why did John try to stop Jesus from being baptized?
- Reread Matthew 3:15. Why did Jesus say He needed to be baptized? How did His baptism "fulfill all righteousness"?

Jesus wanted to obey His Father and identify with God's righteous cause among the people: repentance. Jesus never sinned, therefore, He didn't need to repent, yet He participated in John's baptism of repentance. In doing so, He identified with those He came to save (sinners) and set an example for us.

- What does this teach you about the importance of baptism in a believer's life? Explain.
- How do both passages show the activity of all three Persons of the Trinity?
- How did God the Father affirm Jesus and commission His ministry?

RESPOND
- After reading these verses, what would you say to someone who says, "I believe in Jesus. I just don't understand why I need to be baptized"?
- Baptism does not save you, but it does symbolize the transformation God has begun in you. It also publicly identifies you as a follower of Christ. If you are a Christian but have not been baptized, talk with your parents, pastor, or a Christian mentor. Don't delay in taking this important step.
- Thank Jesus for doing everything necessary to fulfill all righteousness so that you can truly know how He has called you to live.
- For further study of baptism, read Acts 2:38 and 10:48.

TEMPTED

On a scale of 1 to 10, how much would you say Jesus can really relate to your life and problems? Why? Record a few thoughts.

Now, read Matthew 4:1–11 in your Bible like you're reading it for the very first time. Answer the following questions:

- What is something from these verses that stands out to you that you've never really noticed before? Why did it stand out?

- For what reason would the Holy Spirit lead Jesus into the wilderness where He would be tempted by the Devil?

To discover the answer to that question, read Hebrews 2:14–18.

> Therefore, He had to be like His brothers in every way, so that He could become a merciful and faithful high priest in service to God, to make propitiation for the sins of the people. For since He Himself was tested and has suffered, He is able to help those who are tested.—Hebrews 2:17–18

ASK YOURSELF:

- Why does it matter that Jesus became like us and was tempted just as we are?

- How has Jesus helped you in the midst of temptation?

RESPOND

In your journal, list ways you're tempted in the same areas Jesus was: physical desires (bread); importance (reveal greatness); and worldly success (granted kingdoms). Now, considering how Jesus responded to temptation, pray about how He wants you to respond to yours.

LIFE'S PURPOSE

Read Luke 4:14–21 in your Bible. In His hometown synagogue, Jesus was given the honor of reading from the prophet Isaiah. Then, Jesus declared that the text He had just read was about Him. Delve into verses 18–19.

> The Spirit of the LORD is on Me, because He has anointed Me to preach good news to the poor. He has sent Me to proclaim freedom to the captives and recovery of sight to the blind, to set free the oppressed, to proclaim the year of the Lord's favor.—Luke 4:18–19

In the original Isaiah passage, this was the news that God was going to deliver the Jews from captivity in Babylon. How did Jesus accomplish these things in His earthly ministry? List a few examples.

How does sin oppress us? How did Jesus free us from that oppression?

Jesus was declaring that in Him, God was offering His grace and favor to the world. The people would have understood that Jesus was claiming to be the Messiah. Why would it have been hard for them to accept that the boy they'd watched grow up was the Messiah? Explain.

RESPOND

Jesus' words to His parents in the temple when He was 12 show that He understood His mission and purpose by that point. But now, it was time to make it public.

- Jesus knew why He had come and what God was calling Him to do. He understood His purpose. God has a purpose for your life, too: to know Him and play an active role in building His kingdom. What steps will you take to invest in that purpose this week? Record two in your journal.

- Jesus was completely focused on obedience to His Father. Are you? What changes need to happen in your life so you can be? What affect would this kind of obedience have on your witness?

REJECTION

Earlier, you studied Simeon's blessing of Jesus forty days after His birth. Simeon had proclaimed that many people would reject Jesus, and we've now reached the point in Jesus' ministry when that prediction began to be fulfilled. Read Luke 4:20–30 in your Bible. After Jesus used the Isaiah passage to publicly declare He was the Messiah, the people who had watched Him grow up sat there in silence, amazed. Who did Jesus think He was?

Reread Luke 4:23–30. Jesus knew that the people were doubtful of His claims and wanted proof of His divine power. They knew He had performed miracles in Capernaum and wanted Him to do the same in Nazareth. When have you wanted proof that Jesus was at work in a situation rather than trusting Him? Explain.

He also said, "I assure you: No prophet is accepted in his hometown."—Luke 4:24

ANSWER THESE QUESTIONS:

- How did Jesus respond to the peoples' desire for Him to perform on command?

- Jesus performed miracles at God's leading and according to God's purposes, not because people demanded them. Jesus was interested in people who had faith in Him rather than what He could do for them. In response to the peoples' desire, Jesus began listing Old Testament prophets who had to go far away, even outside of Israel, to find people of faith. Why would this have enraged the people? Explain.

- Look at verse 40. Despite the peoples' fury and rejection, Jesus remained focused on God's plan and purpose for His life. How can we remain focused on Jesus and His gospel in a world that rejects Him?

RESPOND

- What are some specific steps you can take to remain focused on your purpose and ministry, even when the world around you rejects Jesus? List two in your journal.

- If someone rejects the gospel when you share your faith, don't take it as a personal failure. You have been faithful to share the hope you have and you are not held accountable for the person's response. Who will you be bold enough to share with this week, even if it means enduring rejection?

SPEED THE LIGHT

Read Matthew 4:12–17 in your Bible. At this point, Jesus began His public ministry. Underline verse 17 as you read.

> From then on Jesus began to preach, "Repent, because the kingdom of heaven has come near!"—Matthew 4:17

DIG DEEPER WITH THESE QUESTIONS:

- According to verse 17, what was the central message of Jesus' ministry? Journal in your own words.

- How is life apart from Jesus described in verse 16? How is life without Jesus "darkness" and "the shadowland of death"? Explain.

- Consider verse 17 once more. What is the primary way Jesus brought light into darkness during His earthly ministry? How does repentance bring us out of spiritual darkness and into the light?

RESPOND

- Think about recent news stories or events in your own school or community. When you look at the world around you, do you see more darkness or light? Are people generally doing okay without Jesus? Journal a few thoughts.

- How does your answer to that question affect the urgency you feel for sharing the gospel?

- What steps will you take this week to shine the light of Christ into a dark world? List two specific action points or the names of two people you will share your story with this week.

- What is one way you can shine the light of the gospel into a world in darkness?

FOLLOWERS WANTED

Read Mark 1:14–20 in your Bible. Underline the phrase *the time is fulfilled* in verse 15. The Messiah God had promised long ago had entered history, and His plan of redemption was being fulfilled. Jesus' first step was to call people to follow Him.

> "Follow Me," Jesus told them, "and I will make you fish for people!" Immediately they left their nets and followed Him.—Mark 1:17–18

DIG DEEPER WITH THESE QUESTIONS:

- The first disciples Jesus called were fishermen, uneducated and unimportant by society's standards. What does that fact teach you about Jesus' kingdom? Explain.

- *Fish for people* was a term Old Testament prophets used to describe gathering people for judgment, but Jesus was inviting Simon and Andrew to join Him in the urgent task of rescuing people from judgment. How does Jesus rescue us from judgment? Explain.

- Think about the disciples' lives before and after their encounter with Jesus. How was their life with Christ different from their life before? How is your life different from the way you lived before meeting Jesus?

RESPOND

Jesus called these men to simply follow Him. He didn't tell them to get it all together or to understand every last detail. He called them to relationship with Him. He is still calling disciples to follow Him today.

- Mull over how quickly the disciples responded to Jesus' invitation. Do you typically follow immediately when Jesus calls you? Why or why not? Ask Him for a heart that desires to follow Him immediately, even when you don't completely understand.

- Following Jesus implies a relationship, allowing Him to be your teacher and guide. In what ways are you allowing Jesus to guide and lead you? In what areas are you trying to be the one in charge? What steps will you take today to give Jesus absolute control? List three in your journal.

UNLIKELY FOLLOWERS

What kind of person do you think would make the ideal disciple? List a few descriptions or characteristics in your journal.

> Jesus replied to them, "The healthy don't need a doctor, but the sick do. I have not come to call the righteous, but sinners to repentance."—Luke 5:31–32

Now, read Luke 5:27–32 in your Bible. At the time of Jesus' earthly ministry, tax collectors were among the most despised people in society. They collected taxes for the Romans, and their profit depended upon how much money they collected, which led them to overcharge. To put it simply, tax collectors were the last people you'd expect Jesus to call to follow Him.

Read through the passage once more and think through these questions:

- Is your concept of the ideal disciple the same as the people Jesus actually called? Why or why not?

- Examine Jesus' response in verses 31–32. How would you write it in your own words?

- Why is it important to understand that Jesus' salvation isn't about what we deserve or what we can earn? Explain.

RESPOND

We are all unlikely followers, yet Jesus has called us to follow Him.

- Reflect on how Jesus has saved you and made you whole. Spend some time in prayer thanking God for the way He reached out to you when you didn't deserve it.

- Because they kept all the religious rules and regulations, the Pharisees and scribes thought they were better than the "sinners." Sometimes, as believers, this attitude can creep into our lives, too. Ask God to reveal any areas in which you've allowed it to. In your journal, list two actions you will take to prevent your heart from becoming like the Pharisees' hearts.

A COMMUNITY BEGINS

Read Mark 3:13–19 in your Bible.

> Then He went up the mountain and summoned those He wanted, and they came to Him. He also appointed 12—He also named them apostles—to be with Him, to send them out to preach.—Mark 3:13–14

List the apostles mentioned in this passage. Next to their names, jot down any facts you may know about them.

THINK THROUGH THESE QUESTIONS:

- Reread verse 14 and underline the things the disciples were being called out to do. Why is spending time with Jesus an important part of being a disciple? Explain your answer.

- The disciples were also called to proclaim God's message of redemption to the world. What does that teach you about the importance of sharing the gospel for modern-day disciples?

- Notice that Jesus called together a core group of men to be His apostles. How does that underscore the importance of community in believers' lives?

RESPOND

Jesus has called you into community just as He did with His apostles.

- How much time do you spend with Jesus? What gets in the way of you doing so? What steps will you take this week to simply spend time with Jesus? Record two action points in your journal.

- Commit to taking a step of deeper commitment to your church community, such as becoming more consistent in attendance, finding a ministry in which you can serve, or meeting with an accountability partner.

THE ONLY WAY

Read John 1:43–51 in your Bible. Answer the questions that follow.

> Jesus responded to him, "Do you believe only because I told you I saw you under the fig tree? You will see greater things than this." Then He said, "I assure you: You will see heaven opened and the angels of God ascending and descending on the Son of Man."—John 1:50–51

ASK YOURSELF:
- How did Jesus' brief interaction with Nathanael show that Jesus knew Nathanael well? Explain.

- The Gospel of John wasn't written as a blow-by-blow account of Jesus' activities; instead, this Gospel is focused on helping people understand the importance of discovering the kind of faith that would transform their lives. How does Jesus' interaction with Nathanael display that focus? Explain.

Now, concentrate on Jesus' comments in verses 50–51. Turn back to Genesis 28:10–22 and skim over the details of Jacob's dream at Bethel.

JOURNAL YOUR THOUGHTS:
- How does John 1:51 relate to Jacob's dream? Be specific.

- What was Jesus declaring about Himself in that statement to Nathanael? Explain.

RESPOND
Jesus declared that He was the only way to know the Father. Jesus' entire discussion with Nathanael was a personal invitation to join Him. If Nathanael followed Jesus, he would have a relationship with God through Jesus, and he would be a part of God's mission and work on earth. Jesus is still inviting people to know Him today.

- Have you personally trusted in Jesus as the only way to know the Father? If you have, thank God for bringing you into relationship with Him. Praise Him for the way He personally called you. Record your prayer of thanks in your journal.

- Jesus invited Nathanael to "greater things" for the kingdom. Ask God to reveal ways He is calling you to build His kingdom on earth. Thank Him for His leadership.

BORN AGAIN

Think about what you studied yesterday: Jesus' invitation to Nathanael to join Him in His work. You learned that true disciples know that Jesus is the only way to have a relationship with the Father. Today, you'll learn that disciples of Christ experience spiritual rebirth and transformation. Read John 3:1–21 in your Bible.

> Jesus answered, "I assure you: Unless someone is born of water and the Spirit, he cannot enter the kingdom of God. Whatever is born of the flesh is flesh, and whatever is born of the Spirit is spirit."—John 3:5–6

PONDER THESE QUESTIONS:

- Jesus told Nicodemus that two births were required to enter the kingdom of God: one physical and one spiritual. How is someone born again? (Hint: look at verses 15–18.)

- Spiritual rebirth is an act of God in which the Holy Spirit makes you brand new. What word or words describe how you feel when you think about how you have been reborn? List a few ideas in your journal.

- Following Christ isn't about following a bunch of rules, behaving better, or doing good works. It's about being transformed. Why is that important for us to understand? Explain.

RESPOND

- If you are a believer, list a few ways you can see the Holy Spirit transforming you. Ask your parents, a Christian friend, or a mentor about ways they see God at work in your life. Thank God for the ways His power is on display.

- Who in your life needs to hear about the good news of what Jesus has done and the transformation they can experience? What steps will you take to share the gospel this week?

BRING SOMEONE WITH YOU

This week, you've learned that Jesus' followers are transformed by the Holy Spirit, called to a new way of life, and humbly aware that their salvation is found in Christ—not their own merit, effort, or good works. Today, you'll learn another important truth about disciples: they bring people to Jesus. Read John 1:35–42 in your Bible.

> He first found his own brother Simon and told him, "We have found the Messiah!" (which means "Anointed One"), and he brought Simon to Jesus. When Jesus saw him, He said, "You are Simon, son of John. You will be called Cephas" (which means "Rock").—John 1:41–42

JOURNAL YOUR THOUGHTS:

- Andrew met the Messiah and couldn't keep the good news to himself. Who has been an Andrew in your life? How?

- Andrew didn't try to reason or argue his brother into believing. He simply invited Peter to come and see. What might be some ways we could invite people to come and experience Jesus for themselves?

RESPOND

- Think about the people who have been Andrews in your life. Thank God for each one. Consider thanking those people personally.

- Who are the people in your life who need to experience Jesus? Pray for each one by name, asking God for opportunities to share your hope in Christ.

- Sharing your faith isn't about browbeating, arguing, or using guilt to force someone to accept Jesus' invitation. It's about presenting Jesus and trusting the Holy Spirit to do the work of changing hearts. Ask God to prepare peoples' hearts and give you the opportunity to talk to them about Jesus.

A WHOLE HEART

Think about a homework assignment, chore, or task you recently completed halfheartedly. What words might describe how you worked? Why did you put so little effort into it? Journal a few thoughts.

With that in mind, read Luke 9:57–62 in your Bible.

> But Jesus said to him, "No one who puts his hand to the plow and looks back is fit for the kingdom of God."—Luke 9:62

ASK YOURSELF:

- After reading these verses, can a true disciple live a life characterized by halfhearted faith? Explain your answer.

- What does wholehearted commitment to Christ look like?

- Look at the excuses the people gave in this passage for not wholeheartedly committing to Jesus. What excuses do you give for halfhearted commitment? What things do you allow to get in the way of obedience?

- Why is it important to understand that faith in Jesus is more than just a simple statement of belief? What do your actions and the way you live your life have to do with it? Explain.

RESPOND

Following Jesus is much bigger than marking off an item on a checklist or going to a weekly event at church. Jesus wants control of every part of your life.

- Evaluate your life. In what ways does your life demonstrate a wholehearted commitment to Jesus? If the Holy Spirit reveals areas marked by a lack of commitment or obedience, confess them immediately. Admit to Jesus once again how much you need Him in every area of your life.

- What steps will you take this week to follow your commitment with action? List two or three in your journal.

- The way you live out your faith is a witness to those around you. When people see that you truly believe Jesus deserves your wholehearted commitment, they will want to know more about the Savior you serve. Ask Jesus to remind you of this truth daily.

LIVING IN POVERTY

Read Matthew 5:3–4 in your Bible. Read verses 3–4 again carefully, then make a list in your journal of those who are blessed.

> "The poor in spirit are blessed, for the kingdom of heaven is theirs. Those who mourn are blessed, for they will be comforted."—Matthew 5:3–4

Known as the Beatitudes, Matthew 5:3–11 describes what it means to be a citizen in God's kingdom. These verses describe the character of true believers.

ASK YOURSELF:

- Consider this quote from Stuart Weber: "The beginning of repentance is the recognition of one's spiritual bankruptcy—one's inability to become righteous on one's own." What does it mean to be spiritually bankrupt?

- How does verse 3 illustrate spiritual bankruptcy?

- Look at verse 4. Believers recognize their sinfulness and their inability to do anything about it. This brings them to a place of repentance. How does verse 4 demonstrate that?

RESPOND

- Have you ever recognized your own spiritual bankruptcy? Journal about that experience. Write Jesus a thank-you for rescuing you from your spiritual poverty.

- Today's verses describe the recognition of sinfulness and repentance that leads to salvation, but as a believer, you know that you still sometimes sin. Ask God to reveal any sin in your life today so that you can confess it and enjoy restored fellowship with God.

STRENGTH UNDER CONTROL

Read Matthew 5:5 in your Bible. Underline what this verse says will happen to those who are gentle.

"The gentle are blessed, for they will inherit the earth."—Matthew 5:5

In today's world, gentleness is often considered a weakness. But in today's Scripture passage, the word *gentle* carries the connotation of strength under control.

THINK THROUGH THESE QUESTIONS:

- Think of what you know about Jesus and the way He interacted with people during His earthly ministry. How did He display strength under control?

- Think about the gentlest Christian you know. How do you see that person submitting his or her life to the Holy Spirit's control? Explain.

- Matthew 5:5 pictures believers who have submitted every part of their lives to Jesus' control. Their lives are characterized by humility, courteousness, self-control, and a tender, compassionate nature. Does that describe you? Why or why not?

- Who is in control of your strength? How do you know? Explain.

RESPOND

- Consider how your understanding of gentleness has changed since studying it today.

- In what ways are you still struggling to submit every part of your life to the lordship of Jesus? In your journal, make a list of reasons He deserves full control of your strength, then spend some time in prayer, asking Him to help you thoroughly submit to Him.

- How has Jesus been gentle toward you? Ask God to help you recall all the times He has been mercifully gentle with you. Praise Him for each instance. Be specific in your praise!

HUNGRY AND THIRSTY

Think about a time when you were extremely hungry or thirsty. What was your mood? Describe how you felt, both emotionally and physically.

With that experience in mind, read Matthew 5:6, then answer the questions that follow.

> "Those who hunger and thirst for righteousness are blessed, for they will be filled."
> —Matthew 5:6

PONDER THESE QUESTIONS:

- People who are hungry or thirsty devote their time and energy to fulfilling those needs. Knowing this, what does it mean to hunger and thirst for righteousness? Explain.

- Continuing with the hunger metaphor, what might keep a person from experiencing spiritual fullness?

- Matthew 5:6 tells us that those who follow Christ have a deep desire to see God's standard established and obeyed in every area of life, particularly in their own lives. Who has been a good example of that kind of righteousness in your life? Why?

RESPOND

- Evaluate your life. Do you exhibit a deep desire to live according to God's standard and pursue righteousness? How does your life display that desire? If that desire feels faint, ask God to ignite your heart with a desire to obey Him in every area of your life.

- Look back at the verses you've read from the Beatitudes so far. Sum up what you've learned from each one. Notice how they build on each other to describe the journey of coming to know Christ.

MERCY!

Reflect on a time when you received something you didn't deserve. What was it? What emotions did you experience? How did you respond? Record a few thoughts in your journal.

Now, read Matthew 5:7 in your Bible.

"The merciful are blessed, for they will be shown mercy."—Matthew 5:7

ANSWER THESE QUESTIONS:

- Mercy is a key aspect of God's character. Ponder the definition of mercy. How has God shown mercy to you?

- If you are a Christian, you have experienced God's overwhelming mercy in Jesus' life, death, and resurrection on your behalf. How does knowing God has given you something you don't deserve affect the way you live? Explain.

- Since God has treated you mercifully, how should you treat others? Why?

RESPOND

- If you are a believer, you have received God's abundant mercy that you in no way deserved. Thank God for His mercy and grace toward you and praise Jesus for willingly laying down His life on your behalf.

- Prayerfully consider if there is anyone from whom you have been withholding mercy. Ask God to help you to show that person mercy, just as He has shown you mercy.

PURE FOCUS

Take a moment to ponder the idea of purity. What kinds of things might you describe as being pure? What colors would you use to symbolize purity in a drawing? Record your response.

Read Matthew 5:8 in your Bible and underline the word *pure* when you read it.

> "The pure in heart are blessed, for they will see God."—Matthew 5:8

PONDER THESE QUESTIONS:

- Based on your understanding of purity, what does it mean to say that someone is pure in heart? Explain.

- Are people naturally pure in heart? If not, how does someone become pure in heart? Explain.

Purity means that something is undiluted, uncontaminated, and clean. Pure gold is 100 percent gold. So, to be pure in heart means that your heart is 100 percent focused on Jesus and His ways.

None of us are naturally pure in heart. Our sinful flesh craves sin. But if we are believers, we have an inner desire for purity and holiness in our lives because the Holy Spirit lives in us. Christians recognize that they belong to God and single-mindedly pursue Him. Those who pursue God and His ways will experience His favor.

RESPOND

- Examine your heart. What sin have you allowed to make it impure? What have you allowed into your life that takes your attention and affection away from God? Confess and repent of these things.

- In your journal, list situations or temptations that distract you from following Jesus with an undivided focus. Jot down ways you will choose to live for God when faced with those situations. Ask God to open your eyes to the way out of temptation He will provide.

PEACEMAKERS

PEACEMAKER (n.)—One who is actively involved in bringing reconciliation between those in conflict.

Mull over the definition of peacemaker above. Who are some famous peacemakers in history? How did they work to bring about peace and reconciliation? Journal a few ideas.

Now, think about your life. Who has been a peacemaker in your life? When has someone helped to bring peace and reconciliation when you were in conflict with someone else?

With those experiences in mind, read Matthew 5:9 in your Bible.

> "The peacemakers are blessed, for they will be called sons of God."—Matthew 5:9

The peace discussed in this verse isn't the end of a battle. It's a sense of wholeness and harmony that can only be achieved through a relationship with Jesus.

ASK YOURSELF:

- Knowing this, what does it mean to be a peacemaker as described in this verse? Explain your answer.

- Christians are peacemakers because they seek to reconcile people to God and each other. Others will see this and know that these people are truly God's children. Who is a good example of this kind of peacemaking in your life? Why?

RESPOND

The only way for people to experience true peace and reconciliation is through a relationship with Jesus.

- Those who don't know Christ are at war with God. Who fits that description in your life? List two names in your journal.

- Only the Holy Spirit can give a person peace with God, but peacemakers can show the way and assist people to understand how to be reconciled to God. What steps will you take this week to be a peacemaker in the lives of those people you listed above? Record two ideas in your journal. Pray that God would give you opportunities to follow through.

PERSECUTED

Think about a time when you were treated unfairly. What happened? How did you respond? Journal a few thoughts.

Read Matthew 5:10–12 in your Bible. Underline the phrase "persecuted for righteousness are blessed."

> "Those who are persecuted for righteousness are blessed, for the kingdom of heaven is theirs."—Matthew 5:10

PONDER THESE QUESTIONS:

- Consider the definition of persecution. Would you ever consider someone going through persecution to be blessed? Why or why not?

- What is the difference between being treated unkindly in general and being persecuted for your faith in Christ? Which is described here? Explain.

- Today's Scripture passage describes persecution that comes into believers' lives because they are living righteously. Why is it important to recognize that persecution is not the result of sin?

- Persecution comes to God's children because their lives contrast with the ways of the world. How does your life and the things that are important to you differ from the things the world values?

RESPOND

- Instead of asking God to keep you safe and happy, ask Him to give you boldness and strength. The early believers prayed for this while under threat of imprisonment (Acts 4:23–31). Pray that you would live boldly for Him, even when it isn't easy.

- Set aside specific time to pray for believers around the world who are being persecuted. See *persecution.org* and *imb.org/pray* for prompts.

MEANT TO SHINE

Read Matthew 5:13–16 in your Bible.

"In the same way, let your light shine before men, so that they may see your good works and give glory to your Father in heaven."—Matthew 5:16

ANSWER THESE QUESTIONS:

- What would happen if you mixed dirt and dust in with salt? Would it still be usable to flavor your food? Explain.

- Salt is meant to flavor and purify. A lamp is meant to shine and guide people. How do these examples help you to understand about what the lives of Christians are meant to do? Explain.

- Read verse 16 once more. According to this verse, what are our good deeds supposed to accomplish? Why is this important to understand?

Just as salt and lamps have a purpose, so do we as followers of Christ. Our lives are meant to point people to God so that He will be glorified, and they will understand and receive His love for them.

RESPOND

We are to reflect His light. Our lives should point to Him. Our thoughts, attitudes, words, actions—everything—should glorify Him so people see Jesus when they look at us. Evaluate your life with these questions:

- Do you try to blend in with what those around you are saying and doing, or do you say no to sin?

- Do you try to hide the fact that you are a Christian from anyone? Or do you live each day confident in His love and determined to show His love to others?

- If your answers reflect that you hide or blend in more than letting your light shine, acknowledge that. Be honest with God about it and ask for His forgiveness for any sin you've committed. Then, ask Him for the courage and strength to live differently this week. Each day is a fresh start, and His mercies are new (Lamentations 3:22–23).

FULFILLMENT

In your journal, write down as many of the Ten Commandments as you can remember without looking them up. Then, turn to Exodus 20 to see if you remembered them all correctly.

PONDER THESE QUESTIONS:

- How many of these commandments have you broken in your life? No one will see this, so you can be honest.

- Why is it so hard to keep all the commandments God gave humanity? Explain.

Read Matthew 5:17–20 in your Bible.

> "Don't assume that I came to destroy the Law or the Prophets. I did not come to destroy but to fulfill."—Matthew 5:17

Why does it matter that Jesus has perfectly kept all these laws? How does that relate to your salvation? Explain.

Jesus accomplished what you could not; He lived a perfect, sinless life that fulfilled the law completely. Even our best efforts to live up to God's commands fall painfully short. That's why Jesus is our only hope. But because Jesus fulfilled the law, we can put our faith in Him and stand before God in righteousness.

RESPOND

- Do you find yourself trying to keep all the rules and earn God's love? Jesus came to set you free from that. Be honest with God about it. Ask Him to help you to rest in what He has already done. Talk to Him honestly today, asking Him to set you free from the temptation to rely on your own good works to earn His favor.

- Write out a prayer, thanking Jesus for His perfect sacrifice and for fulfilling the law in every way. Praise Him for doing what you never could have.

DEALING WITH ANGER

After discussing the qualities that would characterize true believers, Jesus began to detail how their relationship with Him would change the way they interacted with others. First on His list? Anger. Read Matthew 5:21–26 in your Bible to learn more.

> "But I tell you, everyone who is angry with his brother will be subject to judgment. And whoever says to his brother, 'Fool!' will be subject to the Sanhedrin. But whoever says, 'You moron!' will be subject to hellfire."—Matthew 5:22

ANSWER THE FOLLOWING QUESTIONS:

- Jesus equated anger or hatred in your heart toward someone with murder. What does that teach you about Jesus' attitude toward wrath?

- Does this passage mean that it's a sin to get angry? Explain.

- The kind of anger Jesus was talking about here isn't a flash of anger or righteous anger when God's standards have been thwarted. It's the kind of anger you allow to consume your heart and mind, that you hold onto and allow to fester. How can harboring anger and bitterness damage your relationship with God? With others?

- Jesus also included harmful, cutting words that can kill someone's spirit as something believers should refrain from. What does this teach you about the way Christians should treat and value others? Explain.

RESPOND

- Have you been guilty of holding anger like this in your heart? Look up verses in Scripture that talk about anger and how to handle it. (Start with Ephesians 4:26–31, James 1:19–20, and Proverbs 29:11.) Record in your journal one way you will seek to reconcile a relationship that's been broken by anger.

- When temptation comes, rely on Jesus to help you overcome the desire to criticize, hurt, or hold a grudge toward others. Instead, address conflict in your relationships before anger has the opportunity to take root in your heart. Followers of Jesus should be known as people who extend forgiveness, mercy, and grace because of the enormity of sin from which God has forgiven us.

THE HEART

Next, Jesus turned His attention to lust, adultery, and divorce. Instead of focusing on these outward actions, Jesus went straight to the cause: the heart. Read Matthew 5:27–30 in your Bible.

> "But I tell you, everyone who looks at a woman to lust for her has already committed adultery with her in his heart. If your right eye causes you to sin, gouge it out and throw it away. For it is better that you lose one of the parts of your body than for your whole body to be thrown into hell."—Matthew 5:28–29

THOUGHTFULLY ANSWER THE FOLLOWING QUESTIONS:

- How are lust, divorce, and adultery symptoms of a deeper heart issue? Explain.

- In our flesh, we will always subvert, destroy, and twist everything God meant for good, including passion, sex, and marriage. How does today's passage help you better understand the depth of your need for Jesus?

- Why is it important to recognize that without a relationship with Jesus, we will always default to sin and cannot live to please God in any area of our lives?

- Examine verses 29–30. This is hyperbole and is meant to promote the message that believers must do whatever it takes to correct sinful heart attitudes. Why is it vital that we deal with sinful attitudes? Explain.

RESPOND

We're incapable of resisting sin on our own. Even as followers of Jesus, we are still tempted to sin, and we can still choose to disobey Him.

- Ask the Holy Spirit to examine your heart for sinful attitudes that do not reflect Jesus' heart and the way He has called you to live. Confess and repent of these sins today.

- In your journal, list specific actions you will take this week to deal with your heart issues. Be specific and take the drastic steps necessary to cut those attitudes out of your life.

PROMISES

Read Matthew 5:33–37 in your Bible.

> "But let your word 'yes' be 'yes,' and your 'no' be 'no.' Anything more than this is from the evil one."—Matthew 5:37

Reflect upon each statement that applies to you in the list below.

- I committed to helping with a project, but when the time came I stayed home instead.
- I signed up for a church activity, but something else ended up sounding more fun so I went there instead.
- I told my parents I'd clean my room (or another chore), but I ended up hanging out with friends instead.
- I told someone I'd pray for them, but never actually did.

Thinking about your answers and today's passage, consider these questions:

- Have you ever been guilty of breaking a commitment or promise you made to someone? Do you think that was a big deal? Why or why not?
- Children of God tell the truth and live up to their word. Does that describe you? Why or why not?

Jesus' teaching flew in the face of the thinking of the day. He said it was better to make a promise and live up to it than to thoughtlessly use God's name to back up a vow you don't intend to keep.

RESPOND

As Christians, we should be people of integrity.

- Take stock of your life. Does it prove that you are a promise keeper? Do you tell the truth and refuse to twist it so that it benefits you? Would your friends and family members agree with your assessment? Why or why not?
- If God has revealed any areas that do not please Him, confess and repent of them today. Commit once again to live in ways that please Him.
- If you've disappointed someone in the past, how can you rebuild his or her trust? In your journal, record three steps you'll take over the next few weeks to be a trustworthy person in those situations.
- Pray, asking God to help you become a person whose word is trustworthy and honoring to Him.

GOING THE EXTRA MILE

Think about our world today. We live in a culture that craves revenge. The general expectation is that people should pay for every way they've wronged us. How do you see that to be true in society today? Record a few ideas in your journal.

Revenge isn't a new issue. Jesus had something to say about it in the Sermon on the Mount. Read Matthew 5:38–42 in your Bible.

> "You have heard that it was said, An eye for an eye and a tooth for a tooth. But I tell you, don't resist an evildoer. On the contrary, if anyone slaps you on your right cheek, turn the other to him also."—Matthew 5:38–39

ASK YOURSELF:

- Why do you think revenge is such a temptation when someone wrongs us? Explain.
- What does Jesus say we should do instead of exacting revenge on others? Journal in your own words.
- Think about a situation in your life where you might want revenge. How would showing compassion instead of anger point others to Jesus?

RESPOND

- Is there a situation you're facing right now in which you're tempted to hold a grudge instead of extending grace to the other person? Pray over that situation, asking Jesus to fill you with His love so you can respond as He would.
- Journal a prayer, asking God to change your perspective and help you choose love and mercy over revenge.
- Pray by name for the people in your life who are constantly seeking revenge and payback. Ask God to give you opportunities to turn the other cheek or go the extra mile in their lives.

CHOOSE LOVE

Who are some famous enemies? Journal a few that come to mind.

While you may not have a so-called archenemy in your life, there are probably people you don't like or who mistreat you. In the Sermon on the Mount, Jesus even had something to say about how we should treat those people. Read Matthew 5:43–48 in your Bible.

> "But I tell you, love your enemies and pray for those who persecute you, so that you may be sons of your Father in heaven. For He causes His sun to rise on the evil and the good, and sends rain on the righteous and the unrighteous."—Matthew 5:44–45

ANSWER THESE QUESTIONS:

- How did Jesus' command fly in the face of the general thinking of the day? How did it call His followers to a higher standard? Explain.

- Why would He tell us to love those who hurt us? Can we truly do that in our own strength or power? Why or why not?

- What could be the end result of Christians actually living out this command? Explain.

RESPOND

- Think about the people in your life right now. Who are your "enemies," the people who are difficult to love, encourage, or help? Someone who is easy for you to overlook? The genuine test of true Christianity is how believers treat those they dislike or who have mistreated them. Jot down the names that came to mind in your journal. Commit to pray for them, their relationship with Jesus, and for God to help you love them.

- In your journal, list two ways you could begin to show those people the love of Jesus this week. Pray for God to strengthen you and give you the courage to follow through with your ideas. Ask that He would use your interactions to draw these people closer to Himself.

GENUINE GIVING

Earlier in the Sermon on the Mount, Jesus had explained that following Him would affect His followers' relationships. Then, as we'll study this week, He began to detail how that relationship would transform their daily lives and decisions. Read Matthew 6:1–4 in your Bible.

> "But when you give to the poor, don't let your left hand know what your right hand is doing, so that your giving may be in secret. And your Father who sees in secret will reward you."—Matthew 6:3–4

The fact that Jesus' followers would give was a given. Offerings and generosity were already important parts of the Jewish culture. But Jesus wanted His followers to understand that the motivation for giving was just as important as the act.

THINK THROUGH THESE QUESTIONS:

- What does unrighteous giving look like? Why is it important that we are genuine in our desire to give?

- According to this passage, what is our reward when we give because we want others to see how good we are? What is the reward when we give because we want to honor Jesus?

- Think about the people you know. Who is a good example of a genuine, righteous giver? How does that person's generosity help you to know more about Jesus? Explain.

RESPOND

There's no denying that all believers struggle with wanting approval; however, in a heart that has been changed by God, there should be a battle against the sinful desire of seeking the applause of others. Our ultimate goal should be that God be recognized and praised because of our giving. Think about a recent act of giving and ask yourself:

- Did I give to make myself look good or to glorify God?

- If your motives were less than genuine, repent and ask God to change your heart.

- Thank God for His generosity toward you in Jesus. Stress that you wouldn't know what true generosity was if the Father had not sent Jesus.

114

"REAL" PRAYER

As you read Matthew 6:5–8 in your Bible, notice that Jesus was once again challenging the genuineness of a believer's actions. Prayer is supposed to be an intimate conversation with the Father rather than an opportunity to promote our own good works.

> "But when you pray, go into your private room, shut your door, and pray to your Father who is in secret. And your Father who sees in secret will reward you."—Matthew 6:6

THOUGHTFULLY ANSWER THE FOLLOWING QUESTIONS:

- How are we not to pray? Jot down some ideas about what that looks like.

- Write down some phrases you use frequently in your prayers.

In Jesus' name	Be with me today
Bless this food	Other: _____

It's easy to get into the habit of repeating "prayer phrases" without giving much thought to what we're saying. Jesus also cautions us against praying so that others will see how "spiritual" we are. Worrying about what others think of us when we pray aloud turns our focus away from God. When you pray aloud, who are you impressing?

ASK YOURSELF:

- What kind of prayer honors God?

- Prayer is about being intimate with God, holding nothing back. He wants you to be real with Him. Does that describe your prayer life? Why or why not?

RESPOND

- Before you pray, pause to think about the One to whom you're praying. Meditate on God in all His glory, majesty, and power.

- Have a conversation with God. Thank Him, honor Him, confess, and offer your requests, but in all of it, be honest with God. Really focus on what you're saying and don't just go through the motions. Record your prayer in your journal if writing helps you to focus.

- Examine your prayers. Are you repeating phrases or truly seeking to align your heart with God's? Are your prayers more about telling God what to do or asking Him to work in your life and reveal His ways to you?

A MODEL PRAYER

Imagine what it would be like if you were invited to speak to a great king or important authority figure. Would you know what to say? Would you know the proper protocol? Wouldn't you be glad if someone who knew the king well could coach you in what to say? Record a few thoughts in your journal.

Jesus did exactly that when He modeled for believers how to talk to God. As you read Matthew 6:9–15 in your Bible, focus on what this prayer teaches you about who God is and the kind of relationship He wants to have with you.

> "Therefore, you should pray like this: Our Father in heaven, Your name be honored as holy. Your kingdom come. Your will be done on earth as it is in heaven."—Matthew 6:9–10

Examine Jesus' prayer and consider what it teaches about God's character. Jot down which parts of the prayer teach you about those topics. Then, journal a few reasons you know those statements are true.

- He is trustworthy.
- He provides for me.
- He wants me to be honest.
- I must submit to Him.

RESPOND

In your journal, write out a prayer using Jesus' model:

- Praise. Acknowledge God for who He is, expressing your trust in and submission to Him.
- Needs. Pray about your needs and requests. This isn't a time to tell God what to do, but to ask Him to work in your life and trust Him to do so.
- Confession. Repent and confess any sin.
- Praise. End by once again praising God and resting in His authority and goodness.

WHEN YOU FAST

As Jesus explained to His followers the practical ways they would live out their faith, He touched on giving and prayer. Then, He turned His attention to fasting. Fasting was a common practice among Jews, and Jesus expected it of His followers. But, as with giving and prayer, He challenged them to make sure their motives were pure. Read Matthew 6:16–18 in your Bible.

> "But when you fast, put oil on your head, and wash your face, so that you don't show your fasting to people but to your Father who is in secret. And your Father who sees in secret will reward you."—Matthew 6:17–18

THOUGHTFULLY ANSWER THE FOLLOWING QUESTIONS:

- What repeated phrase suggests that fasting is not an option? Explain.
- What motivated the hypocrites to fast?
- Why did Jesus teach that prayer and fasting should be done in secret? Explain your answer.
- Fasting from something that you enjoy is difficult, but it is one way that you can show God that you desire Him more. How could abstaining from food or anything else that you enjoy cause you to seek God?

RESPOND

Fasting isn't a new diet plan. It is a means of drawing closer to God. Whenever you have hunger pangs or your mind drifts to that thing you've given up, let those feelings remind you to pray.

This week, plan one day to fast during lunch. Instead of eating, go to a quiet place. Pray, read your Bible, and fellowship with God. If you have medical reasons that prevent you from going without food, try fasting all day from technology, television, or an activity you really enjoy. The point is to give up something that you enjoy doing, in order to give all your attention to God.

LASTING TREASURE

We live in a culture that is all about getting as much as you can get, so we whine, work, and devote our hearts to going after what the world says we need in order to have value and worth. Read Matthew 6:19–24 in your Bible. Focus on what Jesus said believers should devote their hearts to.

> "Don't collect for yourselves treasures on earth, where moth and rust destroy and where thieves break in and steal. But collect for yourselves treasures in heaven, where neither moth nor rust destroys, and where thieves don't break in and steal."
> —Matthew 6:19–20

ASK YOURSELF:

- What is the difference between an earthly treasure and a heavenly treasure? Explain.

- You can determine where your treasure is by the ways you spend your time, money, and what you think about most often. What does that reveal about the treasures of your heart? Explain.

- Jesus uses the analogy of a master and a slave. How do money and earthly treasures enslave us?

- What does it look like when someone's life is completely controlled by Jesus?

RESPOND

Either your heart belongs to Jesus completely or it belongs to something or someone else.

- Evaluate yourself. What does the way you spend your time, money, and what occupies your thoughts most reveal about where your treasure lies? If this evaluation reveals anything that takes your focus and heart away from God and His work, confess it now. Ask Jesus for a heart that's completely focused on Him.

- In your journal, draw two hearts. In the first heart, list the earthly treasures you struggle with. In the second heart, list things that you can do to store up eternal treasures. Ask God to give you a heart that is totally devoted to Him.

WHAT'S YOUR FOCUS?

What things do you worry about most? List a few ideas.

Worry is a big deal in our relationship with God. Worry displays a lack of faith in God. Instead of trusting Him to meet those needs or work in that situation, we attempt to take control and find the answer ourselves. With that in mind, read Matthew 6:25–34 in your Bible. Focus on the promises of God outlined in these verses.

> "But seek first the kingdom of God and His righteousness, and all these things will be provided for you. Therefore don't worry about tomorrow, because tomorrow will worry about itself. Each day has enough trouble of its own."—Matthew 6:33–34

ANSWER THESE QUESTIONS:

- Jesus lovingly explained that the real problem wasn't anxiety; it was not trusting God. What metaphors did Jesus use to demonstrate how God provides for His creation? Be specific.
- How does the way that God cares for the birds and flowers encourage you to trust Him for your needs?
- Jesus said that our focus in life should be about building His kingdom. Is this your focus? If not, what is getting in the way?

RESPOND

Trusting God to provide for your daily needs may not be a stretch of faith, but trusting Him enough to give up all of your wants in order to devote your life to building His kingdom may be the bigger issue.

- Ask God to give you a greater desire for Him.
- Ask the Holy Spirit to reveal any desires you are allowing to get in the way of helping to build His kingdom here on earth. List what He reveals in your journal and record specific steps you'll take to trust Him and invest in His work.

WATCH YOUR ATTITUDE

Next, Jesus addressed judgmental attitudes. Well aware of the Pharisees' hypocrisy, Jesus didn't want His followers to follow their example. Read Matthew 7:1–6 in your Bible.

> "Or how can you say to your brother, 'Let me take the speck out of your eye,' and look, there's a log in your eye? Hypocrite! First take the log out of your eye, and then you will see clearly to take the speck out of your brother's eye."—Matthew 7:4–5

DIG DEEPER WITH THESE QUESTIONS:

- What is the difference between being judgmental and judging? Explain.

- Jesus wasn't saying that His disciples would never have to make moral judgments or exercise discernment, but that they shouldn't be characterized by an overly critical and fault-finding attitude. Why is it so easy to be critical or find faults?

- Jesus challenged His followers to first examine their own lives and deal with their own sin, recognizing that they were no better than anyone else. Why is that an important part of living out your faith? Explain.

RESPOND

- It's easy to go through life pointing out others' faults, but never dealing with the sin in our own lives. Today, ask God to examine your life and heart and reveal any sin that you need to confess. Repent today.

- Who are the people in your life you most often find yourself being judgmental or critical of? Write their names in your journal and pray over each relationship. Ask God to remind you of the grace He has shown you and pray that He would change your heart toward those people.

- Maybe there is someone in your life who is incredibly critical of you and always ready to point out your flaws and sins. Instead of getting angry, pray that God would empower you to love that person and respond in a way that gives all the glory and attention to Him.

BLESSED TO BE A BLESSING

Read Matthew 7:7–12 in your Bible. As you read, underline the words or phrases that describe God's generosity toward His children.

> "If you then, who are evil, know how to give good gifts to your children, how much more will your Father in heaven give good things to those who ask Him! Therefore, whatever you want others to do for you, do also the same for them—this is the Law and the Prophets."—Matthew 7:11–12

ANSWER THESE QUESTIONS:

- What did this passage teach you about God's generosity? His trustworthiness? Explain.

- This passage points to persistent reliance on God and trust that He will meet our needs. Who is a good example of that in your life? Why?

- Underline verse 12. Because disciples have experienced God's generosity, the least we can do is treat others as we would like to be treated. How does doing so display submission to God and a desire to put His purposes before our own?

- God blesses His children so they can be a blessing to others. How can generously giving to someone open the door to the gospel? Explain.

God desires to give His children good things, but just because we ask for something doesn't mean it is a good gift. The gifts God loves to give are those that will build His kingdom.

RESPOND

- In your journal, list all of the ways that God has been generous to you recently and in the past. Thank Him for each one.

- Think about the needs in your church and community. Pray over each one. What steps will you take this week to help meet those needs through the means God has generously provided for you? Jot down two action points in your journal.

- Memorize Matthew 7:12. You will have many opportunities this week to interact with others. How will you put this verse into action?

ONE WAY

Read Matthew 7:13–29 in your Bible. Focus on the imagery that Jesus used. In your journal, sketch icons that represent that imagery.

> "But everyone who hears these words of Mine and doesn't act on them will be like a foolish man who built his house on the sand. The rain fell, the rivers rose, the winds blew and pounded that house, and it collapsed. And its collapse was great!"—Matthew 7:26–27

PONDER THESE QUESTIONS:

- How do these images all point to the same truth? Write that point in your own words.
- These images help us to understand that there is only one way to be saved, one way to a fruitful life, and only one foundation upon which we should build our lives: Jesus.
- What are some other things that people today think will save them?
- What are the consequences of trusting in something or someone else other than Jesus for salvation? Explain.

We live in a world that thinks there are many ways to God or that it would be more secure to build our lives on things like wealth, power, or popularity. But in the end, the only thing that matters is Jesus.

RESPOND

- Faith in Jesus is not just lip service. If your life doesn't reflect a relationship with Him and you have no inward desire to obey or live to please Him, you need to check yourself. Talk and pray with your parents, pastor, or a mature Christian mentor.
- Think about your friends, family members, acquaintances who are trying to find salvation and meaning in someone or something other than Jesus. Pray for them, asking God for opportunities to tell them about Jesus.

THE REASON FOR PARABLES

Think about your favorite story—whether it's a family story, novel, or the plot of a movie. Jesus often told stories as He was teaching, using imagery to point to greater truths. To discover more about why Jesus told parables, read Matthew 13:10–17 in your Bible. Focus on verses 16–17.

"For this reason I speak to them in parables, because looking they do not see, and hearing they do not listen or understand."—Matthew 13:13

DIG DEEPER WITH THESE QUESTIONS:
- Jesus told the disciples that they were currently seeing things the prophets had longed to see. What did He mean? Explain in your own words.
- Underline Jesus' explanation of why He told parables. Is it confusing? Why or why not?

In simple terms, Jesus told parables to divide the crowd. He wasn't trying to prevent people from understanding His teaching with difficult, mysterious stories. Those who acknowledged Him as Messiah would hear His teaching and understand, applying it to their lives. Those who refused to recognize Him as the Messiah would also refuse to accept His teaching, even going so far as to consciously choose not to believe. Why is it dangerous to hear and understand God's truth, then choose not to believe it? Explain.

RESPOND
- Meditate on Matthew 13:10–17 and the difference between people who listen and understand and those who understand and refuse to let God's truth change their lives. Which category describes you? Why?
- If the Holy Spirit reveals a hard heart toward God's truth, admit this to God. Ask Him to soften your heart to His truth so that you may live accordingly
- Part of being a follower of Christ is knowing His teachings and applying them to your life. In your journal, write two ways you will become a better listener to God's Word.

SMALL BUT SIGNIFICANT

Read Matthew 13:31–33 in your Bible.

> He presented another parable to them: "The kingdom of heaven is like a mustard seed that a man took and sowed in his field. It's the smallest of all the seeds, but when grown, it's taller than the vegetables and becomes a tree, so that the birds of the sky come and nest in its branches."—Matthew 13:31–32

ASK YOURSELF:

- What two items does Jesus compare the kingdom of God to in these verses? What does that help you to understand about the kingdom of God? Explain.

- How much of the flour did the yeast spread through? Why is that important to note?

- The intention of a parable is to use a story to teach one main truth. Knowing that, what truth does the mustard seed and the yeast teach you? Journal in your own words.

RESPOND

Though His message seemed unimportant and His group of followers was small, Jesus declared that His kingdom would spread throughout the world.

- In baking, the work of the yeast can seem insignificant, slow, and small; yet, the tiniest amount of yeast causes entire loaves of bread to rise. How do you see Jesus at work in your heart, even in small ways? How is He changing the way you think or act? Praise God for the ways He is at work in your life, even those no one else might notice.

- Mull over recent headlines or events in the news. It's easy to think that the gospel has no power in today's world, but God is still at work. Ask Him to open your eyes to how He is working to advance His kingdom. Pray that He would guide you to ways you can join Him in that work.

THE GREATEST TREASURE

Think about the most important things in your life, from relationships to actual items. List the top three things you treasure in your journal. Be honest.

Now, read Matthew 13:44–45 in your Bible.

> "The kingdom of heaven is like treasure, buried in a field, that a man found and reburied. Then in his joy he goes and sells everything he has and buys that field."—Matthew 13:44

Reread Matthew 13:44–45 and answer these questions:

- How did the men respond when they found the treasure and the pearl? Why are those reactions important? Explain.

- A parable points to a greater truth, and this parable has to do with the value of God's kingdom. What does it teach you about how valuable knowing Jesus is?

- Jesus used the words *treasure* and *pearl*—both denoting precious, invaluable resources—to describe what it meant to know Him and be a part of His kingdom. Would you use the same kinds of words to describe your attitude toward your relationship with Him? Why or why not?

RESPOND

A relationship with Jesus is so valuable that it reorients believers' lives and becomes their focus. Can you truly say He is the most important Person in your life today?

- If you are a believer and God has used this devotion to help you see other relationships or things you've allowed to take His place in your life, confess those things today. Ask God to center your heart on Jesus.

- Look over the list of things you treasure most. Can you follow God and still treasure those things? If not, what steps will you take to get those things out of your life and make Jesus your focus? List two in your journal.

SOWING MORE THAN SEEDS

Read Matthew 13:1–9 in your Bible. Record in your journal the four different places the seed fell and their results.

Now, read Jesus' explanation of the parable in Matthew 13:18–23.

> "But the one sown on the good ground—this is one who hears and understands the word, who does bear fruit and yields: some 100, some 60, some 30 times what was sown."—Matthew 13:23

PONDER THESE QUESTIONS:

- According to Jesus' explanation, whom or what does the seed represent? Whom does the sower represent? Why is that important?

- The four types of soil describe responses to the gospel: hardened hearts; joyful acceptance with no actual commitment; interest in Jesus that wanes in the face of the world's pleasures or anxieties; and those who receive God's Word, understand it, and seek to fulfill it. Which best describes your response to the gospel? Why?

- Consider verse 22. What are some "worries of this age" that might entice someone away from the truth of the gospel? Explain.

RESPOND

Placing your faith in Jesus is a decision you make in a moment, but is proven by your commitment, perseverance, avoidance of idolatry and anxiety, and the presence of spiritual fruit in your life. Commitment, perseverance, and avoiding idolatry and anxiety are daily struggles. Think about the circumstances in your life in which it seems easier to give up on God and follow after the world. Ask God to focus your heart and mind on Him and remind you of His truth, even when trusting Him seems too difficult.

FINAL JUDGMENT

Think about your favorite movies or books that deal with the battle between good and evil. Jot down a few titles in your journal.

Good and evil aren't foreign concepts in Scripture. As Jesus taught about the kingdom of God, He was clear that a time would come when good and evil would be sorted out. Read Matthew 13:24–30, 36–43 in your Bible. Underline the imagery that symbolizes the good and circle the imagery that symbolizes evil.

> "The Son of Man will send out His angels, and they will gather from His kingdom everything that causes sin and those guilty of lawlessness. They will throw them into the blazing furnace where there will be weeping and gnashing of teeth. Then the righteous will shine like the sun in their Father's kingdom. Anyone who has ears should listen!"—Matthew 13:41–43

According to Jesus' explanation, He identified Himself as the sower and the good seed as "sons of the kingdom" (v. 31), meaning those who believe in Him and are part of His kingdom. The weeds symbolize those who continually do evil and pursue sin.

- Jesus said that the field symbolized the world. Knowing this, what do these verses teach you about good and evil in the world you live in?

- What does this passage teach you about what will eventually happen to those who have placed their faith in Christ? Those who have continually pursued sin?

- How does this passage give you hope and help you to rest in God's faithfulness and trustworthiness? Explain.

RESPOND

- Praise God that no matter how much evil there is, He will eventually triumph over it. Pray about specific examples of evil and sin you see in the world today. Ask Him to give you patience to trust His perfect timing to come and end the evil in this world.

- Record the names of three people in your life who don't know Jesus. Ask God to give you opportunities to share the truth of His Word with them this week.

NO ESCAPING JUDGMENT

Read Matthew 13:47–50 in your Bible. Mull over the analogy used to describe the kingdom of God in today's Scripture passage. Sketch it in your journal.

> "Again, the kingdom of heaven is like a large net thrown into the sea. It collected every kind of fish, and when it was full, they dragged it ashore, sat down, and gathered the good fish into containers, but threw out the worthless ones."—Matthew 13:47–48

ANSWER THESE QUESTIONS:

- How does today's passage relate to yesterday's from Matthew 13:24–30? Explain.

- How is today's passage different from yesterday's passage?

- According to today's Scripture passage, what will the end be for the evil people that the angels separated out in yesterday's devotion?

- How does knowing that those who do not know Christ will face eternal punishment and separation from Him affect the way you interact with others? Your attitude toward sharing the gospel?

RESPOND

- Reflect on how often and how passionately you tell other people about the kingdom of God. How will you let today's passage affect the way you view witnessing? Jot down two ways in your journal.

- Ask God to give you the boldness to verbally tell one person about Him this week. Actively look for opportunities to tell others about Jesus.

- Look over the list of people in your life who don't know Jesus that you created yesterday. Circle one person on that list to invite to come to church or youth group with you. Be in prayer that they will come and hear the truth of God.

WE PLANT; GOD GROWS

Read Mark 4:26–29 in your Bible.

> "The kingdom of God is like this," He said. "A man scatters seed on the ground; he sleeps and rises—night and day, and the seed sprouts and grows—he doesn't know how."—Mark 4:26–27

PONDER THESE QUESTIONS:

- What role did the man in the parable play in making the seeds grow? Explain.

- A faithful farmer plants seeds. He can water the seeds and try to make sure all the conditions are perfect for their growth and success, but he is powerless to actually cause them to grow. If the seed is symbolic of the gospel, what does this parable teach you about the success of the gospel? Explain.

- The success of the gospel isn't dependent on you. Like the sower, you must be faithful to plant the seeds and share the gospel message, but you can't cause people to place their faith in Jesus. You have to share your hope, but trust God to bring the harvest. Why should Christians find it encouraging that we're not in charge of growing the crops? Explain.

RESPOND

The parable of the growing seed teaches us two things: there will be a harvest (demonstrating God's faithfulness), and we must be faithful to share the gospel.

- In your journal, list the names of people you know have heard the gospel, but have not yet trusted Christ as Savior. Commit to pray for these people on an ongoing basis. Ask God to help you to trust Him to bear fruit in those peoples' lives, even if trusting Him to do so is difficult.

- As a believer, you're not responsible for how people respond to the gospel, but you are responsible to share it. Pray that God would provide opportunities to share your faith this week. Ask Him to help you be faithful.

100% DEVOTED

While many of Jesus' parables taught about the kingdom of God, others revealed what following Him actually looks like. Read Luke 10:25–28 in your Bible. As you read, underline any words or phrases that teach you something about what Jesus wants from His followers.

> Just then an expert in the law stood up to test Him, saying, "Teacher, what must I do to inherit eternal life?" "What is written in the law?" He asked him. "How do you read it?" He answered: "Love the Lord your God with all your heart, with all your soul, with all your strength, and with all your mind; and your neighbor as yourself."—Luke 10:25–27

ASK YOURSELF:

- Look at what you underlined in your Bible. What does it mean to love God with all your heart, soul, strength, and mind? Journal in your own words.

- Who in your life is a good example of loving Jesus in this way? Why did you pick him or her? What does that person's life teach you about following Jesus?

- Read verse 28 again. Jesus said, "Do this." What did He tell the expert in the law to do in order to inherit eternal life?

- Why does Jesus want His followers to be entirely committed to Him? Explain.

RESPOND

Jesus wasn't giving His followers a checklist of things they have to do to earn eternal life; He was calling them to submit every bit of their lives and themselves to Him. He wants us to wholeheartedly commit to following Him.

- Your relationship with Jesus and commitment to Him should shape your decisions and values. What does your life declare about your commitment to Jesus?

- If there is anything in your life that is keeping you from completely following after Jesus and walking in His ways, confess it today. In your journal, jot down your action plan to remove those things from your life.

TWO DEBTORS

Read Luke 7:36–50 in your Bible.

> Jesus replied to him, "Simon, I have something to say to you." "Teacher," he said, "say it." "A creditor had two debtors. One owed 500 denarii, and the other 50. Since they could not pay it back, he graciously forgave them both. So, which of them will love him more?" Simon answered, "I suppose the one he forgave more."—Luke 7:40–43.

PONDER THESE QUESTIONS:

- Reread verses 44–46. Compare the woman's response to Jesus with the Pharisee's response to Jesus. How are they different?

- The Pharisees knew only God was capable of forgiving sin, yet Jesus forgave the woman's sins. In doing so, what was Jesus proclaiming about Himself? Why was that so offensive to the Pharisees?

- Skim over the passage once more. Jesus said that the woman's extravagant gratefulness was proper because she truly recognized that she had been forgiven much. What does her example teach you about how those who have been forgiven by Jesus should live? Explain.

RESPOND

- Those who recognize how much they have been forgiven live differently. Love and thankfulness characterize their lives. Do those qualities describe you? Why or why not? If not, what actions will you take to understand the depth of Jesus' forgiveness and cultivate those characteristics in your life? Record two ideas in your journal.

- Evaluate your response to Jesus and His forgiveness. If you're more like the Pharisees, what needs to change in your life so you can express your gratefulness to Jesus? List two ideas in your journal.

UNCONDITIONALLY FORGIVEN

Ponder the cost of a luxury car, a year's tuition to an Ivy League college, or an enormous amount of credit card debt. If you owed that amount of money, how would you feel if someone paid it for you? Jot down a few ideas.

With that in mind, read Matthew 18:21–35 in your Bible.

> "Since he had no way to pay it back, his master commanded that he, his wife, his children, and everything he had be sold to pay the debt. At this, the slave fell facedown before him and said, 'Be patient with me, and I will pay you everything!' Then the master of that slave had compassion, released him, and forgave him the loan."—Matthew 18:25–27

THINK THROUGH THESE QUESTIONS:

- The debt the first slave was forgiven of was enormous, comparable to several million dollars in today's currency. Knowing this, what does this parable help you to understand about the debt you owe because of your sin?

- The slave was forgiven a debt he never could have repaid, even if he'd had several lifetimes to earn the money. The scandal of the gospel is that Jesus has done the same thing for us. Our good works, acts of righteousness, and endless efforts could never make up for the debt our sin created. But Jesus laid down His life and offered Himself as the sacrifice so that our debt could be paid. How does it make you feel to recognize that Jesus laid down His life to pay your debt?

RESPOND

While we were still sinners, Christ died for us (Romans 5:8). Recognize that you are the debtor and Jesus has forgiven you, taking that burden off of you, not because you deserve it or earned it, but because He loves you.

If you're a Christian, ponder the depth of your sin and the great debt Jesus has paid for you. Record your praise in your journal.

JUSTIFIED

Read Luke 18:9–14 in your Bible.

> "Two men went up to the temple complex to pray, one a Pharisee and the other a tax collector. . . . But the tax collector, standing far off, would not even raise his eyes to heaven but kept striking his chest and saying, 'God, turn Your wrath from me—a sinner!'"—Luke 18:10, 13

Read verses 10–14 again. Compare and contrast the hearts and attitudes of the tax collector and the Pharisee in your journal.

The tax collector's prayer was marked by humility and recognition of his standing (as a sinner) before God. The Pharisee's prayer was marked by pride, self-righteousness, and judgment of others.

ASK YOURSELF:
- Whom did Jesus say left justified? Why?
- The Pharisee was a religious leader and the person Jesus' listeners would have expected to be the hero of the story, especially knowing the Pharisees' emphasis on moral excellence. Why is it important to recognize that we aren't justified because of our own goodness or effort, but Jesus' goodness?

RESPOND
Believers are not self-righteous or prideful, pointing hateful fingers toward sinners and proclaiming they are better than them. Believers recognize their need for Jesus, turn to God in repentance, and urge others to do the same.

- Pause to take stock of your life. Which attitude best describes yours: the Pharisee or the tax collector? Confess any sin the Holy Spirit reveals.
- In what ways do you struggle with self-righteousness? What steps will you take this week to deal with this?
- When are you most tempted to judge others for sinful choices? When that happens this week, think about the depth of your sinfulness and your own need for Christ. Let that realization affect the way you respond to others.

KINGDOM RESPONSIBILITY

Consider the definitions of *steward* and *stewardship*. What qualities do you think a good steward possesses? What characterizes someone who's a bad steward? Journal a few thoughts.

Read Matthew 25:14–30 in your Bible.

> "Immediately the man who had received five talents went, put them to work, and earned five more. In the same way the man with two earned two more. But the man who had received one talent went off, dug a hole in the ground, and hid his master's money."—Matthew 25:15–18

ASK YOURSELF:

- Read verses 15–18, 24–27 again. According to these verses, what are some character-istics of a good steward?

- What qualities characterize a bad steward? Explain.

- The slave who hid the talent failed to make any kind of investment with what the master had given him, which displayed a lack of commitment to the master. His desire to be safe overrode his desire to please the master. Has Jesus ever called you to be obedient in a way that would have cost you something? Why is obedience when things don't make sense a good gauge of your commitment? Explain.

The master gave each slave something in this parable. They didn't get the same amount, but no one was left out. The same is true of the kingdom of God. God has placed resources in the lives of every believer—talents, skills, gifts, capabilities—and we must be good stewards of all He has given us.

RESPOND

- Think about the last few days or weeks and the opportunities you experienced to be obedient or faithful to God. What does your obedience (or disobedience) reveal about your commitment to God? Are you truly willing to follow Him wherever He leads, or only when it makes sense?

- Ask God to help you to trust Him entirely and follow Him no matter where He leads, even if it doesn't make sense or scares you.

BECAUSE HE FORGIVES

Skim over Matthew 18:21–35 and remind yourself about what you learned when you studied the parable of the unforgiving servant. In your journal, jot down the main point in your own words.

DIG A LITTLE DEEPER WITH THESE QUESTIONS:

- What does this parable reveal about how God forgives us?

- What does this parable teach you about forgiving others? Explain.

Now, turn to Ephesians 4:31–32. Answer the questions that follow.

All bitterness, anger and wrath, shouting and slander must be removed from you, along with all malice. And be kind and compassionate to one another, forgiving one another, just as God also forgave you in Christ.—Ephesians 4:31–32

- What do these verses have in common with the parable of the unforgiving servant? Explain.

- Underline Ephesians 4:32. As a Christian, you have experienced God's forgiveness for a debt you could never pay. According to these verses, how should that affect the way you interact with others, particularly those who have wronged you?

- Why is it so important that forgiveness characterize the lives of believers? How does practicing extravagant forgiveness testify to the truth of the gospel? Explain.

RESPOND

Because you have been forgiven so much, you must forgive others.

- Think about the people in your life. Are there people you refuse to forgive because you don't think they deserve it? If so, write their names in your journal. Take steps to forgive that person today. Let him or her know you want to forgive because God forgave you of a far greater debt.

- You may need to ask someone to forgive you. If God has used these verses to bring a person to mind, don't delay in seeking his or her forgiveness. List your action plan in your journal. You can't control the person's response, but you can be obedient to God in seeking forgiveness.

WHO IS MY NEIGHBOR?

Just prior to telling the parable of the good Samaritan, Jesus was talking to an expert in the law. Jesus used this interaction to help the crowd see the kind of followers He wanted: people who were wholeheartedly committed to Him. Now, read the parable in Luke 10:25–37. Underline any words or phrases that teach you more about what it means to live for Jesus.

> "Which of these three do you think proved to be a neighbor to the man who fell into the hands of the robbers?" "The one who showed mercy to him," he said. Then Jesus told him, "Go and do the same."—Luke 10:36–37

ASK YOURSELF:

- Ponder verses 36–37 again. At this point in history, a neighbor for most Jews was another Jew, not a Gentile or a Samaritan. How did Jesus define neighbor? Explain it in your own words.

- Read verses 30–35 again. Consider the people who saw the injured man. Whom would you expect to help the man attacked by robbers? Why?

- How did the priest's and Levite's actions display an unwillingness to love others?

- The priest and the Levite were supposed to be representatives of God in the world, yet their actions were unloving and selfish. Why is it so harmful to the gospel when the people of God are selfish and unloving? Explain.

RESPOND

The Jews thought they knew how to please God—with rules and outward actions. But Jesus turned their idea of what was right upside down when He made a Samaritan the hero of His story. Followers of Christ are to be loving, compassionate people—and that love transcends boundaries of race, nationality, economics, or social status.

- Think about your community. Who are the people you are willing to overlook or might consider undeserving of God's grace? List a few ideas in your journal.

- Ask God to change your attitude toward those people today.

JUST ONE SHEEP

Read Luke 15:1–7 in your Bible.

> "What man among you, who has 100 sheep and loses one of them, does not leave the 99 in the open field and go after the lost one until he finds it? When he has found it, he joyfully puts it on his shoulders, and coming home, he calls his friends and neighbors together, saying to them, 'Rejoice with me, because I have found my lost sheep!'"—Luke 15:4–6

Just as the shepherd valued each sheep, God values each person.

Answer these questions:

- In this parable, the shepherd represents Jesus. What does the story reveal about His character? About His love for you? About His desire to have a relationship with you?

- In verse 5, the image of the shepherd putting the sheep on his shoulders meant the sheep was likely injured or weak. What does this tell you about the shepherd's love for the sheep? Explain.

- According to verse 7, how do you think you should react when someone repents?

RESPOND

Remember each person has value to God, including you and me.

- Consider how much the Good Shepherd loves you. Take time to thank Him for His great love.

- In your journal, list the names of a few people you struggle to love. Leave space beneath each name. Pray and ask God to guide you as you write at least one good quality about each person.

- Ask the Holy Spirit to reveal any unconfessed sin in your life. Repent today knowing all of heaven celebrates with you.

THE POWER OF PERSISTENCE

Read Luke 15:8–10 in your Bible.

> "Or what woman who has 10 silver coins, if she loses one coin, does not light a lamp, sweep the house, and search carefully until she finds it? When she finds it, she calls her women friends and neighbors together, saying, 'Rejoice with me, because I have found the silver coin I lost!' I tell you, in the same way, there is joy in the presence of God's angels over one sinner who repents."—Luke 15:8–10

ASK YOURSELF:

- Read verse 8 again. When the woman realized she lost her coin, what did she do? Underline her three actions.

- Ten coins may not sound like much to you, but it was almost an entire day's pay for this woman. Think of a time when you lost something valuable. Did you drop everything to find it? What did you do to look for it?

- Read verse 9 again. The woman made a request to her friends when she found her coin. In the verse, find her request and circle it. Why do you think she wanted to celebrate? Explain.

- What is the similarity between the woman's joy over finding the coin and God's joy when a sinner repents?

- What do the woman's actions teach you about God's persistence in pursuing you?

RESPOND

The woman did not give up until she found her missing coin. She was persistent. Persistence means you continue in an action until it is complete, no matter what circumstances you face.

- How did God pursue you? How did you come to trust Jesus as your Savior? Grab your journal and write about it.

- As a Christian, God continues to pursue you throughout life. How has this helped you grow in your relationship with Him? Explain.

THE INHERITANCE

Look up the definition of *rebel*.

List the names of some authorities or people in positions of power in your life. Have you ever rebelled against any of them? What made you resist their authority?

Now, read Luke 15:11–16 in your Bible.

> "A man had two sons. The younger of them said to his father, 'Father, give me the share of the estate I have coming to me.' So he distributed the assets to them. Not many days later, the younger son gathered together all he had and traveled to a distant country, where he squandered his estate in foolish living."—Luke 15:11–13

Reread Luke 15:11–16 and answer these questions:

- Since an inheritance was usually given after someone's death, what did the son's request say about his feelings for his father? Explain.

- Verse 13 says the son "traveled to a distant country." Think about some of your personal experiences. Do you think distance from the people and things you know can make rebellion easier? Why?

- What were the effects of the son's rebellion? Does your rebellion affect those around you? How does it affect your relationship with God?

RESPOND

Sin is rebellion against God. Rebellion can also mean disobedience, or going against some authority. Because God is holy, sin goes against His very character.

- Take a hard look at your own heart. Do you see any areas of rebellion? Be honest with Him about those things. Journal a prayer confessing your rebellion to God.

- Who can hold you accountable when you feel tempted to rebel?

WELCOME HOME

Think about the longest amount of time you spent away from home. Where did you go? How did it feel to come home? Record your thoughts in your journal.

Read Luke 15:17–24 in your Bible.

"'Father, I have sinned against heaven and in your sight' . . . but while the son was still a long way off, his father saw him and was filled with compassion. He ran, threw his arms around his neck, and kissed him."—Luke 15:18, 20

PONDER THESE QUESTIONS:

- Take a look at verse 18. Highlight the phrase, "I have sinned against heaven and in your sight." How did the son's words represent a repentant heart? Explain.

- The younger son represents those who rebel against God. Because you are a sinner, the younger son represents you. The Father represents God. Why is it important to understand God welcomes us back when we repent?

- Circle the father's actions in verses 20 and 21. What do the father's actions reveal about his character? His love for his son? His desire for his son to return to him?

- Think of the father's character. How does this parable help you understand the love and compassion of the Father? Explain.

RESPOND

Repentance means you realize your sin, confess it to God, and completely turn away from it to follow Him.

- Complete the following in your journal: I am like the rebellious child because I _____. God is like the loving Father because He _____.

- Think about your answers to the statement above. List the son's characteristics from Luke 15:11–20. Do you have any of those same characteristics? What steps can you take to get your heart right with God?

- What does this parable teach you about salvation and the nature of God's redemption? What does it teach you about His eagerness to accept repentant outcasts?

JOIN THE CELEBRATION

Read Luke 15:25–32 in your Bible.

> "But he replied to his father, 'Look, I have been slaving many years for you, and I have never disobeyed your orders, yet you never gave me a young goat so I could celebrate with my friends. But when this son of yours came, who has devoured your assets with prostitutes, you slaughtered the fattened calf for him.'"—Luke 15:29–30

ANSWER THESE QUESTIONS:

- Why was the older son angry at his father's warm welcome of the younger brother?

- How did the older son describe his relationship to his father?

- Skim over Luke 15:1–2. Pharisees and religious leaders believed they were righteous because they did everything commanded by the law. They didn't think sinners deserved the same treatment as them in God's kingdom. How is the older son like the Pharisees and religious leaders? Explain.

- The father responded to his older son in verses 31 and 32. Read the verses and think about the father's response. The father represents God in these verses. What does this tell you about God's character? Explain.

- How do you think the son responded to his father? In your journal, write the way you would respond—your initial reaction.

RESPOND

Self-righteousness is the belief that you are morally better than others. Do you ever act self-righteous, telling God all you've done for Him and how others are undeserving of His love? Write your answers in your journal. Examine your heart toward sinners. Use the questions below as a guide.

- Be honest with God about the way you feel when someone doesn't get what you think they deserve. Ask Him for a heart that rejoices in His mercy and grace.

- Think about your family, school, or community. Who are the people who seem least likely to turn to Jesus for salvation and where do they hang out? Ask God to help you see ways you can be involved in His work in those places.

DESERVING

Read Luke 15:25–32 to briefly review yesterday's devotion. Now read Matthew 20:1–16 in your Bible.

> "'Friend, I'm doing you no wrong. Didn't you agree with me on a denarius? Take what's yours and go. I want to give this last man the same as I gave you. Don't I have the right to do what I want with my business? Are you jealous because I'm generous?'"
> —Matthew 20:13–15

PONDER THESE QUESTIONS:

- What similarities do you see between today's passage and yesterday's Scripture passage?

- Your view of who is worthy of grace is different from God's gracious view. What does today's parable teach about God's grace?

- Imagine you were one of the workers hired early in the day. Would you have a right to be angry? Why or why not? Explain your answer.

Though the early laborers agreed to a denarius for their pay, they were still upset because late arrivers received the same. What God gives to you or someone else is up to God. If God decided to give His grace based upon whether or not someone deserved it, no one would receive it.

RESPOND

- Are you ever jealous over someone's good fortune? Confess this to God with a grateful heart for His grace and goodness.

- How can you have a better attitude toward God's grace for others?

- In your journal, skip to a blank page and write *Thanks for Grace*. Record some specific situations that helped you recognize your need for God's grace. Journal a short prayer of thanks for each one.

CERTAIN JUDGMENT

What do you believe happens after death? What do your friends believe? List a few ideas in your journal. To learn what the Bible has to say, read Luke 16:19–31.

> "'Besides all this, a great chasm has been fixed between us and you, so that those who want to pass over from here to you cannot; neither can those from there cross over to us.'"—Luke 16:26

ASK YOURSELF:

- According to this passage, what happens after death?

- Make two lists: one that describes the rich man, then one that describes Lazarus.

- The rich man wanted to return to share the truth with his family. How did he show he cared about them? How does this compare to the relationship the rich man had with Lazarus on earth?

- What is the relationship between your faith in God and how you treat others? Explain. God's judgment is certain. According to this passage, what are the two options for eternity? How do you choose to spend eternity with God?

RESPOND

The rich man considered his own judgment supreme: He found Lazarus unworthy of love and care. This parable demonstrates the attitude of the heart is more important than the appearance of righteousness.

- Think of the times you've judged others. What steps will you take to stop yourself from doing this in the future? Jot down two steps in your journal.

- Do you overlook some people when it comes to sharing Jesus—people you don't consider important, fail to notice, or simply pretend don't exist? Ask God to help you see and love these people. Pray for opportunities to share the source of your hope with them.

THE STUFF THAT LASTS

Do you always want more—stuff, acclaim, respect, talent—or are you content? Why or why not? Record your response in your journal.

Read Luke 12:13–21.

> He then told them, "Watch out and be on guard against all greed because one's life is not in the abundance of his possessions."—Luke 12:15

CONSIDER THE FOLLOWING:

- According to verse 15, does the amount of stuff you own matter? Why or why not? Explain.

- The rich man focused on his possessions and constantly getting more stuff to enjoy. Read verse 20 again. Circle the word God used to describe the man at the beginning of the verse. Did God consider the man's decision wise? Why or why not?

- Now, read verse 21. The verse says the man kept his wealth for himself and was not "rich toward God." Simply put, the rich man didn't handle his possessions in a way that pleased God. Looking back at verse 21, where should your treasure be? What kind of riches should you have? What does that mean? Journal in your own words.

RESPOND

- Where do you tend to place your confidence? In your journal, write about any that apply:

Your abilities	Money
Good deeds	Possessions
Hard work	Popularity
Jesus	

- By your thoughts and actions this past week, where would you say you're investing the most—the world or eternity? How do you know?

- Why does what you invest in matter? Journal some ways you can choose to invest in God's kingdom.

YOU DON'T HAVE FOREVER

Read Luke 13:1–9 in your Bible.

And He told this parable: "A man had a fig tree that was planted in his vineyard. He came looking for fruit on it and found none. He told the vineyard worker, 'Listen, for three years I have come looking for fruit on this fig tree and haven't found any. Cut it down! Why should it even waste the soil?' But he replied to him, 'Sir, leave it this year also, until I dig around it and fertilize it. Perhaps it will bear fruit next year, but if not, you can cut it down.'"—Luke 13:6–9

PONDER THE FOLLOWING:

- In verses 3 and 5, Jesus spoke the same words. What was the action Jesus told the crowd to take?

- What consequences did Jesus say they would face if they did not act? Why is this important to you today?

Read Galatians 5:22–23. These verses list characteristics of people who have trusted Jesus as their Savior. These characteristics are called fruit of the Spirit. Verses 6, 7, and 9 also use the word *fruit* to describe showing godly characteristics. How does the barren tree illustrate the way many people live their lives today? Explain.

Reread verses 7–9. The vineyard owner was fed up with the tree because it didn't produce fruit like it was supposed to. He ordered the vineyard worker to cut it down. But the vineyard worker interceded and asked the owner to give the tree another chance. In the same way, God's judgment will also come. People must repent before it's too late.

RESPOND

Luke's writing was not only a warning to the people of Israel, but also a warning to you today.

- How does this passage challenge you in the areas of your spiritual life about which you tend to think, *I'll do that when I'm older?* List some of those areas.

- Journal a prayer, asking God to show you specific ways you can live more for Him now.

THE TRUTH ABOUT JESUS

Read Luke 20:9–19 in your Bible. Most biblical scholars believe the vineyard owner in this parable represents God, while the owner's son represents Jesus.

> But He looked at them and said, "Then what is the meaning of this Scripture: The stone that the builders rejected—this has become the cornerstone? Everyone who falls on that stone will be broken to pieces, and if it falls on anyone, it will grind him to powder!"—Luke 20:17–18

CONSIDER THE FOLLOWING:

- In what way do you see God's judgment in this parable? His grace? Explain.

- Read Psalm 118:22, the verse Jesus quoted in today's Scripture. Write your definition of a cornerstone. What does this help you understand about Jesus? Explain.

- Verse 18 upset the religious leaders because they knew Jesus "had told this parable against them." What was their reaction? What stopped them from carrying out their plan? Explain.

RESPOND

- Evaluate your life. Is Jesus the cornerstone, the foundation, and strength of your life? Why or why not?

- Whom or what are you trying to make the focus of your life other than Jesus? Confess these things today. Ask God to help you focus your life on Jesus.

SIGNS

Read Matthew 24:3–36 in your Bible.

> "Now learn this parable from the fig tree: As soon as its branch becomes tender and sprouts leaves, you know that summer is near. In the same way, when you see all these things, recognize that He is near—at the door!"—Matthew 24:32–33

The word *near* doesn't necessarily mean Jesus will return today or even ten years from now; near simply means Jesus has completed what was necessary for people to have access to God through Him and could return at any time.

Reread verses 32–36 carefully and think through these questions:

- No one knows the specific time of Jesus' return. List things in the passage Jesus listed as signs of His return.

- Though no one knows exactly when Jesus will return, you can watch for changes in the world around you. Write the promises about these changes in verses 34 and 35 in your journal.

RESPOND

Many people have tried to predict the day of Jesus' return. Jesus said not even He or the angels know the hour, only the Father (v. 36). Always carefully compare anything you hear (or read) about Jesus' return to the truth of God's Word.

- How would your life change this week if you lived like you really believed Jesus' return was near?

- List at least three things you want to do differently and pray for God to give you an expectant heart as you wait for His coming.

WHAT WILL YOU BE DOING?

Read Matthew 24:45–51.

> "That slave whose master finds him working when he comes will be rewarded."
> —Matthew 24:46

God's timing is not like your timing (2 Peter 3:8–9). He is not late in sending Christ to bring you back to Him, but is patient with those who have not yet repented, giving them a chance to return to Him.

Relate this parable to your life. Draw a picture or write a few words to describe what you would be doing if you were the faithful servant, working when Christ returns, and what you would be doing as the wicked servant, taking advantage of Jesus' delay and pursuing sinful things. What does this parable teach you about what is really important? About how you should spend your life?

RESPOND

A faithful person is someone you can rely on. Faithful people are dependable, meaning they keep their promises. God is the perfect model of absolute faithfulness, even with extremely disobedient people.

- List the qualities of faithfulness mentioned above. Do you have some of those qualities? Pray that God would help you grow in faithfulness.

- Does this parable scare you? Challenge you? Encourage you? Take a look at your life and the qualities you listed above. God knows your heart, so be honest with Him about the areas you struggle with. Journal a prayer confessing your unfaithfulness. Ask God to show you where He wants you to be working.

THE DANGER OF REFUSAL

Now, read Matthew 22:1–14.

"For many are invited, but few are chosen."—Matthew 22:14

You can learn much about God from the king in this parable. Journal what you learned about God from today's Scripture.

The servants represent messengers of the kingdom of God who carry His invitation to all people. In the parable, people were invited to the banquet, but they didn't want to come. What are some reasons people might reject Jesus' invitation today? Explain.

When it comes to knowing God, Romans 1:20 says, "People are without excuse." Matthew 22:12 says, "The man was speechless." He had no excuse for showing up to the wedding improperly dressed. In the same way, no one has any excuse for not knowing God or following His ways.

RESPOND

Pride can blind you to the need to accept Jesus' invitation, as it did for some of the Jews. They thought they were safe because they were God's chosen people and followed the law. But their hearts were not right before God, and they rejected Him.

- Pray for God to help you know if your heart is right before Him. If you aren't sure, you can also talk with a Christian mentor or pastor if you have any further questions or doubts.

- Write the names of any people you know who may be in danger, based on this parable. How might God want to use you to take His invitation to them?

- In your journal, label the top of the page *No Excuses*. Write all the ways God has revealed Himself to you. (Tip: take a look at Job 6:8–9, Matthew 11:27, and 1 Corinthians 2:10 if you need help getting started.)

PREPARE YOURSELF

Read Matthew 25:1–13. Jesus' return is often likened to a wedding, with Jesus as the groom and the church as the bride.

> "Therefore be alert, because you don't know either the day or the hour."—Matthew 25:13

Both the wise and the foolish virgins made decisions on the way. Compare and contrast their actions in your journal.

The foolish virgins were unprepared for the groom's arrival; they represent people who do not know Jesus. The wise virgins were prepared to wait until midnight. The time of both the groom's and Jesus' return is unknown. Like the wise bridesmaids, you must be prepared for a lengthy wait.

ASK YOURSELF:

- What can you do while you wait for Jesus to return? How can you prepare? Explain.

- What does the phrase "the groom was delayed" teach you about God's compassion and desire for people to come to salvation? His love? His patience? Explain.

RESPOND

In this parable, Jesus likely used the term *virgins* to demonstrate the intimate relationship the women had with the bride. Think about how this applies to your relationship with Jesus.

- What situations tempt you to neglect your relationship with Jesus? How do you need to persevere in those situations? Why?

- Besides reading this devotional, what are some steps you're taking to grow in your relationship with Jesus? Are you more or less prepared for His return than you were two years ago? Explain.

READY AND WAITING

Read Luke 12:35–40 in your Bible.

"Be ready for service and have your lamps lit."—Luke 12:35

In verses 35–36, highlight the following phrases: *ready for service*, *have your lamps lit*, *waiting*, and *open the door*. In the parable, the slaves represent Christ-followers. According to the high-lighted words, how should Christ-followers prepare for His return? Explain.

Jesus says more about service in verse 37. In your journal, record similarities and differences between the service mentioned here and in verse 35.

According to verses 37–38, what happened to the servants the Master found readily awaiting His return? In your journal, list some of the blessings they received. What does this teach you about the reward for readily anticipating Jesus' return?

RESPOND

- What does it mean to be ready for Jesus' return? Write seven statements to answer how you will prepare, using the letters below to begin each one. The first one is completed for you.

  Be an example of Jesus' love to everyone I meet.

  E

  R

  E

  A

  D

  Y

- Look at the Be Ready statements you wrote above. Using your journal, examine how those preparations will affect your witness to your non-Christian friends. Make sure to record the names of those friends and pray that each person will be ready for Jesus' return.

- What times in your life have you felt the most spiritually alert? What led to your readiness? Explain. Ask God to continue to prepare your heart for His return.

GOD'S EXPECTATIONS

Read Luke 12:43. Jesus wanted His disciples to be watchful, but He also wanted to find them working. The same is true for you.

> "Much will be required of everyone who has been given much. And even more will be expected of the one who has been entrusted with more."—Luke 12:48

Now, read Luke 12:41–48. Underline any of Jesus' words that remind you that the timing of His return is unknown. Note the different possible results for the slave in verses 43–48:

- If he is working.
- If he is living in blatant disobedience.
- If he is unprepared.
- If he did not know God's will.

Each slave was held accountable for his knowledge and action or inaction. Knowing the Master's will and not doing it is dangerous. What does today's reading tell you about Christian leaders' responsibility to the message of Jesus?

RESPOND

You are accountable to God for completing the tasks He gives to you. No matter how significant or insignificant your task may seem, you are responsible for that task.

- In what ways has God entrusted you with more? Where does God have you working right now? Journal your thoughts about being held accountable to God for those things. Ask Him to help you remain faithful to your responsibilities and to be actively involved where He is at work around you.
- What steps will you take this week to be actively involved in the work of the kingdom? Write them on your mirror or on a sticky note placed on the back of your door.

THERE'S STILL ROOM

Read Luke 14:15–24. Note the excuses people made for not accepting the banquet invitation in verses 18–20.

"Go out quickly into the streets and alleys of the city, and bring in here the poor, maimed, blind, and lame!"—Luke 14:21

ASK YOURSELF:

- Even though the host invited the blind, lame, poor, and maimed, the banquet hall still wasn't full. So, he ordered the servant to go in search of more people. The host represents God. What do these verses help you understand about His love? Explain.

- "Those men" (v. 24) knew their friend was hosting a banquet (v. 16), yet when the banquet was prepared, they made excuses (v. 18). Those men represent the Jews who rejected Jesus. When have you been like "those men"? How did God work in that situation?

RESPOND

If runners miss the sound of the starting gun in a race, the delayed start could cost them first place. In the same way, you settle for second best when you ignore Jesus' invitation to spend time doing His work on earth now. Your other options may not all be bad things, but they can keep you from God's best for you.

- Have you accepted God's kingdom invitation? Journal about your experience.

- Ask God to help see what is most important and help you put Him and His kingdom work first in your life.

- What steps will you take to share the gospel with the people around you this week? Ask a Christian mentor such as a student pastor or parent to hold you accountable by checking in with you at the end of the week.

ETERNAL VIEW

Today's passage describes the beginning of John the Baptist's ministry. His words constantly pointed to the One who would come after him—Jesus. John humbly acknowledged the surpassing greatness of Jesus' work and ministry.

Read Matthew 3:1–12 in your Bible. In your journal, list four messages that John the Baptist proclaimed. What did John's messages encourage people to do? Explain.

> His winnowing shovel is in His hand, and He will clear His threshing floor and gather His wheat into the barn. But the chaff He will burn up with fire that never goes out.—Matthew 3:12

Read verse 12 again. John the Baptist warned of Christ's judgment and gave an illustration of grain and chaff being separated. Record what will happen to the chaff and grain in your journal.

This illustration indicates that no one will escape God's judgment, and He will make no mistakes sorting the believers from the unbelievers. How does this passage help you realize the urgency and importance of sharing Jesus with others? Journal your thoughts.

RESPOND

Have you trusted in Christ as your personal Lord and Savior? Journal your response. If you want to place your faith in Christ, find a couple of trustworthy adults such as a parent, student pastor, or pastor and ask them to share their testimony with you.

COMING DAYS

Read Matthew 8:8–13. The gentile soldier spoke with humility and showed greater faith than the religious leaders in Israel. Why is this important? Journal your response.

"I tell you that many will come from east and west, and recline at the table with Abraham, Isaac, and Jacob in the kingdom of heaven. But the sons of the kingdom will be thrown into the outer darkness. In that place there will be weeping and gnashing of teeth."—Matthew 8:11–12

ANSWER THE FOLLOWING QUESTIONS:

- What comes to mind when you read the words *recline* and *table*? What about *weeping* and *gnashing*?

- Verse 11 gives us a glimpse of eternity with God: believers in fellowship not only with Him, but also with believers from previous generations. Knowing this, how do you envision eternity with God? Sketch a picture.

- There is a clear difference in eternity for those who trust and those who reject the Son of God, Jesus Christ. What does this demonstrate about God's character?

RESPOND

As a believer in Christ, you will always be with God and experience everlasting life. Think of how incredible eternity with God will be.

- In your journal, jot down a few words that describe the glory and character of God.

- For further study on saving faith, read John 3:36 and Romans 10:9.

BELIEVE IN ME

Read John 14:1–6 in your Bible.

> "I am going away to prepare a place for you . . . You know the way to where I am going."—John 14:2, 4

DIG DEEPER WITH THESE QUESTIONS:

- Based on what you read, fill in the blanks below.

  We are to believe in _____, and also in _____.

  Jesus went away to prepare a place for _____.

  Jesus declared, "I am the _____, the _____, and the _____."

- Where was Jesus going? What did Jesus say He would do when He left? Why was it important for Him to go? Explain.

Other passages, such as Matthew 5:12 and 6:19–21, indicate that followers of Christ will receive a reward in heaven. However, today's Scripture focuses on Jesus' personal touch in the preparation of a place for His followers to dwell with Him for eternity.

ASK YOURSELF:

- Jesus came to earth, died for our sins, and left to prepare an eternal place for us to dwell with Him. What does this tell you about Jesus' claim that He was "the way"?

- Look at the end of verse 6. How did Jesus say His followers would get to the place He prepared for them?

RESPOND

In culture, people have many ideas and beliefs about the way to get to heaven. Some say you only have to be a good person, and others believe there is more than one way to get to heaven.

- Meditate on the Scripture you read today. What is the true way to heaven? Are you focused on Jesus and living His way?

- Think about all Jesus experienced and did to enable you to have fellowship with God. Say a prayer of gratitude for Christ's sacrifice and the gift of eternal life with Him.

A REAL RESPONSE

Read Matthew 25:31–46 in your Bible.

> "And they will go away into eternal punishment, but the righteous into eternal life."
> —Matthew 25:46

Look back over what you read and make a list of loving actions the sheep carried out compared to the goats. The sheep in this passage represent the righteous, those who will spend eternity with God. The goats represent those who reject Jesus and will spend eternity separated from Him. According to verses 37–39, how should Christ-followers serve Him? Jot down a few ideas.

RESPOND

Believers are called to care for others as if they are caring for Jesus.

- Are you a sheep or a goat? Why? Journal your response.

- Take a minute to examine your actions, thoughts, and words. Do they honor Christ? Confess any struggles to God and ask Him to help you live in a way that is pleasing to Him.

- What can you commit to today to develop an authentic relationship with Jesus? Journal a few ideas and share them with your student pastor or another mature Christian mentor.

PURE LIFE

Read Matthew 18:8–9.

> "If your hand or your foot causes your downfall, cut it off and throw it away. It is better for you to enter life maimed or lame, than to have two hands or two feet and be thrown into the eternal fire. And if your eye causes your downfall, gouge it out and throw it away. It is better for you to enter life with one eye, rather than to have two eyes and be thrown into hellfire!"—Matthew 18:8–9

Although sin does not cause you to lose your salvation, God takes sin seriously. The vivid metaphors in this passage do not call us to harm ourselves physically, but emphasize the seriousness of sin and the importance of living in righteousness. A Christian's ultimate goal is to respond to salvation in faith, love, and obedience to God.

Living in sin and struggling with sin are two different things. Even after you become a Christian, you won't be perfect; however, you shouldn't continue in sinful habits.

- List a few characteristics of those who live in righteousness and those who have sinful lifestyles.
- Look at the definition of righteousness in your journal. How can believers live lives characterized by righteousness? Explain.

RESPOND

- Consider how God wants us to avoid sin. In your journal, list the people, places, and things that tempt you to sin. How can you avoid these temptations?
- Examine your heart: Do you have any unconfessed sins? Repent and ask God to help you turn from those sins and live for Him.

FREE FROM FEAR

Carefully read Matthew 10:26–31.

> "Don't fear those who kill the body but are not able to kill the soul; rather, fear Him who is able to destroy both soul and body in hell. Aren't two sparrows sold for a penny? Yet not one of them falls to the ground without your Father's consent. But even the hairs of your head have all been counted. So don't be afraid therefore; you are worth more than many sparrows."—Matthew 10:28–31

ANSWER THESE QUESTIONS:

- In your Bible, highlight each phrase that commands you not to fear or be afraid. What are the reasons Jesus tells believers not to fear? Explain in your own words in your journal.

- Whom does today's Scripture say you should fear? Why? Explain.

Fearing God is not about dreading Him, but honoring Him. When you fear God, you recognize His authority and show Him the reverence He deserves. What does it look like to live out a healthy fear of God? Explain.

Judgment will come one day, but believers do not need to be afraid. We can trust God to be true to His word to reward believers and punish His enemies.

RESPOND

- Prayerfully consider your life. Do your actions, words, and heart attitude reflect one who is grateful and secure in their eternity with a Holy God? Why or why not?

- Jot down the name of someone you know who doesn't know Jesus. In your journal, record some ideas on how you can share His love with that person.

BOLDNESS

Read Revelation 21:1–8.

> He will wipe away every tear from their eyes. Death will no longer exist; grief, crying, and pain will exist no longer, because the previous things have passed away.
> —Revelation 21:4

ASK YOURSELF:

- According to verse 1, what will pass away? What will no longer exist?

- Verses 1–7 focus on the reality of eternity for believers. Verse 8 portrays the reality of eternity for those who never sincerely committed their hearts and lives to Jesus Christ. What is the punishment for those who reject Jesus?

- Biblical scholars suggest the "One seated on the throne" (v. 5) is Jesus. He previously spoke as the judge, but in these verses He spoke as Creator. Jesus said He would make everything new. What promises of God will be fulfilled in the new Jerusalem? Hint: Look at verses 3–4.

- According to verse 8, who are the wicked, those who will burn in the lake of fire?

RESPOND

These verses should cause Christians to live with great hope and boldness, knowing that our eternity is sure, our Savior wins, and all will be made right. It should also challenge us to share our faith with others so that they may experience eternity with Christ rather than eternal separation and punishment.

- Have you ever shared with someone about Jesus? Have you ever shared your faith with someone who trusted Jesus as Savior as a result? God desires you to be bold in sharing your faith, not passive. In your journal, jot down some ideas to help you break the ice when sharing Christ.

- Are you compassionate toward people who don't know Jesus? Do you have a burden to share His love with them? Knowing their fate in eternity, offer a prayer asking God to make you more sensitive to the Holy Spirit's leading and to reveal to you anyone you need to share your faith with.

THE BREAD OF LIFE

Read John 6:22–40.

> "I am the bread of life," Jesus told them. "No one who comes to Me will ever be hungry, and no one who believes in Me will ever be thirsty again."—John 6:35

THINK THROUGH THESE QUESTIONS:

- In verses 26–27, notice the two different types of hunger mentioned. Where does "the food that lasts for eternal life" come from? Explain.

- Circle the two required responses (v. 35) to Jesus as the Bread of Life. What does this mean? Explain in your own words.

- The people were amazed by the signs Jesus performed, but still refused to believe He was the Son of God (v. 36). Read verses 39–40. Jesus mentions two things that are God's will. Highlight those two things. What does this teach you about salvation? Eternal life?

- Jot down a few things, other than Jesus, that people often look to for meaning and purpose.

RESPOND

Bread is necessary for survival. Just like God provided manna to satisfy the Israelites' hunger in the wilderness, He gave Jesus to sustain us spiritually. Faith in Jesus is necessary for eternal life.

- Do you think of Jesus as necessary to your everyday life? Why or why not? Journal your response.

- The good news of Christ affects us in practical and spiritual ways. How can you share Christ's love today to meet someone's physical and spiritual needs? Jot down some ideas in your journal.

THE LIGHT OF THE WORLD

Read John 1:1–5 and 3:19–21.

ASK YOURSELF:

- Who is the Light and who sent that light to men?
- Why did the people like darkness (v. 19–20)? Are people still this way today?
- According to verse 21, those who live by the truth will do what?

Read John 8:12–20.

> Then Jesus spoke to them again: "I am the light of the world. Anyone who follows Me will never walk in the darkness but will have the light of life."—John 8:12

Jesus wasn't saying He provided light or enlightenment; He was the Light. Since God was the light that guided the Israelites through the desert, the religious leaders would have immediately understood that Jesus was also claiming divinity.

ASK YOURSELF:

- When the Jews questioned Jesus' claim of divinity, what was His response (v. 19)? Journal in your own words.
- How was Jesus' promised light different from the light provided by the golden lamps during the Festival of Tabernacles? Explain.

RESPOND

When you need to do something well, you find a place with good lighting. The same should be true in your walk with Christ—when you want to live well, draw close to Him. Are you seeking Christ in all you do? Talk honestly about this with God and ask Him to help you draw near to Him.

THE DOOR

Read John 10:1–10. In Jesus' day, people would have understood that the gate to the sheepfold was a shepherd or watchman lying across the opening in the wall. As you will study more tomorrow, Jesus was also known as the Good Shepherd. Put simply: Jesus is the leader and protector of His people.

> "I am the door. If anyone enters by Me, he will be saved and will come in and go out and find pasture."—John 10:9

THINK THROUGH THESE QUESTIONS:

- Circle the phrase "the door" throughout the passage. What does Jesus' identity as the door tell you about the way to eternal life? About your salvation? Explain.

- Jesus is the only way to enter eternal life. He provides salvation to all who place their trust in Him. When you trust Jesus as Savior, you become His. Your salvation and your place with Him in eternity is secure. In verse 9, Jesus promises three things to those who enter through Him. List them in your journal.

- Read verse 10 again. What did Jesus promise here? Write His promise in your own words.

- What does Jesus' promise in verse 10 reveal about His character?

RESPOND

- Jesus didn't only promise life after we die. He also promised abundant life while we're here on the earth. How has He provided abundant life to you? Journal a prayer of thanks to God for all He has done for you.

- Doors let things in and keep things out. For further study on the function of doors in Scripture, read Genesis 4:7, Psalm 141:3, Colossians 4:2–3, and Revelation 3:20.

THE GOOD SHEPHERD

Reread John 10:1–5 from yesterday's devotion.

The shepherd in this passage knew his sheep, called them, and led them. Notice that the shepherd didn't just call his sheep with a command to follow, but he called them by name—pointing to the intimacy of the relationship between shepherd and sheep. Biblical scholars suggest this metaphor demonstrates the relationship between Jesus and His people.

Now, read John 10:11–21.

> "I am the good shepherd. I know My own sheep, and they know Me, as the Father knows Me, and I know the Father. I lay down My life for the sheep."—John 10:14–15

ASK YOURSELF:

- Read verses 11–15. List some characteristics of a good shepherd in your journal.

- Jesus called Himself the Good Shepherd and believers are referred to as His sheep. Look at the characteristics you listed above. How would you describe Jesus' relationship with us? Explain.

- Read verse 11 again. Underline the words "I lay down my life for the sheep." How does this show Jesus' love for you? How does it point to Jesus' death on the cross?

RESPOND

Jesus wants a personal relationship with you—He wants to know you. You are so important to Jesus that He died for you to have the chance to know Him. He invites you to an intimate relationship built on love and trust.

- Relationships provide you with many good things, but usually require things of you as well. In your journal, draw a line down the middle of a clean page. At the top of the page, write the headings *Given* and *Required*. Under the appropriate heading, jot down some things God provides for us and some things He requires of us.

- Jesus loves us enough to die for us. He takes care of us. Is there someone in your life today who needs to hear this? Pray that the Holy Spirit would help you discern how to share the truth with them.

THE RESURRECTION AND THE LIFE

Read John 11:17–27.

> Jesus said to her, "I am the resurrection and the life. The one who believes in Me, even if he dies, will live. Everyone who lives and believes in Me will never die—ever. Do you believe this?"—John 11:25–26

CONSIDER THE FOLLOWING QUESTIONS:

- Read verses 22 and 24. Highlight the phrase *I know*. What do these words indicate about Martha's faith? Do you think she trusted Jesus? Why or why not?

- Martha believed and had faith in Jesus, but she did not understand the scope of His power. Even though Lazarus had been in the tomb for four days, Jesus had the power to give Him life physically as well as spiritually. Why is this concept so important?

Jesus asserted His power over death, stating that He was the source of resurrection power and eternal life. Only He has the power to give us real, meaningful, and abundant life.

RESPOND

- Have you accepted Jesus' invitation to spend eternity with Him? Thank Him for His gift of salvation. If you haven't trusted Jesus as Savior, find a couple of trustworthy adults such as a parent, student pastor, or pastor and ask them to share their testimony with you.

- Jesus sees the bigger picture (v. 4). Have you experienced a time when God seemed to delay a response, but later revealed His "big picture" to you? Journal what stands out to you most about that time.

- If you know people who are grieving, pray for them. Ask God to help you show His love to those who are hurting.

THE WAY, THE TRUTH, THE LIFE

Read John 14:1–11.

> Jesus told him, "I am the way, the truth, and the life. No one comes to the Father except through Me."—John 14:6

ASK YOURSELF:

- What did Jesus mean when He said, "I am the way, the truth, and the life" (v. 6)?

- It is only through Jesus that you can be reconciled to God, know the truth about how to live, and experience new life. According to the last part of verse 6, what is the way to be reconciled to God? How did Jesus make this possible? Explain.

- Many people believe that there is more than one way to get to heaven. Circle the words *except through me*. How do Jesus' words go against that view?

- Reflect on verse 7. Jesus said if the disciples knew Him, they would know the Father. In verse 9, Jesus repeated Himself, once again declaring that He and God are one. How does knowing this affect your view of Jesus' authority? His promises to you?

RESPOND

- Journal a prayer, thanking God for providing a way for you to be reconciled with Him through Jesus.

- Do you struggle to believe Jesus is the way, the truth, and the life? Confess your struggle to God. If you have questions, ask your student pastor or another pastor at your church.

- Ask God to help you to stand firm in your beliefs. Pray that He will give you wisdom as you talk to people who have different beliefs.

- Look at the definition of the word *reconciled* in your journal. Examine your heart. Are you reconciled to the Father?

THE VINE

Read John 15:1–8.

> "I am the vine; you are the branches. The one who remains in Me and I in him produces much fruit, because you can do nothing without Me."—John 15:5

ANSWER THE FOLLOWING QUESTIONS:

- A vine sustains—fruit will not grow unless connected to the vine. What does it mean that Jesus is the vine? Explain.

- In verse 4, Jesus said a branch cannot produce fruit on its own. Look back at the first part of the verse. How does a branch produce fruit? How does this relate to a Christian's relationship with Jesus?

- In verses 3–4, Jesus was speaking to His disciples. Why was it important for them to remain in Him? How does this apply to you? Explain.

- Throughout His ministry, Jesus focused on bringing glory to God. Look at verse 8. What does this tell you about the importance of producing fruit as a follower of Jesus?

- How could remaining connected to Jesus and producing fruit help others recognize their need for Him?

RESPOND

If you want to truly live out your faith, you must remain connected to Jesus. When you remain in Jesus, your life will bear the fruit of your relationship with Him. Put simply: if you truly love and follow Jesus, others will be able to see Him working through you. Jesus said to remain in Him five times throughout verses 1–8. Does this describe your relationship with Jesus? Why or why not? How are you growing in your faith? Journal your response.

CHRIST ALONE

Read through Matthew 3:1–12.

> "Therefore produce fruit consistent with repentance. And don't presume to say to yourselves, 'We have Abraham as our father.' For I tell you that God is able to raise up children for Abraham from these stones."—Matthew 3:8–9

ASK YOURSELF:

- What is John's message in verse 2? Explain in your own words what it means to repent.
- In verses 8–9, John cautioned the religious leaders of two things. List them in your journal.

No background and no amount of rule following can make you right with God—only true repentance and Jesus have that power. The leaders trusted in their own good works and in their lineage links with Abraham to bring them into God's covenant. Why would John's teaching fly in the face of their beliefs?

The Pharisees knew they needed to repent, but they only partially repented. Outwardly, they did what they needed to do to show others that they were repentant; however, they continued to sin while denying their guilt.

RESPOND

Many people still believe they only have to be good or follow rules to get to heaven. What about you? Journal a prayer asking the Lord to show you ways you might be trusting something or someone other than Jesus for salvation.

RULE FOLLOWER

Read Matthew 15:1–20.

> "These people honor Me with their lips, but their heart is far from Me. They worship Me in vain, teaching as doctrines the commands of men."—Matthew 15:8–9

ANSWER THESE QUESTIONS:

- Jesus railed against the Pharisees for two reasons: Their love of tradition was greater than their love for God and they believed corruption came from breaking the law instead of a sinful heart. Highlight where you see evidence of these two issues throughout the passage. In your journal, explain them in your own words.

- The Pharisees were so caught up living in line with the law that they failed to recognize their own sinfulness. This can also happen for believers today. List a few ways you can guard against this in your own life.

- Why is it important to recognize that we are sinful people and cannot save ourselves?

RESPOND

- When has following rules been more important to you than following Jesus? Evaluate the things you say and do. Be honest with God. Pray and ask Him to help you see following Jesus as the most important thing.

- People have sin in their hearts, and Jesus came to replace that sin with His righteousness. If you haven't trusted Jesus as Savior, find a couple of trustworthy adults such as a parent, student pastor, or pastor and ask them to share their testimony with you.

BLINDED

Have you ever asked God to send you a sign to prove that He was there? To prove He loved you or that you were on the right path? Journal your experience.

Read Matthew 16:1–12.

> The Pharisees and Sadducees approached, and as a test, asked Him to show them a sign from heaven.—Matthew 16:1

The Pharisees witnessed Jesus' miraculous feeding of the four thousand yet they wanted something more—another sign. The question asked in verse 1 is more a question of Jesus' authority than a request.

The sign of Jonah, referenced in verse 4, is a reference to Jesus' resurrection. Jonah was in the belly of a fish for three days, and even compared the experience to death (Jonah 2:2, 6–7). This parallels with Jesus being in the tomb for three days before His resurrection.

CONSIDER THESE QUESTIONS:

- The Pharisees directed their focus and faith to the wrong places. They questioned Jesus, ignored His authority, and denied Him as the Messiah. They refused to accept His authority in their lives. When have you been like that?

- How can this kind of thinking lead others astray? What is a modern-day example of that?

RESPOND

- Some things appear to be good on the outside but actually go against what Scripture teaches. Are there influences in your life that are dangerous to your relationship with Christ? What can you do to minimize or eliminate those influences? Journal your response.

- To better understand the sign of Jonah read Jonah 1:17 and Matthew 12:40.

FALSE SECURITY

Read Matthew 23:1–15.

> "They do everything to be observed by others . . . They love the place of honor at banquets, the front seats in the synagogues, greetings in the marketplaces, and to be called 'Rabbi' by people."—Matthew 23:5, 6–7

ANSWER THESE QUESTIONS:

- Jesus identified the Pharisees as hypocrites who burdened people with strict rules and regulations; they claimed that abiding by these rules would help people find favor with God. They loved the structure of religion, but they didn't know God.

- Ponder verse 12. What does it mean to be humble? Why is this important? Explain.

- The Pharisees had a false understanding of salvation and were setting others up for hardship and heartache by teaching that salvation came from following rules. When you talk about your faith with someone, should you focus more on the rules you follow or what Jesus did for you? Why?

- Why is it important to recognize that your relationship with Jesus is not a checklist or long list of rules?

RESPOND

Without a relationship with Jesus, you can't experience salvation or true reconciliation with God. You can know about God and even talk about God without knowing Him personally. Explore your own thoughts about your relationship with Jesus. Do you believe your salvation is based on how well you follow the rules or solely on the work of Jesus? Why? Journal your answer.

HYPOCRITES

Read Matthew 23:25–28 and answer the following questions:

- Underline the word *hypocrites* each time it appears, and write down the definition in your journal. Define the term in your own words.

- Jesus pointed out that the Pharisees were living a life of hypocrisy—they didn't live for the God they proclaimed to love. Why is this so damaging to the name of God even today?

- When have you heard someone claim to love Jesus, but act in ways that failed to match up with those words? What did you learn from that experience?

"In the same way, on the outside you seem righteous to people, but inside you are full of hypocrisy and lawlessness."—Matthew 23:28

The Pharisees were overly concerned with their outward appearance and gave little attention to their inner purity. Scripture however tells us that righteousness flows from the inside out and results in Christlikeness.

- How does knowing Jesus encourage you to pay attention to your inner purity?

- Look at verse 26. How does a person walk in righteousness? Describe this process in your own words.

RESPOND

- Evaluate your own life and ask the Holy Spirit to examine your heart. Are you guilty of acting one way at church and another way around your friends at school?

- What changes do you need to make in your life today to get rid of sin and truly live in a way that honors Jesus? In your journal, list the steps you will take to make these changes.

WHAT REALLY MATTERS

Read Matthew 23:23–24.

> "Woe to you, scribes and Pharisees, hypocrites! You pay a tenth of mint, dill, and cumin, yet you have neglected the more important matters of the law—justice, mercy, and faith. These things should have been done without neglecting the others. Blind guides! You strain out a gnat, yet gulp down a camel!"—Matthew 23:23–24

ASK YOURSELF:

- These Pharisees tediously counted out a 10 percent tithe of everything they owned—even garden herbs. List the three things they neglected.

- The act of tithing was not bad; God actually commanded us to tithe. The Pharisees' issue was that they focused intently on the outward aspects of this command while missing out on important things God's law revealed. How do you see this in the church today? Give a specific example in your journal.

- Jesus continually pointed out that the Pharisees followed rules, but did not allow God to transform their hearts. They misjudged what was important to God. You can easily place your entire focus on doing things and fail to recognize the heart behind your actions. What are "gnats" in your life that hog your focus? What are the "camels" in your life? Explain.

RESPOND

Evaluate your own life and answer these questions in your journal.

- How can you remain focused on what is truly important to God?

- How can you be a person of justice, mercy, and faithfulness to those around you?

TWO COMMANDS

Now, read Matthew 22:34–40 and do the following:

- In verse 36, underline the word *greatest*. Phrase the expert's question in your own words and journal it.

- Verses 37–40 contain Jesus' response. List the two commands Jesus indicated.

- What does it mean to love the Lord with all your heart, soul, and mind? Why is this the most important command?

> He said to him, "Love the Lord your God with all your heart, with all your soul, and with all your mind. This is the greatest and most important command. The second is like it: Love your neighbor as yourself."—Matthew 22:37–39

When you love God with all our heart, you are compelled to love others. By loving others like this, you show them the love of God.

In today's Scripture, Jesus addressed the heart of the issue with the Pharisees. The attitude of your heart matters. If we do not have love for God, we become legalistic like the Pharisees—focusing on the laws instead of the God who gave them.

RESPOND

Journal your response to the following questions:

- Is your life characterized by His love?

- List some ways you can live out these commands this week.

- How does placing importance on loving God and others affect those around you?

- Think especially about people who don't know Jesus. List some ways you can obey these two commands and be a light for Christ to them.

PLEASING FAITH

Don't skim this passage lightly. Look carefully at what this conversation revealed about the motives of both Jesus and the woman.

Read Mark 7:24–30.

> Then He told her, "Because of this reply, you may go. The demon has gone out of your daughter."—Mark 7:29

THINK THROUGH THESE QUESTIONS:

- In verse 26, highlight the word *kept*. The Gentile woman absolutely believed Jesus could do something about the demons possessing her daughter. How did that display the woman's faith in Jesus?

- Why is it important that the woman recognized Jesus could do something about the evil spirits that possessed her daughter?

It may seem at first that Jesus was callous to this woman's cry for help, but this exchange actually sheds light on the gospel in a historical context. Jesus came first for the Jews, but ultimately salvation would be available for all.

Jesus told the woman that it was not yet her turn for salvation (v. 27). Her response showed that she understood Jesus' power had no boundaries (v. 28). In this way, her faith surpassed many of the Jews'. Not only did this Gentile woman acknowledge Jesus as her Lord, but she was content with just a crumb of His mercy. How did Jesus honor her undaunted trust in Him?

RESPOND

You can't be a Christ-follower without faith. Salvation can't be earned and we can't be saved from sin if we don't have faith in the God who saves.

- This woman had faith that Jesus could heal her daughter from the demons that possessed her. Think about how you approach Jesus. Would you describe your faith as absolute? Why or why not?

- Can you think of someone who shows this kind of faith? In your journal, list some characteristics of people who seem to have unshakable faith.

FAITHFULLY FOLLOW

Read Matthew 19:16–22. The young man seemed to know he lacked something. He assumed he could do more to earn salvation, but salvation can't be earned.

> "I have kept all these," the young man told Him. "What do I still lack?" "If you want to be perfect," Jesus said to him, "go, sell your belongings and give to the poor, and you will have treasure in heaven. Then come, follow Me."—Matthew 19:20–21

ASK YOURSELF THESE QUESTIONS:

- Jesus told the young man, "There is only One who is good" (v. 17). What did He mean?
- Jesus said the young man had to keep the commandments to enter eternal life—but Jesus was the only one able to do that perfectly. Why did Jesus direct the man to examine his obedience to the Ten Commandments?

This ruler thought he was doing all the right things, but Jesus proved otherwise. Still, Jesus gave the ruler a chance to reveal his heart and follow Him. When faced with his own insincere motives, the man walked away from this encounter disappointed.

Read verse 21 and Matthew 6:19–21. Journal some things you treasure, both worldly treasures and treasures in heaven.

RESPOND

The man allowed his earthly wealth to get in the way of knowing Jesus. Sometimes we do the same.

- What things in your life do you choose to prioritize over spending time with Jesus? What evidence in your life reveals your priorities? Journal your response.
- Journal some obstacles to your relationship with Jesus and ways to overcome them.

LIKE A CHILD

Read Mark 10:13–16 in your Bible.

> When Jesus saw it, He was indignant and said to them, "Let the little children come to Me. Don't stop them, for the kingdom of God belongs to such as these. I assure you: Whoever does not welcome the kingdom of God like a little child will never enter it."—Mark 10:14–15

Childlike frailty and dependence can be seen as a burden or weakness. Jesus saw this group of children as worthy recipients of His time, as well as a perfect illustration for the disciples. They still hadn't grasped that the only way to share in His blessings would be to confess total weakness and dependence upon Him.

ASK YOURSELF:

- How would you compare your faith in Christ to the dependence of a child?

- What would it take for you to have childlike faith, remaining completely dependent on Him?

- Why is it important that Christians realize that redemption isn't dependent upon them keeping rules or being good, that instead they must totally rely on Jesus?

RESPOND

- Do you remember when you first realized your need for Jesus? Journal about your experience.

- In your journal, list a few areas of your life you struggle to give over to Jesus. Pray and ask God to show you how to live completely dependent upon Him.

- For further study on dependence on God, read Proverbs 3:5; Jeremiah 17:7–8; and Philippians 4:19.

DOING VS. BEING

Read Luke 10:38–42 in your Bible.

> The Lord answered her, "Martha, Martha, you are worried and upset about many things, but one thing is necessary. Mary has made the right choice, and it will not be taken away from her."—Luke 10:41–42

PONDER THE FOLLOWING:

- Based on the events recorded, how would you describe Mary and Martha?

- If you were Martha, would you have been upset with Mary? Why or why not?

- How did Jesus help Martha see beyond her own priorities to what was truly important? Explain.

Jesus didn't demean Martha's desire to serve Him, but He gently reminded her that it was more important to spend time with Him and learn from Him. Sometimes even good things can distract you from connecting with Jesus on a deeper level.

RESPOND

Serving God and doing good things in His name should never take the place of your relationship with Him.

- Think about some of the ways you serve God and jot them down in your journal.

- How might these responsibilities or commitments become a distraction from spending time learning from Jesus?

- Examine your heart—is Jesus your top priority? Spend some time in prayer and ask the Holy Spirit to guide you as you answer this question.

- Close your eyes and reflect on your day. Would people see Jesus through the way you live? How do you interact with others? React to frustrations? What do you consider most important? Journal your thoughts.

SEEKING TO SAVE

The words Jesus said and the deeds He did during His ministry served to prepare people and help them understand what He would soon accomplish on the cross. As you read today's Scripture, pay attention to how His encounter with Zacchaeus revealed the true purpose of His earthly ministry.

"Today salvation has come to this house," Jesus told him, "because he too is a son of Abraham. For the Son of Man has come to seek and to save the lost."—Luke 19:9–10

Read Luke 19:1–10 in your Bible and do the following:

- Underline the words "running" and "climbed." These actions were considered undignified for a grown man in that day. How do these actions reveal Zacchaeus' desperation to see Jesus? Explain.

- Circle the word "must" (v. 5). Now, read verse 10. Why was it so important for Jesus to go to Zacchaeus' house?

- How was Zacchaeus changed after this personal encounter with Jesus? What evidence do you see of conviction?

- How do the words of verses 9 and 10 reveal the purpose of Jesus' ministry? Journal your thoughts.

RESPOND

Jesus sought out a tax collector, a notorious sinner, and went to His house. Jesus didn't ask Zacchaeus to repent before He stayed with Him. Jesus took the gospel to Zacchaeus. Today Jesus continues to pursue the lost, seeking to win their hearts with the offer of salvation. In your journal, draw a line down the middle of the page to create two columns. On one side, record Jesus' actions in the passage—He sought, invited, lodged with, and brought the gospel. In the other column, list ideas for how you can do these same things to help others see how Jesus loves and pursues them.

RELIGION OR RESPONSE?

Read Luke 10:38–42 in your Bible.

> "For God loved the world in this way: He gave His One and Only Son, so that everyone who believes in Him will not perish but have eternal life. For God did not send His Son into the world that He might condemn the world, but that the world might be saved through Him."—John 3:16–17

Read John 3:1–21.

A Pharisee named Nicodemus approached Jesus by night and called him "Rabbi," which can also mean Master. He was respectful of Jesus, but his questions revealed his uncertainty of Jesus' claims. Jesus immediately directed the conversation to the fact that religious knowledge doesn't earn salvation.

ASK YOURSELF:
- What does Nicodemus' conversation with Jesus reveal about his understanding of who Jesus was?

- Think about how Jesus' gospel contradicted the legalistic beliefs of the Pharisees. What are the main differences between religion and a saving faith in Christ?

- What does this passage reveal about the personal nature of the gospel? Eternal life? God's love for you? Explain.

RESPOND
- Salvation isn't free—God sent His own Son to pay the price for your reconciliation. As you go through the rest of the week, meditate on God's gift to you.

- How would you personally explain what it takes to be saved? Journal the story of when you trusted Jesus as Savior. Then, pray and ask God to help you know how to tell someone else about Him.

LIVING WATER

Read John 4:1–26 in your Bible.

> Jesus said, "Everyone who drinks from this water will get thirsty again. But whoever drinks from the water that I will give him will never get thirsty again—ever! In fact, the water I will give him will become a well of water springing up within him for eternal life."—John 4:13–14

Use the questions below to help you study.

- Jesus called Himself "the gift of God" (v. 10). How does this reveal God's character? His love for you?

- Highlight the phrase "living water" in verse 10. What does this mean? Explain the concept in your own words.

- What does it mean to thirst for Jesus? How does He quench this thirst?

- Jesus' ministry was characterized by meeting physical needs in order to illustrate spiritual truths. This encounter was no different.

- What does Jesus' conversation with this woman teach you about salvation? About eternal life?

RESPOND
Just as Jesus offered this woman living water, He offers us the same gift.

- Whom or what do you look to for satisfaction? Do you look to Jesus? Confess your answer to God and ask Him to help you be fully satisfied in Him.

- Think of a few ways Jesus specifically satisfied your spiritual needs. Thank Him for providing for you.

GOOD NEWS TRAVELS

Read John 4:39–42.

> And they told the woman, "We no longer believe because of what you said, for we have heard for ourselves and know that this really is the Savior of the world."—John 4:42

This woman wouldn't even draw water at the same time as the other women in her town. Her shame kept her isolated. After encountering Jesus, she entered town and shared her testimony with anyone who would listen.

ASK YOURSELF:

- In today's Scripture, we see a drastic change in the woman's life. What was the reason for her change? How does this show the way people should respond to God's gift of salvation? Explain.

- What was the town's reaction to the woman's testimony? Why is it important that they believed her?

- What did the town's people do when they heard her testimony? Do people respond this way today when they hear of Jesus changing someone's life? Why or why not?

RESPOND

- If you are a Christian, imagine how your life would be different if you never trusted Jesus. How has your encounter with Jesus given you confidence to face your culture? Journal your response.

- Remember only God can save people—we can't. Still, people can come to know who He is by your testimony. Find time this week to share with someone the story of Jesus and how you came to know Him. Trust the results to God.

FULLY FORGIVEN

As you have seen through your devotions this month, the Pharisees often tried to trap Jesus into blaspheming God. This Scripture is yet another account of the Pharisees asking questions related to the law in hopes of finding a way to accuse Jesus of breaking God's law.

Read John 8:1–11 in your Bible.

> When Jesus stood up, He said to her, "Woman, where are they? Has no one condemned you?" "No one, Lord," she answered. "Neither do I condemn you," said Jesus. "Go, and from now on do not sin anymore."—John 8:10–11

This encounter confirms two things about the gospel. First, no sinner is beyond Jesus' power to forgive. Second, Jesus wants us to remember our own need for His mercy when we are tempted to judge those who have not yet trusted Him.

ASK YOURSELF:

- How does Jesus' response disarm the woman's accusers?
- Have you ever seen a Christian show love to someone most people would rather not associate with? What happened? How did that experience affect you? Explain.
- Read Romans 3:10–12, 23. How does Jesus' treatment of this woman demonstrate the truths in these verses? How should you treat those who don't know Jesus and live differently?

The woman was caught in sin and she deserved the punishment outlined in the law. Jesus is the only One who can claim true perfection, yet He extended grace and forgiveness to the woman while urging her to stop her sinful behaviors. He does the same for us today.

RESPOND

No one is beyond Jesus' power to redeem and forgive. As Christ-followers, knowing that we are repentant, forgiven sinners, we must reach out with compassion and mercy to those living in sin. How do you respond to people living sinful lifestyles? Do you tend to lean toward grace or judgment? Talk to God about it honestly and ask Him to help you to view others the way He intended.

WATER TO WINE

Read John 2:1–11 in your Bible.

> Jesus performed this first sign in Cana of Galilee. He displayed His glory, and His disciples believed in Him.—John 2:11

ASK YOURSELF:

- Highlight the phrase "do whatever He tells you" (v. 5). How does this show Mary's faith in Jesus? How does this instruction apply to you today?

- Jesus demonstrated His authority over nature by doing something that seemed impossible—changing water into wine. Biblical scholars suggest that the sign could also be considered a manifestation of His glory. Knowing this, what was the point of Jesus turning water into wine at the Cana wedding?

- What was the result of Jesus' displaying His glory (v. 11)? How does reading this account help you to see His glory? Explain.

RESPOND

- The general definition of *glory* includes words like *magnificence, renown,* and *honor.* In your own words, describe actions that display these characteristics today.

- When have you seen God's glory through something He accomplished in your life? Journal about that experience.

- For further study on the glory of God revealed through Jesus, read Philippians 2:9–11.

POWER AND PEACE

Read Mark 4:35–41 in your Bible.

> He got up, rebuked the wind, and said to the sea, "Silence! Be still!" The wind ceased, and there was a great calm. Then He said to them, "Why are you fearful? Do you still have no faith?"—Mark 4:39–40

Imagine yourself in the disciples' predicament: you're in a boat, the wind starts whipping, the waves are crashing into the boat, the boat is starting to sink, and the One who can save you is asleep. How would you react?

Mark's gospel account of Jesus calming the storm mentioned Jesus was in the boat, "sleeping on the cushion" (v. 38). Although the disciples had not seen the storm coming, nothing about their situation caught Jesus off guard. He had confidence in His Father's power and was able to sleep. Highlight the question "Don't You care . . . ?" (v. 38). Consider Jesus' response in verses 39–40. How does His response indicate His concern for His disciples? How did this situation strengthen their faith? Explain.

Jesus commanding the wind and waves demonstrated His ability to handle anything; even bringing peace to anxious hearts. We have to believe in God's incredible power and ability to take care of us—there's nothing He can't handle. However, we also have to remember that faith in God requires more than simply believing He exists; it requires trusting in Him completely.

RESPOND

- Close your eyes for a minute and think about your life. What tough things are you facing at school or at home, with your friends and your family? List a few in your journal.

- Much like He calmed the storm recounted in Mark's gospel, Jesus has the power to bring calm and peace to your life. He knows what you're going through now and what you'll face ahead. How can you trust Him to be with you during difficult times? What are some ways He's proven faithful in the past? Journal your thoughts.

A FEW LOAVES AND A WILLING HEART

Read John 6:1–13 in your Bible.

> Then Jesus took the loaves, and after giving thanks He distributed them to those who were seated—so also with the fish, as much as they wanted.—John 6:11

Although Jesus asked the disciples to come up with a solution for feeding a multitude of people (v. 5), verse six indicates Jesus already had a solution in mind. Read Philip's reply in verse seven and Andrew's reply in verses 8–9. Restate each response in your own words in your journal.

Notice both disciples were focused on how impossible the task seemed—they doubted they could find enough food for such a large group of people. How would you respond if Jesus asked you for a solution? Explain.

Verse 11 tells us that Jesus gave the people as much bread and fish as they wanted, and verse 13 says the disciples collected twelve baskets of leftovers. They had more than enough to feed the people. The disciples tried to solve the problem with logic, but Jesus has the power to do more than we can imagine.

RESPOND

The young boy offered five loaves and two fish to feed a crowd of about five thousand, but the disciples didn't see how such a small gift would help their predicament. We all have something to offer to the kingdom of God: time, talents, money, or even a social media platform. Maybe those gifts seem small, but no matter how insignificant you believe they are, God can use them for His kingdom.

- List two gifts you can use for the kingdom of God.
- Look at the list you created. Pray for the faith to give your gifts completely to the Lord and expect Him to multiply them for His glory.

ORDINARY AND EXTRAORDINARY

Read Matthew 17:24–27 in your Bible.

> "But, so we won't offend them, go to the sea, cast in a fishhook, and take the first fish that you catch. When you open its mouth you'll find a coin. Take it and give it to them for Me and you."—Matthew 17:27

Jesus indicated that He didn't have to pay the tax because He was God's Son, and that His followers didn't have to pay the tax because the king doesn't tax his sons. This emphasizes the voluntary nature of giving to God, consistently highlighted in the New Testament. This particular tax was collected by the temple; however, we must remember that Jesus also instructed us to obey the laws of the land.

THINK THROUGH THE FOLLOWING:
- What is so extraordinary about the way Jesus provided the coin? Explain.
- Would Jesus and Peter experience difficulty paying the tax? Why or why not?
- Peter had to trust Jesus to provide for them, and trust that the first fish he caught would have the coin for the temple tax. If you were in Peter's position, what would you do? Explain.

RESPOND
- In what ways have you seen God provide for your needs, or the needs of your friends and family? Has He ever provided for you in a way that seemed extraordinary?
- Invite God to meet your needs in whatever ways He sees fit, and pray that He gives you the faith to see His care for you no matter what method He uses.

STEP OUT OF THE BOAT

Read Matthew 14:22–33 in your Bible.

> "Lord, if it's You," Peter answered Him, "command me to come to You on the water."
> "Come!" He said. And climbing out of the boat, Peter started walking on the water and
> came toward Jesus.—Matthew 14:28–29

- List the two commands Jesus gave in verses 27 and 29.
- Why do you think it's important that Jesus told the disciples to have courage? Explain.
- What did Peter do that caused him to sink? Explain.

Peter is often criticized for taking his eyes off Jesus, but notice that Peter did step out of the boat. Jesus' power and Peter's faith allowed him to do something that seemed impossible. Examine Jesus' statement in verse 31. How does He indicate the outcome could have been different if Peter would have kept faith?

RESPOND

Is Jesus calling you to step out in faith? Draw a simple boat and label it with the area of comfort or safety that applies to you (popularity, laziness, self-centeredness, unbelief). What is holding you back from meeting Jesus where He called you?

STRANGE REQUESTS
AND FULL NETS

Read Luke 5:1–11 in your Bible.

> "Don't be afraid," Jesus told Simon. "From now on you will be catching people!" Then they brought the boats to land, left everything, and followed Him.—Luke 5:10–11

ASK YOURSELF:

- Highlight the word *Master* in verse 5. What is the significance of Peter recognizing Jesus as Master before the miracle occurred?

- Peter was a fisherman by trade and Jesus was a carpenter. Why do you think Peter took Jesus' advice on where to cast the nets? Explain.

- Jesus asked Peter to do something that seemed illogical. Peter obeyed even though He might not have understood Jesus' command. The result? They caught so many fish the boat began to sink. Jesus often asks us to do things that do not necessarily make sense, but His commands always line up with God's plan. We can trust and obey, knowing His ways are best. When have you seen an example of this in your life? Explain.

- What was the result of Jesus providing the fish (vv. 10–11)?

RESPOND

A common theme in many of Jesus' miracles was that He exceeded expectations. At the wedding at Cana, the wine was described as the best of the event. When He fed the five thousand, they collected twelve baskets of leftovers. In today's miracle, the disciples caught so many fish that hauling in the nets almost sunk the boat.

- Do you trust in God's Word? His promises? Talk honestly with God and confess any mistrust you may feel. Ask Him to help you trust completely in Him and to obey Him without hesitation.

- Think of a time when you obeyed God and He blessed you in abundance. Jot down some key things you learned from that experience.

- What expectations do you have for what Christ might want to do in your life? Do you have faith that He might exceed those expectations? Journal your thoughts.

AUTHORITY AFFIRMED

Review yesterday's devotion. The first time the disciples obeyed Jesus and caught an abundance of fish was at the beginning of His earthly ministry. Today's story is similar, but occurred after Jesus' resurrection.

Read John 21:1–14 in your Bible.

> "Cast the net on the right side of the boat," He told them, "and you'll find some." So they did, and they were unable to haul it in because of the large number of fish.
> —John 21:6

Consider these questions:

- How does this story connect to the miracle in Luke 5:1–11? Jot down a few ideas.

- Jesus revealed Himself to His disciples for a third time through this miracle, which was similar to the one He performed when He called Peter and John to be His disciples. Notice John's and Peter's reactions in verse seven. Why is this important? Explain.

- When they arrived on shore and sat down to eat breakfast with Jesus, the disciples didn't have any doubts about who He was. Would you respond the same way? Why or why not?

RESPOND

Each of Jesus' post-resurrection appearances proved the truth of His resurrection, showed that He defeated death, taught the disciples their mission, and emboldened them to do as He commanded. It is also important to note the significance of these events for us today—He is still alive and we have the opportunity to have a personal relationship with Him.

- Think about the first time you heard that Jesus died for your sins. Do you still look at His sacrifice the same way? Why or why not? Record your response in your journal.

- Take a minute and meditate on Jesus' patience with us and His desire to use us as a part of His plan. How do you see His patience? How do you know He wants you to be a part of His plan? Journal your thoughts.

THE POWER TO SPEAK

Read Isaiah 35:5–6. The prophet Isaiah told of Jesus' healings in the Old Testament. Throughout the Book of Isaiah, physical illness was often a metaphor for a spiritual issue. The complete healing indicated in theses passages parallels new life in Christ.

Read Matthew 9:32–24.

> Just as they were going out, a demon-possessed man who was unable to speak was brought to Him. When the demon had been driven out, the man spoke. And the crowds were amazed, saying, "Nothing like this has ever been seen in Israel!" But the Pharisees said, "He drives out demons by the ruler of the demons!"—Matthew 9:32–34

- Circle each variation of the word *speak* or *say*. Underline the word *demon* each time it appears.

- Look back at the Scripture in Isaiah. Why is it important that the man spoke? Explain.

- The Pharisees thought Jesus' authority came from the ruler of demons (v. 34). Read Luke 11:17–19. What was wrong with their theory? Explain.

RESPOND

The Pharisees sought every excuse to believe that Jesus was not from God. He had turned their world upside down by interpreting the Scriptures with authority and performing great signs. Instead of seeking God, they sought to prove they were right.

- When God turns your world upside down, do you struggle to trust Him? Do you have faith that no matter the circumstances He has your best interests in mind? Why or why not? Journal your thoughts.

- List two ways you can trust God's ultimate authority in your life.

EVIL COWERS

Read Luke 4:31–37 in your Bible. Highlight the word *authority* throughout the passage. What does it mean that Jesus' message had authority? Explain.

> They were astonished at His teaching because His message had authority. . . . Amazement came over them all, and they kept saying to one another, "What is this message? For He commands the unclean spirits with authority and power, and they come out!"—Luke 4:32, 36

In the Old Testament, God was often called the Holy One. In this passage, the demons' referring to Jesus as the Holy One of God shows their recognition of Him as the Son of God.

The demons asked Jesus if He had come to destroy them; even they recognized His authority over evil and were terrified. Biblical scholars suggest that the demons weren't just afraid of Jesus' preaching and purpose, but that they feared His presence. Why do you think the demons feared Jesus' presence? Why is this important?

RESPOND

- What does Jesus' power over evil mean for you? Jot down a list of prayer requests about your future, your community, and the world that appeals to Jesus' sovereignty. Pray for those requests each day this week.

- Examine your heart. Do you recognize Jesus' sovereignty? Have you fully surrendered your life to Him? Journal your thoughts.

CROSSING THE LINE

Read Mark 7:24–30 in your Bible.

What does it mean to have bold faith? Journal your thoughts.

> Then He told her, "Because of this reply, you may go. The demon has gone out of your daughter." When she went back to her home, she found her child lying on the bed, and the demon was gone.—Mark 7:29–30

ASK YOURSELF:

- What is your first impression of this story? Explain.

- At first glance, it may seem that Jesus' response to this woman is curt and uncaring. However, Jesus acknowledged that the priority of His mission was to bring salvation to the Jews. He did not completely exclude the Gentiles, but said that the Word of God must go to the Jews first, and then to the Gentiles. Underline the word *kept* in verse 26. What kind of faith did she show? Explain.

- Why did the woman's reply cause Jesus to grant her request for His healing? Explain.

RESPOND

During Jesus' time, men and women did not interact like this in public. This encounter crossed cultural and religious boundaries. The woman took a risk in faith, and Jesus responded to her belief and courage.

- What are some ways that you can be courageous in your faith? Jot down a few ideas in your journal.

- What's one thing you can do tomorrow to demonstrate your compassion for someone who is different from you?

- Think of a time when you persistently asked God for something and your faith was rewarded. Journal about that experience.

A DESPERATE PLEA

Consider the word *unbelief*. What does this mean? When have you experienced unbelief and what did God do to help you believe? Journal about your experience.

Read Mark 9:14–29 in your Bible.

> "And many times it has thrown him into fire or water to destroy him. But if You can do anything, have compassion on us and help us." Then Jesus said to him, "'If You can'? Everything is possible to the one who believes." Immediately the father of the boy cried out, "I do believe! Help my unbelief."—Mark 9:22–24

Answer these questions: What did Jesus request of the boy's father before He drove out the demon? Why is this important? Explain in your own words.

The father had the faith to come to Jesus and request help for his son, but he needed both faith and belief in Jesus for true spiritual healing to take place.

Although the disciples were unable to cast out this demon, Jesus had given them the power to do so, and they had experienced success before this encounter. List the two reasons Jesus gave for the disciples' inability to drive out the demon.

RESPOND

- Have you ever fasted? What was it like? How did the experience draw you closer to God? Journal about your experience.

- Think of two people who have strong faith. List the two names and record characteristics that demonstrate each person's faith in your journal.

(REST)ORATION

Read Luke 13:10–17 in your Bible.

> "Satan has bound this woman, a daughter of Abraham, for 18 years—shouldn't she be untied from this bondage on the Sabbath day?" When He had said these things, all His adversaries were humiliated, but the whole crowd was rejoicing over all the glorious things He was doing.—Luke 13:16–17

ASK YOURSELF:

- Jesus' healing involved not only the physical healing of the woman's disability, but also spiritual healing by casting out the evil spirit. Not all physical ailments were caused by demons. Bible scholars suggest this was a rare case in which both occurred simultaneously. Why did the leader of the synagogue complain about Jesus healing on the Sabbath? Why is that significant?

- Jesus considered changing this woman's life as more important than the religious leaders' imposing rules. He respected the Sabbath, but didn't refrain from doing God's work on that day either. Despite the Pharisees' anger at Jesus for healing a woman on the Sabbath, God was glorified through His actions. Look at verse 17 and complete this sentence. Jesus' _____ were humiliated, but the _____ rejoiced. Why?

RESPOND

When Jesus healed this woman, people rejoiced. The religious leaders used the law to bind people, but Jesus came to change people's hearts by setting them free from sin. He did not nullify the law, but fulfilled it. God's law still guides our behavior even though Jesus provides our righteousness.

- Examine your heart. What are some of your thoughts and actions that need to change? Ask Jesus to continue to change your heart and help you see your need for Him.

- For further study on God's law, read Exodus 20:1–17. How does God's law guide your behavior as a believer? Explain.

FREEDOM FROM OPPRESSION

Read Luke 8:26–37 in your Bible.

> When He got out on land, a demon-possessed man from the town met Him. For a long time he had worn no clothes and did not stay in a house but in the tombs. . . . Then people went out to see what had happened. They came to Jesus and found the man the demons had departed from, sitting at Jesus' feet, dressed and in his right mind. And they were afraid. Meanwhile, the eyewitnesses reported to them how the demon-possessed man was delivered.—Luke 8:27, 35–36

Think through the following questions:

- Circle instances of the words *beg, permit,* and *permission.* Why do you think the demons made requests of Jesus?

- What does the description of the demons' power over the man—and the demons' terrible fear of Jesus—tell you about Jesus' authority?

When the people saw the healed man calmly seated at Jesus' feet, they were afraid (v. 35). Before, He had worn chains and shackles, living among the tombs. Jesus' power delivered the man from the demons and into new life. He has the power to free us from darkness and give us new life as well. (See Ephesians 5:8 and 2 Timothy 1:10.) What does it mean to have new life?

RESPOND

The demon-possessed man did not do anything deserving Jesus' presence or His mercy; Jesus came to him to set him free. In the same way, He meets us where we are—so we don't have to be "cleaned up" before we can come to Him.

- How does your own spiritual transformation compare to that of the man in this story? What has Jesus freed you from? Journal your thoughts.

- How has Jesus changed your life? Think of ways you can tell your story to others.

TELL ALL

Read Luke 8:38–39 and complete the following.

- Examine this Scripture carefully. Jot down Jesus' actions and the reaction of the man.

- In other healing accounts, Jesus asked the people He healed not to tell about their experience, yet He commanded this man to do the opposite. Why is this significant?

The man from whom the demons had departed kept begging Him to be with Him. But He sent him away and said, "Go back to your home, and tell all that God has done for you." And off he went, proclaiming throughout the town all that Jesus had done for him.—Luke 8:38–39

The man begged to go with Jesus. He was desperate to stay with the One who freed Him. However, Jesus wanted the man to go and tell others what He did for him, and the man obeyed.

CONSIDER THE FOLLOWING:
- Why did the man's transformational experience require action? Explain.

- Highlight the word *proclaiming*. Look at the definition of *proclaim* in your journal. How important was Jesus' authority over evil in this man's life? How important is Jesus' authority over evil today?

RESPOND
- What Jesus did for you is worth sharing with others. In your journal, jot down the names of a few people you can tell about Him.

- Have you practiced telling people what God has done for you? In your journal, record your story and commit to telling one person from your list about it this week.

- For further study on redemptive stories, read about Paul's conversion in Acts 9.

MOTIVE AND HEART

Consider the many ways Jesus has proven Himself to be the authoritative, powerful, Son of God. List some ways in your journal, then circle those that are most meaningful to you.

Read Mark 2:1–12 in your Bible.

> Right away Jesus understood in His spirit that they were thinking like this within themselves and said to them, "Why are you thinking these things in your hearts?"
> —Mark 2:8

THINK THROUGH THESE QUESTIONS:

- In verse 8, Jesus' question revealed that He knew what the Pharisees were thinking in their hearts. Why is this important?

- God is omniscient. When Jesus revealed the Pharisees' inner state, He showed His power, authority, and oneness with God. In what other ways did Jesus show His power and authority in verses 9–10?

- Look at verse 12. How did the people react to Jesus' revealing His authority through healing the man and forgiving His sin? Why did they react this way? Explain.

RESPOND

God wants a relationship with us, but it is important to remember who He is—He's not just the Giver of unconditional love—He has power over all things.

- Jesus determined the Pharisees' thoughts and knew their hearts before they said a word. He knows you the same way. Ask the Holy Spirit to guide you as you examine your heart. Are there things you need to confess to God? Be honest with Him and ask Him to help you keep your heart pure.

- For further study, read Mark 9:14–27. Journal about how you identify with this father—you want to believe, but still struggle and sometimes doubt Jesus' power to overcome all things.

DESIRE TO HEAL

Read Mark 5:24–34 in your Bible.

> For she said, "If I can just touch His robes, I'll be made well!" Instantly her flow of blood ceased, and she sensed in her body that she was cured of her affliction.
> —Mark 5:28–29

ASK YOURSELF:

- Take a closer look at verses 25–27. List four things that happened to the woman as a result of her sickness.

- Though the doctors couldn't heal the woman, her sickness was not beyond the reach of God's power or compassion. Jesus stopped in the middle of a pressing crowd to acknowledge this woman. What does this say about her value to Him? Your value to Him?

- In verse 34, Jesus said, "your faith has made you well." How did this woman show faith by going to Jesus for healing? Explain.

RESPOND

The woman was an outcast because of her condition, yet Jesus didn't rebuke her for touching Him; He rewarded her faith with healing.

- You may find yourself thinking that God has more important concerns to listen to or more significant healings to perform and that your concerns aren't important. This woman—hurting, penniless, desperate, and unimportant—somehow recognized that Jesus could and would heal even her. Confess to Jesus any doubts you have about His care for you and others.

- Journal a few areas in which you or people you know need healing. Pray for those requests daily. In your journal, record dates any of those prayers are answered.

MYSTERIOUS

Read John 9:1–5 in your Bible.

Like we often do, the disciples sought a reason for the man's sickness. Do you ever ask God why something happened? Can you think of a specific example? Journal your experience.

> "Neither this man nor his parents sinned," Jesus answered. "This came about so that God's works might be displayed in him."—John 9:3

Read John 9:1–12 in your Bible and think through these questions:

- During this time, religious leaders taught that any misfortune such as this man's blindness was brought about by sin. Look at verse 3. What did Jesus' response to His disciples reveal about sin and sickness? Explain.

- Jesus demonstrated His power while also demonstrating compassion toward the man. Today He has the power to work in our lives and the lives of those around us no matter what the situation. When has God used something negative in your life to demonstrate His power? Explain.

- Jesus completely healed the man to display God's power in his life. Think of a time when God's power was displayed in your life. Did you live differently after that experience? Why or why not?

RESPOND

In John 9, Jesus chose to heal the man's longtime blindness to bring glory to Himself. Sometimes, He chooses to glorify Himself by not healing. Think of a time when you asked God for healing and the person remained sick. What were your thoughts? Journal about that experience and ask God to help you see the situation in light of His plan and His glory.

With what current situation is God asking you to trust Him? Journal a prayer to God. Be honest with Him about your difficulty trusting Him and ask Him to help you trust Him completely.

THE ONLY HOPE

Read John 5:1–15 in your Bible.

> "Get up," Jesus told him, "pick up your mat and walk!" Instantly the man got well, picked up his mat, and started to walk.—John 5:8–9

ANSWER THESE QUESTIONS:

- People with all kinds of ailments came to Bethesda to be healed. This particular man had been sick for thirty-eight years, and Jesus knew the man had been there for a long time. How did this show His compassion?

- Reread verse 6. Jesus didn't ask the many why he wasn't well; He asked if the man wanted to get well. How does the man's response indicate His misunderstanding of Jesus' question? Explain.

- What was Jesus' response to the man's complaint (v. 7)? Journal in your own words.

- How do Jesus' words in verse 14 give hope? Explain.

RESPOND

- The sick man trusted in a myth about the pool of Bethesda as the only possible means for healing. What "good" things are you placing your hope in, instead of Christ? Jot down a few ideas in your journal.

- What good things are you trying to do to earn God's favor?

- What can you change this week to demonstrate a full trust in Jesus as your only source of hope and healing? List three ideas in your journal.

THE TOUCH OF A HAND

Read Mark 1:29–31 in your Bible.

> So He went to her, took her by the hand, and raised her up. The fever left her, and she began to serve them.—Mark 1:31

- After leaving the synagogue, Jesus and His disciples went to Capernaum where Jesus was "at once" (v. 30) made aware that Peter's mother-in-law had a fever. Being omniscient, Jesus likely already knew about her sickness but allowed His disciples to come to Him with their concern. What were the three actions Jesus took after the disciples brought Him their news (v. 31)?

- Jesus could have spoken healing over Peter's mother-in-law from where He was, but He chose to go to her, touch her, and help her get up. How does this healing show Jesus' compassion and love for His people? Explain.

- What does this tell you about His character? His relationship with you?

RESPOND

Although Jesus knows what we need—He still wants us to come to Him. He wants relationship.

- We all have needs and pain. What are some things you're struggling with right now? Talk honestly with God and ask Him to help you overcome your struggle.

- Think about a specific situation where you needed God's help or healing and His response strengthened your relationship with Him. What happened? How did you respond? Journal your response.

- In your journal, list a few people you know who are going through a tough time or are enduring sickness. Pray over those people every time you see their names.

WHEN WORDS ARE ENOUGH

Read John 4:46–54 in your Bible.

This was not Jesus' first miracle in Galilee. During both miracles, the people who came to Jesus for help were required to trust Him at His word that He would provide.

"Go," Jesus told him, "your son will live." The man believed what Jesus said to him and departed.—John 4:50

ASK YOURSELF:

- Jesus answered the royal official's plea by accusing the crowd of only looking for signs and wonders. In this case, He didn't give them a miracle to witness. What did He do instead? Why is that important?

- Examine Jesus' promise to the official in verse 50. The word *go* here is a command. Jesus didn't just give the official permission to leave; He told him to go and promised healing for the man's son. What kind of faith did Jesus require from the official? Explain.

- Imagine what you would do if you were the official: would you leave behind your one chance at healing with a promise? Why or why not?

RESPOND

Today, people love to rely on their own wisdom for answers to tough questions, but as believers we should rely on the truth of God's Word. It can be difficult to obey His commands without assurance that the outcome will be what we want, but we have to trust in God and in the truth of His Word, knowing that His way is best. Think of a time when you had to choose to obey God based only on a promise in His Word. At the time, maybe it made more sense to go against God's Word, maybe you were afraid of how others would react, or maybe you didn't trust God to take care of your situation. What was the most difficult thing about that situation? Do you still struggle to trust in His Word no matter what? Journal your thoughts.

WILLING AND ABLE

Read Luke 5:12–16 in your Bible and think through the questions that follow.

> He saw Jesus, fell facedown, and begged Him: "Lord, if You are willing, You can make me clean."—Luke 5:12

- In today's passage, Jesus and the man with the skin disease both took a risk. What risk did each one take? Explain.

- Looking at verse 12, what three things did the man do?

- Consider the man's request to Jesus. Highlight or circle the word *willing*. Why is this word important? Explain.

- In this passage, the man with the skin disease showed humility. The opposite of humility is pride. Record some characteristics of a humble person and one who is prideful.

RESPOND

We all have a reason to follow Jesus, but we must be willing to let Him cleanse us and prepare our hearts for His kingdom.

- On a sticky note, complete the following statement: Lord, if You are willing, You can . . .

- Stick the note on your mirror or the back of your door, where you'll see it often. Even if Jesus doesn't take away that circumstance, heal that sickness, or change that situation, know that it isn't because He wasn't able.

- For further study, read Isaiah 55:8–11. Meditate on these verses, considering the faith it takes to believe that God's ways are better, even though we can't always comprehend them.

FAITH THAT GIVES LIFE

Read Matthew 9:18–19 in your Bible. Many Jewish leaders didn't follow Jesus because His teachings were radically different. Today's reading focuses on one Jewish leader, Jairus, who came to Jesus for help when his daughter was sick. Read Jairus' statement at the end of verse 18. What does this tell you about his faith?

Read Mark 5:22–24 in your Bible.

> One of the synagogue leaders, named Jairus, came, and when he saw Jesus, he fell at His feet and kept begging Him, "My little daughter is at death's door. Come and lay Your hands on her so she can get well and live."—Mark 5:22–23

Consider the following:

- As you read, underline any words that indicate Jairus' feelings about his daughter's illness. What does his persistence reveal about the urgency of his situation?

- Review both accounts of Jairus' encounter with Jesus. List some things that revealed his faith in Jesus.

- Why is it important to believe that Jesus can overcome anything? Explain.

RESPOND

- Terminal illness and death are often difficult to address, so prayerfully think about a time in your life when you lost a loved one or knew someone with a terminal illness. How did you respond? Journal your about your experience.

- Jairus showed faith by going to Jesus with his dying daughter, believing His touch alone would heal. On a scale of 1–10, how strong is your faith during times of crisis?

- Do you believe that Jesus is strong enough today to work miracles like He did with Jairus' daughter? Confess any doubts to God and ask Him to help you trust Him with the tough situations in your life.

OBSTACLES TO OPPORTUNITIES

Review yesterday's devotion before you read today's Scripture. As you continue reading about Jairus' encounter with Jesus, consider how Jesus used a seemingly hopeless situation to show more of His power. Think of a time when Jesus gave you hope in a situation that seemed impossibly grim. Journal about that experience.

Now, read Matthew 9:23–26.

> When Jesus came to the leader's house, He saw the flute players and a crowd lamenting loudly. "Leave," He said, "because the girl isn't dead, but sleeping." And they started laughing at Him. But when the crowd had been put outside, He went in and took her by the hand, and the girl got up. And this news spread throughout that whole area.—Matthew 9:23–26

Next, read Mark 5:35–43 in your Bible.

ANSWER THESE QUESTIONS:
- In verses 35–36, Jairus received news that His daughter had died. How did Jesus respond? Why is this important?
- Jesus' words "only believe" (v. 36) were meant to encourage Jairus' to keep believing that Jesus could still save his daughter. What does this teach you about your own belief when circumstances seem beyond hope? Explain.
- Jesus used the word *sleeping* to describe the girl's condition, and the people in Jairus' house laughed at Him. Why do you think they responded this way? How would you respond?

RESPOND
We don't have the benefit of seeing the bigger picture, but God does. We sometimes find ourselves feeling completely hopeless, filled with anxiety and sadness, and wanting to give up the belief that God can change our situation. Today's passage teaches us that nothing and no one is beyond God's power. What circumstances in your life seem hopeless right now? Journal a prayer to God, placing your fears and hope in His hands. Confess your need for His help and thank Him for using difficult circumstances to draw you into a deeper relationship with Him.

MESSAGE OF HOPE

Over the next few days, you will read about Jesus raising Lazarus from the dead. Quickly read through the complete story in John 11:1–44.

> When Jesus heard it, He said, "This sickness will not end in death but is for the glory of God, so that the Son of God may be glorified through it."—John 11:4

ASK YOURSELF:

- Jesus had a strong bond with Lazarus. As you focus your attention on verses 1–6, underline any words or phrases that help you better understand their relationship.

- Despite Jesus' relationship with Lazarus and his sisters, He waited to go to them. Jesus knew that God would demonstrate His power and authority by raising Lazarus from the dead. He even told His disciples that the outcome of Lazarus's sickness would not be death, yet Lazarus was in the tomb when Jesus arrived. In your own words, explain Jesus' statement in verse 4.

- Jesus' timing assured that there would be no mistaking that Lazarus was dead when He arrived. How did Jesus' timing bring glory to God? Explain.

- List a few ways Jesus showed His authority and power by waiting until Lazarus was dead to perform a miracle.

RESPOND

Before the story completely unfolded, Jesus told His disciples the outcome—Lazarus wouldn't stay in the tomb. While we have access to the end of this story, Jesus' disciples questioned His choice to remain where He was because they knew He could heal Lazarus. Jesus doesn't always work in ways that we understand or provide healing when we think He should, but He has the power to do more than we can imagine. When have you questioned something God allowed in your life? Maybe a loved one died, but you prayed for healing. Talk honestly with God about any doubts or fears you had. Ask Him to help you see how He worked things for good in that situation.

SPELL IT OUT

Review yesterday's devotion. Examine Jesus' use of the word *sleep* throughout this week's devotions.

Read John 11:11–16 in your Bible.

> So Jesus then told them plainly, "Lazarus has died. I'm glad for you that I wasn't there so that you may believe. But let's go to him."—John 11:14–15

COMPLETE THE FOLLOWING:

- Highlight each occurrence of the word *asleep* or *sleep* by Jesus and the disciples.

- Circle the phrase "so then Jesus told them plainly" (v. 14). What does that mean? Write the statement in your own words.

- Check out Jesus' words in verse 15. Why would Jesus be glad He wasn't there when Lazarus died? How would Jesus' absence at the time of Lazarus' death later help the disciples to believe in Him? Explain.

RESPOND

It's difficult to understand how God works, but you can know His ways are perfect. Jesus had to spell this out for His disciples when they didn't understand, and He will do the same for you as you walk with Him.

- Has God ever used a difficult situation in your life to help you believe in Him, trust Him, or understand more about Him? Journal about that experience.

- Thank God for revealing to you what you need to know to trust and believe in Him. Ask Him to continue to strengthen your faith.

LIFE GIVER

Jesus' resurrection defeated death. He knew this would happen—through His death, He extended the gift of eternal life to all people.

Jesus offered Himself as a sacrifice for the sins of everyone who would ever believe in Him, but we still have to choose to accept His gift and enter into a relationship with Him.

Read John 11:17–27 in your Bible and consider the following:

- How does Martha's response in verse 24 reveal her misunderstanding of Jesus' promise that her brother would rise again? Explain.

- What did Jesus declare about Himself in verses 25–26? Explain it in your own words.

- How did Martha respond after His declaration? How should you respond to His declaration?

- Martha assured Jesus she understood Him as the resurrection and the life. How does her response to His request to roll away the stone from Lazarus' tomb (v. 39) indicate differently?

Jesus said to her, "I am the resurrection and the life. The one who believes in Me, even if he dies, will live. Everyone who lives and believes in Me will never die—ever. Do you believe this?"—John 11:25–26

RESPOND

- Read aloud and meditate on John 11:25–26. Consider the fact that the One who is life is able to restore life.

- Have you accepted that Jesus is the only way to eternal life? If you haven't, let today be the day you trust in His saving power. If you have given your life to Christ, take some time now to thank Him for the incredible gift of salvation.

- For further study on salvation in Christ, read Romans 10:9–10 and Hebrews 7:25.

FOR GOD'S GLORY

Before you read today's devotion, review this week's devotions about Lazarus. In your journal, write down thoughts that stick out most to you from those passages of Scripture. Next read John 11:38–44.

> So they removed the stone. Then Jesus raised His eyes and said, "Father, I thank You that You heard Me. I know that You always hear Me, but because of the crowd standing here I said this, so they may believe You sent Me."—John 11:41-42

THINK ABOUT THE FOLLOWING:

- Read verse 39 again. Compare Martha's reaction here to her reaction in verse 27. Does her response indicate the same kind of faith? Why or why not?

- What did Jesus' prayer before he performed the miracle indicate about His mission? What did it reveal about God's plan? Explain.

Jesus' prayer showed intimate knowledge of His Father's plan for Lazarus. Jesus thanked God because God "heard" (v. 41) Him, the past tense pointing to their connection and God's foreknowing of the event taking place. Jesus prayed aloud as proof to those standing around that God really did send Him and accomplish His will through Him—He wanted them not just to observe the miracle, but to believe in Him.

RESPOND

- Are you quick to give God glory when you see Him work in mighty ways? This is how you can let the world know what a great God you serve—by telling others of His works. In your journal, come up with a few ways you could tell someone about Jesus and what He did for you.

- Glance over your journal entry. Do you know people who need to hear your story? List their names in your journal.

- Find an older Christian mentor, such as your student pastor or a small group leader and ask them to hold you accountable to share your story with one of those people this week.

OBEY TO HONOR

Read John 5:21–24 in your Bible.

When people hear the word *honor*, they think of battles, soldiers, winning awards, or being in a respected career. What does the word *honor* mean? Do you think you honor Jesus? Why or why not? Journal your response.

> "And just as the Father raises the dead and gives them life, so the Son also gives life to anyone He wants to."—John 5:21

ASK YOURSELF:

- What does this passage reveal about the relationship between Jesus and His Father? Why is that important?

- List specific roles of Jesus named in this passage. Who gave Him permission and authority over all people?

- Jesus honored God by obeying Him and fulfilling His purpose. How can you do the same? How does living for Jesus acknowledge His power and authority in your life?

RESPOND

You can honor Jesus in your relationship with Him by living and speaking in ways that glorify God and show He is Lord of your life.

- Reflect on verse 21 for a moment. How has Jesus brought life to you? Are you quick to share this with people around you? Journal your response.

- Think of people in your circle who need to hear about Jesus and list them in your journal. Ask God to show you how to be more intentional about sharing His truth with them.

COMPASSION LEADS TO ACTION

This miracle was the first account of Jesus raising someone from the dead. As you studied earlier this week, He also raised Jairus' daughter and Lazarus.

Look up and write down the definition of *compassion* in your journal. Define the term in your own words.

Read Luke 7:11–15 in your own Bible.

> When the Lord saw her, He had compassion on her and said, "Don't cry." Then He came up and touched the open coffin, and the pallbearers stopped. And He said, "Young man, I tell you, get up!"—Luke 7:13–14

Think about the following:

- This lady had nothing. She was a widow and about to bury her only son—she probably had no other means of financial support. Knowing this, how does Jesus' reaction to her plight reveal His compassion?

- What was the outcome of this miracle (v. 16)? How would you react?

- List some ways Jesus raising this young man from the dead mirrors the salvation Christ offers to believers.

RESPOND

During Jesus' earthly ministry, He only raised three people from the dead. Why not more? These miracles weren't about people, they were about Him—to show that He was the Son of God and to offer salvation to the world.

- When have you experienced Jesus' power in your life? Have you experienced Him work a miracle for you? Is there one you need to ask for now? Journal your response.

- Do you know people who need compassionate love? In your journal, list some places you can go to show compassion to the hurting and needy people around you. Then, record how you will carry out your plan.

DEATH IS DEFEATED

Read Matthew 28:1–7 in your Bible.

> But the angel told the women, "Don't be afraid, because I know you are looking for Jesus who was crucified. He is not here! For He has been resurrected, just as He said. Come and see the place where He lay. Then go quickly and tell His disciples, 'He has been raised from the dead. In fact, He is going ahead of you to Galilee; you will see Him there.' Listen, I have told you."—Matthew 28:5–7

CONSIDER THESE QUESTIONS:

- What did the women find when they reached the tomb? Why is that important?

- Describe the women's initial reactions to the angel. How would your reaction be similar? How would it differ?

- In verse 6, the phrase "just as He said" referred to Jesus' prophecy of His coming death and resurrection. Why is it important that the angel confirmed Jesus' words? Explain.

- The angel gave the women three commands in verses 5–7. What were they and why are they significant?

- What did the angel's final command reveal about Jesus' love for His disciples? Explain.

RESPOND

Jesus had the power to take on sin and overcome the grave, but His resurrection also showed God's love and that He keeps His promises. Consider how deeply Jesus loves you—so much that He died for you!

- Have you ever felt overwhelmed by Jesus' love for you? Journal about that experience.

- Praise God for sending Jesus to die on the cross for you. Praise God for His love. If you don't know where to begin, try praying Psalm 103.

ULTIMATE VICTORY

Read 1 Corinthians 15:12–19.

First-century believers were often persecuted for their faith in Christ, so there was little earthly gain for their choice to follow Jesus.

> For if the dead are not raised, Christ has not been raised. And if Christ has not been raised, your faith is worthless; you are still in your sins. Therefore, those who have fallen asleep in Christ have also perished. If we have put our hope in Christ for this life only, we should be pitied more than anyone.—1 Corinthians 15:16–19

ASK YOURSELF:

- What was being preached that didn't line up with the gospel? Why didn't this teaching make sense in light of God's plan for Jesus and believers?

- If Jesus' resurrection had never happened, according to Paul, what would that mean for the Christian faith? Explain.

- Focus on verses 16–19 for a moment. Think about why Paul said believers "should be pitied more than anyone" (v. 19). Are believers today "pitied" for belief in Christ? Why or why not? Explain.

- How does your faith hinge on the resurrection? Explain.

RESPOND

- Jesus still has the power to bring the dead to life today. Do you know people who need the power of Jesus to break the chains of sin in their lives? Commit to pray for these people, asking God to use you as a light for Him.

- Living life with an eternal perspective means you live life focused on your future with Jesus and helping other people know how to spend eternity with Him, too. In your journal, explain eternal perspective in your own words.

- Because of Jesus' power over death, you will spend eternity with Him if you trust Him as your Savior. How can you live with an eternal perspective this week? Jot down a few ideas in your journal.

ETERNAL JESUS

What does it mean to say that Jesus is eternal? Describe the concept in your own words.

Read John 8:56–59 in your Bible.

> Jesus said to them, "I assure you: Before Abraham was, I am."—John 8:58

Jesus used the phrase "I am" in John 8:58 to refer to Himself. This phrase was first used in Exodus 3:14 when Moses asked God who he should say sent him to the Israelites. Why do you think it bothered the Jews that Jesus claimed to exist before Abraham?

Now, read Colossians 1:15–20 in your Bible.

> He is the image of the invisible God, the firstborn over all creation.—Colossians 1:15

Consider this: Jesus isn't only like God; Jesus is God. The death of an ordinary man on a cross would have no ramifications for the rest of us—the One to die had to be perfect, spotless, without blemish. Only Jesus, fully God and fully man, could take on the sins of the world and offer us the opportunity to be restored to a right relationship with God. Through Jesus, we are able to see the invisible attributes of God and witness His character. In your journal, list some of Jesus' characteristics that help you understand more about who God is.

RESPOND

The reason Jesus came to earth in human form was to restore our relationship with God and to help us know Him on a deeper level.

- Think of some people who need to experience restoration in their relationship with God. List their names and commit to pray for them this week.

- In your journal, record some steps you can take to share Jesus with the people you listed above.

THE SAVIOR WE NEED

Read John 1:10–13 in your Bible.

> But to all who did receive Him, He gave them the right to be children of God, to those who believe in His name, who were born, not of blood, or of the will of the flesh, or of the will of man, but of God.—John 1:12–13

- John painted a picture of Jesus as One who was fully God and yet willingly humbled Himself by taking on flesh as He came to humanity to be the Savior for those who would receive Him. Verse 11 says Jesus "came to His own." The Jews were God's chosen people. Why do you think the Jews rejected Jesus? Explain.

- Why is it important to note that Jesus created the world, but the world did not recognize Him? What hindered their recognition?

- What do you think it means to receive Jesus? Why is that important?

Only God has the power to save. He sent Jesus to provide salvation and offer a way for people to be restored to God. However, people must still respond by trusting Jesus as Savior.

RESPOND

Each car has a blind spot, or place where the driver can't see by using side or rearview mirrors. We all experience spiritual blindness in our lives. Before we know Christ, we are unable to clearly see Him for who He is. Once we trust Him as Savior, our eyes are opened and we are able to know Him.

- In your journal, list some things in your life that helped you realize your need for a Savior.

- Consider the story of how Jesus opened your eyes to who He is. How did you respond to Him? Whom can you share this story with? Journal your response.

IN REMEMBRANCE OF ME

Read Matthew 26:17–30 in your Bible.

> "For this is My blood that establishes the covenant; it is shed for many for the forgiveness of sins."—Matthew 26:28

- While observing the Passover with His disciples, Jesus explained the significance of the Passover meal, which we know as the Lord's Supper. What was the significance of the first Lord's Supper?

- What does this symbolic event help Christians to remember?

- Verse 28 says that Jesus' blood was shed for our forgiveness. Our redemption rests in Christ and was made possible through His blood. (See Ephesians 1:7). Explain in your own words the new covenant that would be established through Jesus' blood.

- How does the Lord's Supper help you acknowledge God's love for you?

- Read Romans 6:22–23. We are all slaves to sin before we trust Jesus as Savior. Describe how the Lord's Supper demonstrates freedom from slavery to sin.

RESPOND

- Think back to the first time you took part in the Lord's Supper. Journal about that experience.

- Develop a plan for how you will observe the Lord's Supper differently next time. How will you prepare your heart? Include prayer points and Scriptures to meditate on.

PURIFIED

Read Mark 11:15–19 in your Bible.

> Then He began to teach them: "Is it not written, My house will be called a house of prayer for all nations? But you have made it a den of thieves!"—Mark 11:17

ASK YOURSELF:

- How was Jesus portrayed in this story? How does this relate to the character of God in regards to purity?

- Why did Jesus overturn tables and throw out the people who were buying and selling in the temple complex? Explain.

- Compare and contrast "house of prayer" and "den of thieves" (v. 17). Journal your thoughts.

Jesus cleared out the money changers and those selling animals for sacrifice. They defiled the temple, which was designed as a place of prayer and worship. These businesspeople set up their tables in the court of the Gentiles—a space intended to allow non-Jews to worship. The people lost sight of the temple's purpose. Can you think of an example of this today? When have you lost sight of your main purpose as you follow Jesus?

RESPOND

The Bible says that our bodies are sanctuaries of the Holy Spirit (1 Corinthians 6:19). Impurity comes in many different forms and affects different people in different ways.

- Do you struggle to keep your mind pure? Your body? Your heart? Journal your response, confessing your need for Jesus to help you stand strong in the face of temptation.

- List three ways you can guard your heart against impurity.

WORSHIP THE KING

Read Luke 19:28–44 in your Bible.

> Now He came near the path down the Mount of Olives, and the whole crowd of the disciples began to praise God joyfully with a loud voice for all the miracles they had seen: The King who comes in the name of the Lord is the blessed One. Peace in heaven and glory in the highest heaven!—Luke 19:37–38

- Sketch a picture of the scene described in verses 37–38.

- Jesus humbly entered Jerusalem on a donkey, but was greeted by a royal procession worthy of a king. His triumphal entry moved His people to praise. These people recognized that Jesus came in God's name. Why is that significant?

- The Pharisees asked Jesus to rebuke His disciples for calling Him "the blessed One" and "King." Examine Jesus' response and journal in your own words.

- Read through the passage again and note how the crowd worshiped Jesus.

RESPOND

- Examine your heart. What words describe the way you worship God?

- List attitudes and actions in your own life that need to change to enhance the way you worship God.

TRUE DEVOTION

Read Luke 7:36–50 in your Bible.

> "Therefore I tell you, her many sins have been forgiven; that's why she loved much. But the one who is forgiven little, loves little." Then He said to her, "Your sins are forgiven."—Luke 7:47–48

CONSIDER THE FOLLOWING:

- Look at verses 37–38 and 43–46. Compare and contrast the woman's actions to those of the Pharisee.

- The Pharisees considered this woman an outcast—she was labeled as a sinner. But she approached Jesus and anointed His feet with an expensive perfume. How does her gift demonstrate her thankfulness for Jesus' forgiveness? Her faith?

- Though the woman's gift may seem extraordinary, the greatest gift in this story is Jesus' forgiveness of the woman's sins. Even before His death on the cross, Jesus had the authority to forgive. What is significant about the phrases "your sins are forgiven" (v. 48) and "your faith has saved you" (v. 50)? Explain.

RESPOND

True gratitude leads to action. Jesus died to forgive the sins of all people for all time. Those who choose to receive His forgiveness and trust in Him as Savior will spend eternity with Him.

- In what ways have you responded to Jesus' sacrifice for your sins? Journal a prayer thanking Jesus for His forgiveness.

- How will you show gratitude to Jesus this week? In the way you prioritize your time and resources? Serve God and others? Worship? List a few ideas on an index card and place it in your book bag, purse, or wallet. Glance at the card throughout the week to remind yourself to show gratitude to Jesus in all you do.

THE DARK BEFORE THE DAWN

In today's passage Satan directly challenged God by entering Judas. Although we can't ignore the fact that Judas was still responsible for choosing to plot against Jesus, we have to acknowledge that Judas gave in to temptation.

Read Luke 22:1–6, 47–53 in your Bible.

> While He was still speaking, suddenly a mob was there, and one of the Twelve named Judas was leading them. He came near Jesus to kiss Him, but Jesus said to him, "Judas, are you betraying the Son of Man with a kiss?"—Luke 22:47–48

- Why do you think Judas betrayed Jesus to the priests and religious leaders? Explain.
- The soldiers and religious leaders likely expected Jesus to fight back. Instead, He went with them peacefully and willingly. What does this tell you about His character and the importance of God's plan?

Jesus referred to Judas' betrayal and Jesus' arrest as "the dominion of darkness" (v. 53). The events that followed Jesus' arrest probably caused the disciples to feel hopeless, but God was victorious—He raised Jesus from the dead.

RESPOND
- List a few areas you're currently struggling with giving over to God. Then, ask Him to help you trust Him no matter what you face.
- How can you focus on the victory we already have in Jesus as you face difficult situations? Record some ideas in your journal.

FREEDOM ISN'T FREE

Look up the definition of *sacrifice*. What does sacrifice look like to you? What does it look like to God? Journal your thoughts.

Read Hebrews 9:12–14 in your Bible and think through these questions:

- What did the sacrifice of bulls and goats purify (v. 13)? Do you notice anything these sacrifices failed to cover?

- Old Testament law required that sacrificial animals be without blemish (Leviticus 1:3 and 3:1). In what way was Christ a sacrificial lamb?

- What did Christ's sacrifice cleanse (v. 14)?

- Compare and contrast the Old Testament animal sacrifices and Christ's sacrifice.

How much more will the blood of the Messiah, who through the eternal Spirit offered Himself without blemish to God, cleanse our consciences from dead works to serve the living God?—Hebrews 9:14

RESPOND

- In your journal, list specific words that describe the freedom you experience because of Christ's sacrifice. Thank Him for the sacrifice He made for you.

- Do you know people who don't know that Jesus gave His own life to offer them freedom from sin? List a few names in your journal and commit to pray for those people this week.

INNOCENT UNTIL PROVEN GUILTY?

Which is worse—incredible physical pain or humiliation? Why?

Read Luke 22:63–71 in your Bible.

> They all asked, "Are You, then, the Son of God?" And He said to them, "You say that I am." "Why do we need any more testimony," they said, "since we've heard it ourselves from His mouth?"—Luke 22:70–71

CONSIDER THE FOLLOWING:

- Leading up to the trial, the guards holding Jesus did not protect or treat Him fairly. Instead, how did they treat Him?

- List the questions the Sanhedrin asked Jesus (vv. 67, 70).

- The Sanhedrin unfairly condemned Jesus because of their unbelief. When they mistreated Jesus, they demonstrated their lack of faith in Him and in God's plan. However, Jesus continued His journey to the cross, offering salvation to all people. In what ways do you, like the Sanhedrin, wrestle with unbelief? Explain.

- How can we know the truth about Jesus and God's plan?

RESPOND

- Ask God to help you look to His Word for truth about His identity and character.

- Find Jesus' "I am . . ." statements recorded in the Gospels. List two of the statements in your journal. Then, read the context surrounding each statement. Journal about any new insights into Jesus' character.

FULFILLED

Read Luke 22:37 and John 19:31–37 in your Bible.

"For I tell you, what is written must be fulfilled in Me: And He was counted among the outlaws. Yes, what is written about Me is coming to its fulfillment."—Luke 22:37

- After reading these Old Testament references, record the prophecy made about Jesus. In your journal, note the way Jesus' trial and crucifixion fulfilled that prophecy.

Old Testament	New Testament
Psalm 34:20	John 19:36
Isaiah 53:12	Luke 22:37
Zechariah 12:10	John 19:37

- The Old Testament prophecies fulfilled in these verses were written hundreds of years before Christ was born. What does that tell you about God's knowledge of the future? His omnipotence?

The day of preparation mentioned in verse 31 was the day before the Sabbath of Passover week. This was a significant day for the Jews—it was the day the lambs would be sacrificed for the people's sins. When the high priest sacrificed the lambs for the sins of the Jewish people, Jesus sacrificed Himself as payment for the sins of all people.

RESPOND

The Old Testament prophecies fulfilled in Christ remind us that His sacrificial death was God's plan all along. Journal a prayer of thanks to Him for planning so far in advance to rescue you from the slavery of sin.

TROUBLE'S COMING

Read Matthew 26:52–56 in your Bible.

"But all this has happened so that the prophetic Scriptures would be fulfilled." Then all the disciples deserted Him and ran away.—Matthew 26:56

ASK YOURSELF:

- Why didn't Jesus try to stop the events leading toward His death (vv. 53–54)? Explain.

- Jesus knew what was about to happen to Him and didn't fight the arrest. What does this indicate about Jesus' understanding of the Father's plan? His trust in His Father? His love for you and me?

Read John 18:1–11 in your Bible. Think through the following:

- In what ways did Jesus immediately take control of the situation?

- What was "the cup" Jesus referred to in verse 11? Explain.

- Compare the two passages from today's devotion. List Jesus' words and actions that indicate His willingness to fulfill His Father's plan.

RESPOND

- As you go through your day, consider this: Jesus knew He would be arrested as part of His Father's plan, yet He didn't fight it. Would I be willing to be arrested for living out my faith?

- Jesus followed His Father's plan completely and willingly. Examine your own life and ask the Holy Spirit to guide you as you check your heart. Do you obey God not matter the cost? Honestly talk with God about any struggles you may have when it comes to following His plan.

- In what way are you like Peter, fighting against God's difficult and painful plan? Ask God for strength to help you respond to difficult situations in a way that honors Him.

IN MY PLACE

Read Mark 15:21–37 in your Bible.

But Jesus let out a loud cry and breathed His last.—Mark 15:37

COMPLETE THE FOLLOWING:
- List the details (who carried the cross, where He was crucified, etc.) Mark recorded about Jesus' crucifixion.

- According to verse 27, describe the types of people typically sentenced to death by crucifixion.

- Look closely at verses 26, 29–30. What's so ironic about the "crime" Jesus was charged with? What about the people's mocking and questioning why Jesus couldn't save Himself?

- Reread verses 30–32. Underline the phrase "He saved others; He cannot save Himself!" Consider the statement in light of what you know about Jesus. Did Jesus have the power to save Himself? Why do you think He remained on the cross? Explain your answer.

Jesus' words in verse 34 expressed His humanity and revealed what He knew to be true—in the end God would triumph over evil. By choosing to save you and me, Jesus chose not to save Himself. His choice to remain on the cross provided all people who believe in Him the only means to live free from sin if they trust Him as Savior.

RESPOND
Jesus endured separation from God for a time, as He became sin, in order to offer us freedom from and forgiveness for our sins. When did the significance of Jesus' death on the cross make a difference in your life? Journal about your experience.

AN HONEST PRAYER

Read Matthew 26:36–46 in your Bible.

> Going a little farther, He fell facedown and prayed, "My Father! If it is possible, let this cup pass from Me. Yet not as I will, but as You will."—Matthew 26:39

ANSWER THESE QUESTIONS:

- List the emotions Jesus experienced in this passage.

- What traits did Jesus model for believers in this passage?

- In your own words, describe what Jesus asked of God.

- Jesus humbly submitted to God's will (vv. 39, 42). What was God's will in this situation?

- How might Jesus' response to God in this situation encourage believers who are struggling?

RESPOND

- What situation have you repeatedly asked God to take away from you? What happened as a result? Journal about that experience.

- In what way is God currently asking you to submit to His will? Are you excited? Scared? Angry? Unsure? Be honest with God, admit how you feel, and then ask Him to help you submit to His perfect will.

- In Gethsemane, Jesus asked His disciples to pray with Him—He instructed them to do so for their own strength. Who can you ask to pray with you in tough situations? List a few names in your journal.

THE LOUDEST VOICE

Journal a few things that might distract you from hearing God's voice or seeking His will.

Now, read Luke 23:1–24 in your Bible.

> But they kept up the pressure, demanding with loud voices that He be crucified. And their voices won out.—Luke 23:23

Reflect on the following:

- Underline each statement in this passage that declared Jesus' innocence.
- Why did the officials send Jesus back and forth (vv. 14–15)?
- Whom did Pilate listen to in the end? Why?
- Who appeared to have the most power in this situation? Herod? The people? Pilate?
- Who actually held the power? (See John 19:11.) Why is that important?

RESPOND

Jesus was innocent, yet He was sentenced to die because the Jews angrily and incessantly insisted He was a criminal of the highest order. Just like Pilate and Herod Antipas, sometimes we hear others' voices louder than God's. When we focus on others' opinions and words more than God's will and His Word, it's easy to obey the wrong voice.

- In what ways are you tempted to follow others' opinions rather than God's truth? Pray, honestly confessing any struggles to God. Ask Him to give you the strength to overcome the struggles in your life.
- Journal three specific things you will do this week to help you focus on obeying God, instead of living to please others.

PASSOVER LAMB

Our world is full of symbols. Road signs use symbols to warn us of potential danger. We use emojis to communicate to our friends. We identify things through symbols and understand their intended meaning.

In today's passage, Jesus changed the disciples' understanding of the Passover when He used the elements of the meal to symbolize His death on the cross. From that point on, every element of the Passover meal would remind those who participated about Jesus' sacrifice and atonement for sins.

Read Matthew 26:26–29 in your Bible.

> As they were eating, Jesus took bread, blessed and broke it, gave it to the disciples, and said, "Take and eat it; this is My body."—Matthew 26:26

ANSWER THESE QUESTIONS:

- In the Old Testament, the bread represented God's provision for His people in the desert. In using the bread (v. 26) and cup (v. 27) as symbols, how did Jesus reinterpret their message?

- Why was it necessary for Jesus to become the sacrifice for sin? Explain.

- Read Jeremiah 31:31–34. In verse 33, underline the phrase "I will put My teaching within them and write it on their hearts." Then, look closely at the end of verse 34. In your own words, journal the difference between the old and new covenants.

RESPOND

- Meditate on Jesus as the Passover Lamb—what that means for you, those you love, and those you don't know.

- Journal a prayer of thanks to God for sacrificing His only Son to pay for your sins.

- List four ways you can show your thankfulness for Christ's sacrifice.

REDEEMING SACRIFICE

Read 1 Peter 1:18–19 in your Bible.

> For you know that you were redeemed from your empty way of life inherited from the fathers, not with perishable things like silver or gold, but with the precious blood of Christ, like that of a lamb without defect or blemish.—1 Peter 1:18–19

Redemption requires one person paying a price to ensure another's freedom or release. Redemption breaks bonds of oppression and slavery to sin. In this verse, we see that we were purchased or released from slavery to sin into a living hope in salvation through Jesus Christ.

- Reflect on the definition of redemption above. Explain the term in your own words.

- The Jews would recognize the concept of redemption in God's deliverance of His people out of Egypt. For us, it is the picture of a person who was enslaved to sin and set free by Christ's death on the cross. Why is it so important to realize that we were enslaved to sin and in need of being set free? Explain.

- Peter described life without Christ as "empty" (v. 18). List some things people often try to fill that emptiness with.

RESPOND

We can only experience redemption because of the blood of Christ. He was the perfect sacrifice because He lived His whole life without sin. The gospel—the way Jesus' life, death, and resurrection unfolded—was always God's plan for bringing redemption to us.

- In your journal, jot down the story of how you came to know Jesus. Practice sharing your story with a parent or friend.

- List two people you know who need to hear the gospel message. Commit to sharing your story with them.

ONCE AND FOR ALL

Read Hebrews 9:11–28 in your Bible and thoughtfully answer these questions.

> According to the law almost everything is purified with blood, and without the shedding of blood there is no forgiveness.—Hebrews 9:22

- Reread verses 12–13. Describe the process used by priests in the Old Testament to atone for the people's sins and the ways Jesus replaced the need for those sacrifices.

- In verse 14, highlight the phrase "how much more." Reread the entire verse and describe the main idea in your own words.

- What had to take place (v. 15) for redemption and the establishment of the new covenant? Why?

- Review today's passage. Explain the concept of salvation.

RESPOND

Christ's death on the cross was God's plan all along—Jesus shedding His blood to cover our sins fulfilled the Old Testament law to the fullest extent. Jesus was not a victim of the Roman government; instead His death was the perfect sacrifice and exactly what we needed to be forgiven. Take a few minutes and journal a prayer of thanks to Jesus. Here are some things you may consider thanking Him for: living a perfect life, enduring such tremendous pain physically and spiritually as He hung on the cross, shedding His blood so you could be forgiven, and conquering death and sin for those who place their faith in Him.

FULL OF LIFE

What comes to mind when you hear the word *thief*? Think of famous thieves from movies, TV shows, or books, and jot down some of their characteristics in your journal.

Now, read John 10:9–11 in your Bible.

> "A thief comes only to steal and to kill and to destroy. I have come so that they may have life and have it in abundance."—John 10:10

ASK YOURSELF:

- How do believers "enter" (v. 9) through Jesus?
- What did Jesus mean by "life . . . in abundance" (v. 10)? Explain.

When we repent and believe, Christ gives us a new life, an abundant life. Therefore, every genuine Christian believer has been redeemed from an empty existence to a full life in Christ. Jesus didn't just call us to this kind of life—He lived out an example through His perfect fellowship with God.

We have to remember that having life in abundance doesn't mean we will have everything that we want—it means we have everything we need in Christ Himself. In plain terms, explain what Jesus said in verse 11.

RESPOND

Jesus' blood sacrifice for our lives has supreme value. Our lives should be lived in testimony to that—He is far more precious than earthly wealth.

- In your journal, list a few things you tend to value above Jesus. Confess those struggles to the Lord, and ask Him to help you recognize His value and give Him the highest place of honor in your life.
- Consider the point of today's devotion. Ask yourself: What do the words *abundant life* mean to me personally? Journal your thoughts.

UNLIMITED ACCESS

People are separated from God because of their sin. Before Jesus' death on the cross, priests interceded for the people by offering yearly sin sacrifices, but the people did not have direct access to God.

Read Matthew 27:50–54 in your Bible.

> Suddenly, the curtain of the sanctuary was split in two from top to bottom; the earth quaked and the rocks were split.—Matthew 27:51

EXPLORE THE FOLLOWING:

- List the events that occurred when Jesus died.

- The high priest was the only person allowed beyond the curtain that separated the people from God's presence. Why is it important that the temple veil was torn? What is the significance to you today?

- In your own words, explain the guards' exclamation in verse 54.

- Describe the guards' reaction when all of these things occurred. Imagine you were at the cross; would your reaction be like the guards'?

RESPOND

Before Jesus' death, people only had access to God through the priest. Now, Jesus is our High Priest—constantly interceding for us at the right hand of God in heaven.

- Meditate on today's Scripture. Praise God for giving you direct access to Him through Jesus.

- Prayerfully consider what Jesus' death on the cross means to you personally. Then, record your thoughts in your journal.

- Does Jesus' death on the cross affect the way you live your life? On a scale of 1–10, how much does His sacrifice affect your daily life?

A HOLY CHALLENGE

Think about your favorite sports team, the armed services, police, and nurses. These people all have one thing in common—they wear uniforms and their uniforms represent the people they serve. In the same way, when you trust Jesus as Savior, you bear His name; you represent Him. The way you live should call others to "taste and see that the Lord is good" (Psalm 34:8).

Read 1 Peter 1:22–23 in your Bible.

> By obedience to the truth, having purified yourselves for sincere love of the brothers, love one another earnestly from a pure heart.—1 Peter 1:22

ANSWER THE FOLLOWING QUESTIONS:

- Underline the word *obedience* (v. 22). How did Peter call believers to obey God?

- What does it mean that believers are "purified" (v. 22)? Explain.

- What does the word *earnestly* indicate about the way we should love each other?

- According to Peter, how are believers empowered to love one another?

RESPOND

Our relationships with others point to our relationship with Christ. Do we truly love others from a pure heart? Do we love them as He loves us? This may sound difficult, or even impossible, but this is the life God calls us to live.

- In your journal, create three columns with the headings *God's Love*, *My Love*, and *Love Better*. Under the appropriate heading, record ways God demonstrated His love to you, how you show love to others, and the names of people you need to love better.

- Glance at the names you listed in the third column of your journal page. Ask God to help you have the courage to seek or extend forgiveness in those relationships. Pray for those people to see God's love as well.

FOLLOW ME

Read John 1:35–42 in your Bible and think through these questions.

> When he saw Jesus passing by, he said, "Look! The Lamb of God!" The two disciples heard him say this and followed Jesus.—John 1:36–37

- Highlight the phrase *Lamb of God* (v. 36). Describe what this means in your own words.
- According to verse 37, what happened after the two disciples heard John's claim?
- Jesus called the disciples to come and they went with Him, but they went beyond following Jesus. List Andrew's actions after he stayed with Jesus.
- When Christ changes your life, He changes your identity. Believers are adopted into God's family, trading in their own agenda for His—and He commands us to go and tell others about Him. After only a few hours in Jesus' presence, how did Andrew demonstrate an understanding of Jesus' message? How can believers follow Andrew's example today?
- Read Luke 6:40 and explain the main idea of this verse in your own words.

RESPOND

We are not exempt from God's missionary mandate. He was sent, and now He sends us. Sound intimidating? Through the saving power of the gospel and the filling of our hearts with God's Holy Spirit, we are empowered to join God's rescue mission—one person at a time. In your journal, name a few people you know who don't know Jesus. Pray over them, asking God to help them see their need for a Savior and to give you the opportunity to share the gospel with them.

SOVEREIGN AND ETERNAL ONE

Read Revelation 22:12–13 in your Bible.

"I am the Alpha and the Omega, the First and the Last, the Beginning and the End."—
Revelation 22:13

- Summarize verse 12 in your own words.

- All people will experience a final judgment and Jesus will be the Judge. List the words Jesus used to describe Himself in verse 13.

- The Alpha and Omega begin and end the Greek alphabet. When Jesus called Himself the Alpha and Omega, He pointed to His eternal and sovereign nature. God was first called the Alpha and Omega (Isaiah 44:6; Revelation 1:8), but here Jesus made it clear that He, too, is eternal and sovereign. Explain what Jesus claimed about His nature and His relationship with God by the titles He gave Himself in verse 13.

Put simply: Jesus has the final say. From the beginning, He was God's plan to reconcile His people. From the beginning, Jesus knew He would return for all believers and righteously judge all people for their response to how they either received or rejected Him. Knowing Jesus has the final say, do you need to change your lifestyle? Why or why not?

RESPOND

Jesus is all the righteousness of God, and believers are completely covered by His righteousness. So when you approach Jesus during the final judgment, you can be confident in knowing that Jesus will see His own righteousness instead of your sin.

- Meditate on Jesus as "the Alpha and the Omega." Praise Him for being the all-powerful, all-knowing, ever-present God.

- Have you trusted in Jesus as Savior? If so, journal about the ways He changed your life and examine any areas that need to change.

THE PERFECT ONE

Earlier this month, you learned that *redeemed* means to pay the ransom or price for somebody—like paying for someone to be released from slavery. Keep this definition in mind as you read today's devotion.

Read 1 Peter 1:18–25 in your Bible and explore the following.

> He was chosen before the foundation of the world but was revealed at the end of the times for you who through Him are believers in God, who raised Him from the dead and gave Him glory, so that your faith and hope are in God.—1 Peter 1:20–21

- Sin enslaved all people and in order to be free from our sins, we would have to be perfect. In a world ruled by sin, we couldn't save ourselves. We needed a substitute because God needed a perfect sacrifice. Jesus was the only one able to die for our sins, a "lamb without defect or blemish" (v. 19). Why was it so important for the sacrifice to be perfect?

- According to verses 18–21, what was God's plan for redemption?

- Read Ephesians 2:8–9. Why do people need a Savior?

- Jesus' perfect life redeemed us from an empty, sinful life and eternal separation from God. He redeemed us for a relationship with God.

RESPOND

- In your journal, list any sins you struggle with. Now, draw a cross over the list. Let this be a reminder to you that these sins do not control you anymore—Jesus paid the price for your sins on the cross and set you free from their hold on your life.

- Spend some time in prayer, thanking God for sending Jesus to set you free from your sins and redeem you from your empty way of life. Ask God to help you live in His freedom.

THE IMAGE RESTORER

Read Genesis 1:27–28 and Psalm 8:3–5 in your Bible and complete the following:

- Rewrite Genesis 1:27 in your own words. What does this tell you about God's plan for people? His love for us?

- Focus on Psalm 8:5. What do you think it means that God crowned us with glory and honor? Explain.

The world we live in seems to say that souls vary in importance. God's Word disagrees—all of humanity was created in His image. Every life has value and worth because it bears the image of God, the glory of God. However, sin marred that image and only Jesus' death could restore it.

We all, with unveiled faces, are looking as in a mirror at the glory of the Lord and are being transformed into the same image from glory to glory; this is from the Lord who is the Spirit.—2 Corinthians 3:18

Read 2 Corinthians 3:18 and Colossians 3:9–10 in your Bible and answer the following.

- In 2 Corinthians 3:18, did Paul describe this change as immediate or gradual? Explain.

- Reread the previous question. In your Bible, underline any key words that helped you determine your answer.

- Summarize Colossians 3:9–10. List some differences between the old and new self. (See Ephesians 4:22–24 for guidance.)

- According to Colossians 3:10, explain how we are renewed.

RESPOND

Glorifying God isn't just about what you do, but who you are as His image-bearer. The more time you spend with God, the more you will reflect Him in the way you live. In your journal, jot down some specific ways you notice God's transformation in your own life.

PERFECT HIGH PRIEST

Read Hebrews 7:23–28 in your Bible.

> For this is the kind of high priest we need: holy, innocent, undefiled, separated from sinners, and exalted above the heavens. He doesn't need to offer sacrifices every day, as high priests do—first for their own sins, then for those of the people. He did this once for all when He offered Himself.—Hebrews 7:26–27

- Record the differences between Jesus and the Levitical high priests listed in today's Scripture.

- In order for the high priest to permanently intercede for the people, he had to be holy, innocent, undefiled, separated from sinners, and exalted above the heavens. Why was this impossible for the high priests but completely possible for Jesus?

- In summary, what does Jesus offer that the high priests of the Old Testament could never offer?

RESPOND

Jesus is supreme—a new kind of priest—perfect and flawless in every way. He established the new covenant with His blood and acts as our High Priest, continually going before God on our behalf. His priesthood is permanent because He is alive forever. Explore this idea: *Jesus' sacrifice paid for all my sins, even the ones I haven't committed yet. His sacrifice was enough to cover my mistakes forever.* How does this help you handle your mistakes? Journal your thoughts.

THE SUPREME ONE

Define the term *reconcile* in your own words.

Read Colossians 1:15–20 in your Bible and consider these questions.

> For God was pleased to have all His fullness dwell in Him, and through Him to reconcile everything to Himself by making peace through the blood of His cross—whether things on earth or things in heaven.—Colossians 1:19–20

- List all the characteristics of Jesus that Paul mentioned in these verses.

- These descriptions of Jesus indicate that there is nothing and no one greater than Him. He is the image of God, Creator of everything, and sovereign over all.

- Rewrite verse 19 in your own words. Pay special attention to the words *fullness* and *dwell*.

- Look at verse 20. What does Jesus' sovereignty make Him completely qualified to do?

- We were created to have a relationship with God, but sin fractured our bond. Only Jesus has the power to restore our relationship with God, to reconcile us. Explain in your own words how Jesus heals that relationship (v. 20).

RESPOND

Jesus is uniquely qualified to bring about reconciliation between God and people and the entire universe. The reconciliation He offers is 100 percent complete; you only have to trust Him as Savior. He already finished the work on the cross.

- On a sticky note write the following truths: *I am completely forgiven, completely loved, and eternally secure in Jesus Christ.* Place the note on the back of your door or your mirror so you can see it every day.

- Journal a prayer of thanks to God for sending Jesus to reconcile your relationship with Him.

THE SAVING ONE

People stood as enemies against God because of their sinful actions. Jesus' death provided a way for all people to become friends of God through trusting Him as Savior.

Now, read Ephesians 2:12–13 and Colossians 1:21–23 in your Bible.

> Once you were alienated and hostile in your minds because of your evil actions. But now He has reconciled you by His physical body through His death, to present you holy, faultless, and blameless before Him.—Colossians 1:21–22

- In your journal, list characteristics of people's lives before and after reconciliation.
- Explain in your own words what Paul meant by "you who were far away" (Ephesians 2:13).

Our sin separated us from God, and the only way to be free from sin was through the blood of Jesus sacrificed for us. Those who don't accept His gift of grace will spend eternity paying for their sins by receiving the fullness of God's wrath rather than His kindness and love. What did it take for you to be presented to God "holy, faultless, and blameless" (Colossians 1:22)?

RESPOND

Redemption is at the heart of what Jesus did for us. At the moment you trusted Him as Savior, you became a friend of God and all of your sin was completely forgiven. Do you ever struggle to believe you're completely forgiven? In your journal, write out Colossians 1:22 and replace the word *you* with *me*. Read it aloud several times and ask God to help you believe the truth of His words.

COMPLETELY JUSTIFIED

Mentally list changes that happen over time, for example, the erosion of a mountain. Now, think of changes that occur instantly, like flipping a switch to fill a dark room with light. Journal a few more instant and slow changes.

Trusting Jesus as Savior results in instant change. The moment you placed your faith in Him, you were declared righteous.

Now, read Romans 4:25 in your Bible.

> He was delivered up for our trespasses and raised for our justification.—Romans 4:25

EXPLORE THE FOLLOWING:

- What does it mean that Jesus was "delivered up" for our sins? Explain.

- Justification means to be declared righteous by God because of Christ's death and resurrection on our behalf. The payment for our sin was accomplished in His death, and the promise of eternal life was cemented in His resurrection.

- Christ's death and resurrection, not our actions, bring us into right standing with God. List some ways people often try to justify themselves.

RESPOND

Simply put: sin declared us guilty before God, but Jesus' death and resurrection declared believers as not guilty.

- All believers are justified. Do you sometimes feel unholy, unrighteous, and less than perfect because of your struggle with sin? Journal your thoughts.

- Is there any unconfessed sin in your life? Be honest with God about your struggle and ask Him to help you stand firm against temptation.

LIVE TRANSFORMED

Review yesterday's devotion before digging into today's Scripture. At the moment of your salvation, the resurrection of Christ reconciled you back to God.

Read 1 Peter 1:22–25 in your Bible.

> Since you have been born again—not of perishable seed but of imperishable—through the living and enduring word of God.—1 Peter 1:23

ASK YOURSELF:

- How should believers live out the change brought about by Christ's presence in our lives?

- According to these verses, how should believers treat one another?

Now, read Isaiah 40:6–8 in your Bible.

> The grass withers, the flowers fade, but the word of our God remains forever.—Isaiah 40:8

CONSIDER THE FOLLOWING:

- In these verses, humanity is described in terms of the temporary and insignificant. List the two things the Book of Isaiah compared to humanity in verse 6.

- According to verse 8, what quality does God's Word possess? Explain.

RESPOND

Christ's resurrection changed everything, so when Christ redeems us, everything about our lives should change as well. His resurrection leads to us living a new life.

- In your journal, quickly list anything in your life that comes to mind when you see the words *temporary* or *insignificant*. Pray, asking God to help on focus on meaningful things.

- Prayerfully examine your life and your heart. What does it mean to live a transformed life? In what ways does your life need to change as you live out your faith? Journal your response.

LIVE HUMBLY

Read Philippians 2:1–13 in your Bible and explore the following.

> For it is God who is working in you, enabling you both to desire and to work out His good purpose.—Philippians 2:13

- In verses 1–2, Paul reminded the Philippians that they were one in Christ. List the ways Paul said believers could be encouraged in that oneness.
- According to verses 3–5, how do people treat each other when they live humbly?
- The world tells us to live for ourselves. However, Jesus' teaching was countercultural and He perfectly modeled a humble life. Using verses 5–11, describe Christ's humility.
- Living in full obedience to God isn't easy. In fact, without Jesus' presence in our lives, there is no way we can follow His example for living. In what way does verse 13 encourage believers?
- When you become a Christian, God gives you new life, changes the way you think and act, and gives you the power to live out all He commanded you to do. How should these verses challenge believers?

RESPOND

- Ask the Holy Spirit to guide you as you examine your heart. Typically, what is your attitude toward serving God? Do you live in constant obedience to Him? Journal your thoughts.
- Do you live in full obedience to God? Talk honestly with Him, confess any disobedience in your life, and ask Him to help you obey His commands no matter what.
- Journal some ideas of different ways you can show Jesus' love to others. Under your list of ideas, name a few people who need to know His love. Using both lists, choose a way to show Jesus' love to one of those people this week.

MESSAGE SENT

The moment you trusted Jesus as Savior you were fully forgiven and your relationship with God was restored. Your restoration did not happen because of anything you did, but because of what Christ did for you.

Read Colossians 1:20 in your Bible. According to this verse, what is the only way people can find true peace?

Now, read 2 Corinthians 5:15–21 in your Bible.

> Therefore, we are ambassadors for Christ, certain that God is appealing through us. We plead on Christ's behalf, "Be reconciled to God."—2 Corinthians 5:20

ANSWER THE FOLLOWING:

- Verses 17 and 21 are like bookends, reminding us of what God did for us through Christ. Summarize these verses in your own words.

- According to Paul, after Jesus reconciled believers to God, what ministry did God give to us (vv. 18–20)?

- Highlight the word *plead* (v. 20). What does this word indicate about the urgency of sharing God's message of reconciliation?

- Explain what reconciliation means. What is Paul's challenge to people who have experienced reconciliation?

RESPOND

We can be ambassadors of reconciliation through our interactions with others—how we treat them and what we say to them.

- Are you pleading on Christ's behalf for your friends and family to be reconciled to God? In your journal, jot down the names of those you know who need to know Jesus as their Savior. Pray for each person on your list and look for ways to show His love to them.

- Ask yourself this question: Am I acting as an ambassador for Jesus by pursuing reconciliation with those around me? Journal your response.

- Think of people you may need to reconcile with. Ask God for the strength and wisdom to reach out to them.

PROPHECIES FULFILLED

Read Luke 24:1–8 in your Bible and think through these questions.

> He is not here, but He has been resurrected! Remember how He spoke to you when He was still in Galilee, saying, "The Son of Man must be betrayed into the hands of sinful men, be crucified, and rise on the third day?"—Luke 24:6–7

- Why did the women go to the tomb?
- Summarize the angels' message to the women in verses 5–7.
- Luke's account of resurrection morning emphasizes that the events of Jesus' death and resurrection fulfilled His prophecies. Luke recorded three times that Jesus predicted His betrayal, death, and resurrection. Describe each of the predictions in your journal.
- Jesus clearly articulated to His disciples how His life would end. Why do you think they were still surprised when His prophecies came true?

RESPOND

Instead of finding Jesus' body, the women found an empty tomb. This caught them off guard, but signified the truth of Jesus' words about His resurrection. The empty tomb meant that He was no longer dead, but alive forever.

- Think about the words *alive forever* in the statement above. What does it mean to you personally that Jesus is alive forever? Journal your thoughts.
- Have you ever doubted that God would fulfill His promises? Honestly confess your struggle to Him and ask God to help you trust Him no matter what.

EVIDENCE: AN EMPTY TOMB

Have you heard the phrase "you have to see it to believe it"? List some things that are difficult to believe without seeing any physical evidence.

Why do you think people struggle to believe in what they can't see? Explain.

Read John 20:1–10 in your Bible.

> The other disciple, who had reached the tomb first, then entered the tomb, saw, and believed.—John 20:8

- List the details about Mary's visit to the tomb and what she found (v. 1).

- In your own words, explain Mary's conclusion about the empty tomb in verse 2.

- Do you think the women and disciples expected to find Jesus in the tomb? Why or why not?

Despite all of Jesus' teachings about His resurrection, most of the disciples rejected Mary's report. Of the two disciples who accompanied her on a return to the tomb, the Bible says they "saw and believed" (v. 8), meaning they likely believed Jesus did rise from the dead as He foretold. However, verse 11 indicates that the disciples didn't fully understand the connection between Jesus' resurrection and the fulfillment of Old Testament prophecy.

RESPOND

- Think about your own life. Would you have overlooked the fact that Jesus had been raised from the dead? Why or why not?

- Many people today still don't believe Jesus rose from the grave. How would you respond to someone with this belief? Journal your thoughts.

- Do you know people who are skeptical when it comes to believing Jesus' resurrection? List their names in your journal. Then, throughout the week, pray that God would open their hearts to His truth.

NO REASON FOR FEAR

As the women walked toward the tomb, they were convinced of what they would find—the tomb, sealed by a large boulder, with Jesus' body inside.

Imagine you were walking with the women that day. Journal what you would have thought.

Now, read Mark 16:1–8 in your Bible.

> "Don't be alarmed," he told them. "You are looking for Jesus the Nazarene, who was crucified. He has been resurrected! He is not here! See the place where they put Him. But go, tell His disciples and Peter, 'He is going ahead of you to Galilee; you will see Him there just as He told you.'"—Mark 16:6–7

COMPLETE THE FOLLOWING:
- In verse 5, Mark said the women were amazed and alarmed. Why do you think they reacted this way?

- What were the first three words the young man said to the women? What's the significance of his statement?

- Why do you think the angel encouraged the women to look at Jesus' empty tomb for themselves? Explain.

Biblical scholars suggest that the angel's command for the women to go and tell the disciples demonstrated Jesus' love and concern for them. They were dejected and afraid—their Master had been crucified! How would physical proof of His resurrection reassure the disciples? Show them Jesus' love?

RESPOND

Just like the women in today's passage, you have also heard about Jesus' resurrection—the empty tomb signified His conquering of death.

- Consider what Jesus' resurrection means to you. Journal a prayer of praise to God for raising Jesus to life.

- In your journal, jot down the names of two people who need to know God's truth. Commit to sharing Jesus' message of salvation with them this week.

MOURNING TO REJOICING

Read Matthew 28:1–8 in your Bible.

So, departing quickly from the tomb with fear and great joy, they ran to tell His disciples the news.—Matthew 28:8

COMPLETE THE FOLLOWING:

- Jot down details about the physical appearance of the angel of the Lord (v. 3).

- No human deception could have mimicked an earthquake and the appearance of the angel. In your journal, sketch a picture depicting the scene in verses 2–4.

- Think back to previous accounts of this scene. With the inclusion of the angel's appearance and the earthquake, why is the angel's statement in verse 5 so important? Explain.

- These were extraordinary events that caused the guards to faint in fear. However, when the angel spoke to the women, they had a different reaction. Describe their actions upon hearing the angel's good news.

RESPOND

- Jot down the last piece of great news you received. Who brought the message?

- Now, think about the first time you heard about Jesus' resurrection. Who told you about Him? How did they tell you? Describe the conversation in your journal.

- Hearing that Jesus had risen from the dead was the best piece of news these women received. How did the news of His resurrection change your life? Journal about your experience.

- If you have placed your faith in Jesus, pray for an opportunity to tell this news to others this week.

BRIBES AND LIES

The women obeyed the angel's command to go tell the disciples the good news that Jesus had been raised from the dead. For followers of Jesus, this was terrific news that caused great rejoicing. However, for those who opposed Jesus, this created a problem. Why?

Now, read Matthew 28:4, 11–15 in your Bible.

> After the priests had assembled with the elders and agreed on a plan, they gave the soldiers a large sum of money and told them, "Say this, 'His disciples came during the night and stole Him while we were sleeping.'"—Matthew 28:12–13

ASK YOURSELF:

- List the priests' actions upon hearing the guards' testimony.

- What did the priests' reaction indicate about the importance of Jesus' message?

- What plan did the priests devise in order to quiet the news of Jesus' resurrection?

- The priests didn't want the soldiers to admit that Jesus had been raised from the dead because that would have affirmed His identity as the Son of God. So, the priests who had sentenced Jesus to death bribed the guards to lie.

RESPOND

- How would you have responded if you were one of the Roman guards bribed by the priests? Journal your thoughts.

- Have you been asked to lie before? How did you respond? Record your experience in your journal.

- Consider this: The truth of Jesus' resurrection was so powerful that the Jewish religious leaders bribed elite Roman soldiers to lie about the occurrences outside the tomb. Ask yourself: *Do I understand the powerful message represented by the empty tomb?*

- Look back at the previous question. Ask God to continue to help you understand the truth of the resurrection and what it means for you.

NO NONSENSE

Read Luke 24:9–12 in your Bible and think through the following.

Returning from the tomb, they reported all these things to the Eleven and to all the rest.—Luke 24:9

- Record the differences between Peter's and the rest of the disciples' responses to the women's testimony.

- At this time, the testimony of women was highly disregarded. When the disciples heard their story about Jesus being resurrected, they thought the women were babbling nonsense. What are some things that cause us to disregard others' testimony today? Why?

- Peter raced to the tomb to discover the truth for himself. How did his actions support the importance of testimony? Explain.

RESPOND

- Believing that Jesus was resurrected is crucial to the Christian faith. How would you explain the resurrection to someone else? Practice what you would say in the mirror.

- Ask God to bring to mind a few people in your life who don't believe Jesus rose from the dead. Jot down their names in your journal.

- Look back over your list of names. Prayerfully consider how you can share Jesus' love with them this week. Ask God to give you the opportunity and courage to speak.

AS YOU GO

Quickly list some of the truths you've learned as you studied the narrative accounts of the resurrection this week. At the beginning of this week, we studied Jesus' promise that He would be betrayed, put to death, and raised again. How should these truths affect the way believers live?

Read Mark 16:14–18 in your Bible.

> Then He said to them, "Go into all the world and preach the gospel to the whole creation."—Mark 16:15

COMPLETE THE FOLLOWING:
- Underline the words *go* and *preach* in verse 15.
- Highlight the phrases *all the world* and *the whole creation* (v. 15). Why is it important that disciples not leave out anyone when sharing the message of Christ? Explain.
- Record what Jesus said about the two different types of people in verse 16 (believers and non-believers).

Now, read Matthew 28:16–20 in your Bible. Journal the four commands Jesus gave to His followers (vv. 19–20).

The word *go* can better be translated with the phrase *as you are going*. This small difference carries huge implications. Yes, God calls us to go on mission trips, but He also calls us to make disciples as we go about our normal routine. Record the promise Jesus made at the end of verse 20 in your own words.

RESPOND
Understanding that the God who has all authority on heaven and earth will be with us as we go is a great comfort to believers. His presence within us, the Holy Spirit, enables us to make disciples. He goes with us and gives salvation only He can give.

- Meditate on what it means that the Holy Spirit dwells within us, enabling us to do God's work.
- Journal a prayer of thankfulness to God for His constant presence and help in your life.

A LOVING INVITATION

The women and Jesus' disciples likely thought this chapter of their lives was over—Jesus' earthly ministry was finished. In reality, Jesus showed them the beginning of a new kind of life. Read Matthew 28:8–10 to see how Jesus introduced this new life to His followers.

> Then Jesus told them, "Do not be afraid. Go and tell My brothers to leave for Galilee, and they will see Me there."—Matthew 28:10

DIG DEEPER WITH THE FOLLOWING:

- Examine the women's reactions to the angel's news in verse 8. Circle any words that describe their reactions to the angel's news.

- The women were on their way to deliver the angel's message to the disciples when Jesus met them. Describe the women's response to seeing Jesus alive.

- Compare and contrast the women's reactions to the angel's message (v. 8) and seeing Jesus alive (v. 9).

- Why is it important to note the difference of these two reactions? How does this point to the way Jesus' presence affects our lives?

- Read verses 16–17. Explore the disciples' response to seeing Jesus alive. Why is this significant?

RESPOND

Like He did for the disciples, Jesus extends a loving invitation for you to come and see the risen King. The question is how will you respond to that invitation? Today Jesus calls you to meet with Him through Scripture, prayer, and placing your faith in Him for salvation. Have you responded to Jesus' invitation to spend eternity with Him? Journal about that experience using the following questions as a guide.

- What caused you to realize your need for a Savior?

- Who told you about Jesus?

- How did your life change after salvation?

AN ASSURING PRESENCE

Read Mark 16:9–10 in your Bible and consider the following.

> Early on the first day of the week, after He had risen, He appeared first to Mary Magdalene, out of whom He had driven seven demons.—Mark 16:9

- What encounters caused Mary to report back to the disciples that Jesus had risen? Explain.

- Jesus revealed Himself to Mary Magdalene, affirming the promise given to her before His death and the angel's message at the tomb. The reassurance of Jesus' presence allowed her to overcome her fear and report the good news to others. How did this encounter with Jesus provide assurance to Mary to believe that Jesus was the promised Messiah?

- Jesus appeared to His disciples to encourage them when they were full of doubt. In what ways does He encourage believers today?

RESPOND

Many times the further we stray from Jesus, the more our doubts increase. The closer we come to Jesus, the more His presence removes our fears and doubts.

- Have you ever doubted one of God's promises? Journal about that experience, considering the following: What caused you to doubt? How did God help you overcome your doubt?

- Consider your relationship with Jesus. Ask yourself: Am I spending time in His presence every day?

- If you answered yes to the question above, journal a few ways you spend time in His presence. If you answered no, journal a few ideas of ways you can make time to spend in His presence.

MISSING THE POINT

Even though the disciples spent time with Jesus during His earthly ministry and heard Him speak of His coming death and resurrection, they still didn't fully understand all that took place—they didn't recognize Jesus.

Now, read Luke 24:13–35 in your Bible.

> He said to them, "How unwise and slow you are to believe in your hearts all that the prophets have spoken! Didn't the Messiah have to suffer these things and enter into His glory?" Then beginning with Moses and all the Prophets, He interpreted for them the things concerning Himself in all the Scriptures.—Luke 24:25–27

These two disciples were so focused on the way they thought the Messiah would redeem Israel, they failed to understand what Scripture taught about Him.

- What caused the men to doubt that Jesus was the Messiah? Explain.
- Summarize Jesus' response to their uncertainty.
- Explain verses 31–32 in your own words.
- Consider the way people treat Scripture today. List some ways people trust in their own ideas and knowledge rather than the authority of God's Word.

RESPOND

Jesus suffered and died for your sins, offering you the gift of salvation should you choose to trust Him as your Savior. Sometimes it's easy to overlook the fact that His suffering included experiencing the wrath of God in the form of momentary separation from God as Jesus bore our sins. Do you remember the first time you heard about what Jesus did for you on the cross? Journal about that experience.

REJOICE, HE IS RISEN!

Read John 20:11–20 in your Bible and answer these questions.

> Having said this, she turned around and saw Jesus standing there, though she did not know it was Jesus. . . . So the disciples rejoiced when they saw the Lord.—John 20:14, 20

- List Mary's four actions in verses 16–18.
- What kind of transformation happened for Mary and the disciples when Jesus revealed Himself to them?
- Look at verse 20. What proofs did Jesus give for the truth of His resurrection?
- When Jesus revealed Himself to His disciples, John said they "rejoiced" (v. 20). When you rejoice, you show your joy. Why is it important to rejoice over Jesus' resurrection?
- Neither Mary nor the disciples recognized Jesus until He revealed Himself to them. What might keep people from recognizing Jesus today?

RESPOND

Multiple accounts in Scripture teach that encounters with the risen Jesus resulted in a transformed life. Though we don't encounter Jesus face-to-face like the disciples, we encounter Him through His Spirit, His Word, and prayer.

- Have you encountered the risen Jesus? How did He transform your life? Journal your response.
- On the next page of your journal, record ways Jesus continues to reveal Himself to you as you study His Word and spend time in prayer. Do you respond to Him in the same way as when you first trusted Him as your Savior?

WITNESS

Read Luke 24:36–49 in your Bible.

> Then He opened their minds to understand the Scriptures. He also said to them, "This is what is written: The Messiah would suffer and rise from the dead the third day, and repentance for forgiveness of sins would be proclaimed in His name to all the nations, beginning at Jerusalem. You are witnesses of these things. And look, I am sending you what My Father promised. As for you, stay in the city until you are empowered from on high."—Luke 24:45–49

THINK THROUGH THESE QUESTIONS:

- In verses 41–42, what additional physical proof of life did Jesus show the disciples?
- Rewrite verse 45 in your own words. Why is this important?
- What did Jesus reveal about the disciples' purpose (v. 48) and mission (v. 49)?
- How have you seen Christians today being a witness for Jesus?

RESPOND

In a court trial, witnesses are those who saw an event take place and provide firsthand testimony of that event. Witnesses are also used to identify people. Being a witness for Christ involves living life with Christ. In other words, you can't talk about Christ or show others His love if you don't know Him.

- In your journal, jot down a few names of people you know who don't know Jesus as Savior. Commit to pray for those people this week.
- Journal ideas of ways you can be a witness for Christ over the next week.
- After you come up with a few ideas, prayerfully consider sharing Jesus' message with one of the people on your list.

JUMP IN!

Distractions come in different forms—sports, social media, TV shows, and so forth. List some things that might distract you from seeing God's work in your life.

Now, read John 21:1–14 in your Bible.

> "Cast the net on the right side of the boat," He told them, "and you'll find some." So they did, and they were unable to haul it in because of the large number of fish. Therefore the disciple, the one Jesus loved, said to Peter, "It is the Lord!" When Simon Peter heard that it was the Lord, he tied his outer garment around him (for he was stripped) and plunged into the sea.—John 21:6–7

THINK THROUGH THE FOLLOWING:

- Jesus doesn't always reveal Himself in ways we expect. Describe the way Jesus made Himself known to His disciples in this passage.

- Compare and contrast Peter's and John's responses to recognizing Jesus.

- Give an example of the way people often respond to recognizing Jesus today.

- In what ways are we accountable for our response to Jesus?

RESPOND

Jesus revealed Himself to His disciples, they recognized Him, and then they responded by going to Him.

- Ask the Holy Spirit to guide you as you examine your heart. Have you responded to Jesus?

- Consider Peter's response to seeing Jesus on the shore. How do you respond when you recognize Jesus' presence in your life?

- In your journal, list three ways you can get rid of the things that distract you from recognizing Jesus' presence in your life.

RECONSTRUCTED

Before you begin reading today's devotion, read Acts 13:9. Saul was also called Paul. Keep that in mind as you read.

Now, read Acts 9:1–8, 19–21 in your Bible.

> Immediately he began proclaiming Jesus in the synagogues: "He is the Son of God." But all who heard him were astounded and said, "Isn't this the man who, in Jerusalem, was destroying those who called on this name and then came here for the purpose of taking them as prisoners to the chief priests?"—Acts 9:20–21

Saul's "proclaiming" Jesus as the Son of God could also be called preaching. Proclaiming means unashamedly, publicly declaring something one believes is important. Preaching is the means by which humans present God's truth through the power of the Holy Spirit.

Dig deeper with the following: Saul encountered Jesus on the road to Damascus, where he planned to imprison more of Jesus' followers. Summarize Jesus' words to Paul in verse 5.

Notice Saul responded to Jesus' call on His life immediately. He got up, was led to Damascus, stayed with the disciples for a time, and then began preaching Jesus as the Son of God.

- Describe the people's response to Saul's conversion and message.
- How should Saul's response to salvation inspire you?

RESPOND

When Saul encountered Jesus on the road to Damascus his mission was simple—arrest followers of Jesus. But when Jesus appeared to Saul, He changed Saul's heart and mission—"take My name to Gentiles, kings, and the Israelites" (Acts 9:15). As believers, Jesus also changed our hearts and called us to tell others about Him.

- Imagine your life before knowing Jesus. In your journal, list a few differences between your life then and now.
- Think of two people who need to hear the gospel message. Prayerfully consider how you can share your story with them this week.

MOVING ON

What comes to mind when you hear the words *touch* and *cling*? List some similarities and differences in your journal. Review John 20:1–16. Summarize what occurred in these verses.

> "Don't cling to Me," Jesus told her, "for I have not yet ascended to the Father. But go to My brothers and tell them that I am ascending to My Father and your Father—to My God and your God."—John 20:17

Think through the following.

- Underline the words *ascended to the Father* (v. 17). What did this phrase indicate about the upcoming change in the way the disciples would experience relationship with Jesus?

- Jesus wasn't preventing Mary from actually touching Him and verifying His life. He helped her remain connected to the present, to a new job He had for her to do. What was the mission Jesus gave to Mary in today's passage?

- Soon, Jesus wouldn't physically be with His disciples and Mary. How would this moment prepare her for that time?

RESPOND

- We often hold on tightly to our relationship with Jesus and like it the way it is. Why do you sometimes struggle to move on to the greater things He has planned for you? Journal your thoughts.

- In your journal, jot down a few things you know God has called you to do. Ask Him to continue to direct you and help you follow and carry out His plan and mission for your life.

- In what ways do you try to keep your relationship with Jesus the same? Prayerfully consider how He might be calling you to move forward.

LAST LESSONS

Teachers instruct us about certain topics and act as a guide through the subject material. List a few characteristics of your favorite teachers in your journal.

Read Acts 1:1–5 in your Bible.

> After He had suffered, He also presented Himself alive to them by many convincing proofs, appearing to them during 40 days and speaking about the kingdom of God. —Acts 1:3

DIG DEEPER WITH THE FOLLOWING:

- Jesus remained on earth how many days after His resurrection?
- According to verse 3, what did Jesus teach His disciples? Why is this significant?
- Jesus commanded the disciples to stay in Jerusalem. Why?
- What was "the Father's promise" (v. 4–5)?
- Why is this promise important (v. 4)? Explain.

RESPOND

The "kingdom of God" (Acts 1:3) referred to God's rule over His people. Jesus' earthly ministry, including His parting instruction to His disciples in today's passage, focused on the central theme of the kingdom of God. As God's people, the disciples had an important calling to continue God's work on earth. Believers today have the same calling on our lives.

- On a sticky note, list some talents and passions God has given you that can help you do His kingdom work here on earth. Place the note on the back of your bedroom door or on your mirror where you'll see it every day.
- Meditate on the kingdom of God. Ask yourself: *How am I making the most of my time to daily prepare for God's call on my life?*

TO THE RIGHT

Read Mark 16:19–20 in your Bible and explore the following.

> Then after speaking to them, the Lord Jesus was taken up into heaven and sat down at the right hand of God.—Mark 16:19

- Being seated at the right hand of God indicated Jesus' position as one of honor, power, and authority. Though the ascension marked the end of Jesus' earthly ministry, it didn't mark the end of His ministry. Record Jesus' actions in verse 19 and then examine the disciples' actions in verse 20. How are these actions connected? Explain.

- Why is this significant?

- Matthew 26:64 mentioned Jesus' being seated "at the right hand of the Power." What mental picture does this bring to mind?

- Read Psalm 110:1. What did the Psalmist say would happen when Jesus sat down at the right hand of God?

- The writer of Hebrews also identified Jesus as our High Priest who continually intercedes for us (Hebrews 7:24–25). Why is this important?

RESPOND

Jesus still works in believers' lives even though He ascended to be with the Father. He works through His Holy Spirit and intercedes for us with God.

- Consider your own sinfulness. How does this help you see your need for a Savior? For someone working on your behalf? List a few ideas.

- How does knowing that Jesus intercedes for you with the Father change your outlook on stress, the future, and pain? Journal your thoughts.

EXPECTANTLY

Review yesterday's devotion before you dig into today's Scripture. Jesus' ascension was the rising, or ascending, of Jesus into heaven on the fortieth day after His resurrection.

Read Luke 24:50–53 in your Bible.

> And while He was blessing them, He left them and was carried up into heaven. After worshiping Him, they returned to Jerusalem with great joy.—Luke 24:51–52

ASK YOURSELF:

- What did Jesus do for His disciples as He ascended into heaven? Why is this significant?
- Describe the disciples' response to Jesus' ascension.
- Why do you think they responded this way? Would your response be similar? Explain.

Now, read Acts 1:9–11 in your Bible and think through the following:

- Examine the question the two men asked the disciples in verse 11. How do you think this question was meant to propel the disciples into action? Explain.
- In your own words, jot down the promise given at the end of verse 11.

RESPOND

Many Christians glance over passages about the ascension without giving much thought to its implications. However, it was a monumental point in the faith of the disciples. Jesus' ascension proved Jesus was who He claimed to be and caused them to worship and rejoice. Consider all the benefits of Jesus' ascension. Journal a prayer of praise to God for faithfully providing an advocate for you.

SECOND CHANCE

Recall a time when you messed up but received a second chance. Did you deserve it? How did you respond to the gift of a second chance? Describe your experience.

Read Luke 22:60–62 in your Bible. Based on this passage, did Peter need restoration? Why or why not?

Now, read John 21:15–19 in your Bible.

> When they had eaten breakfast, Jesus asked Simon Peter, "Simon, son of John, do you love Me more than these?" "Yes, Lord," he said to Him, "You know that I love You." "Feed My lambs," He told him. . . . After saying this, He told him, "Follow Me!"—John 21:15, 19

THINK THROUGH THE FOLLOWING:

- In your own words, rewrite Jesus' command to Peter in verses 15–17.
- How did Jesus restore Peter's leadership? Explain.

RESPOND

Peter betrayed the One whom he promised to follow forever. But Jesus didn't give up on Peter; instead, He gave Peter the opportunity to confess aloud his love for Jesus and reaffirm his commitment to follow Jesus' calling on his life.

- Consider your own life. Ask yourself: Have I ever denied Jesus through my words or actions? Have I expressed my love and devotion to Him through my love and service?
- List a few ways Jesus has called you to teach others about Him.
- Journal a prayer of thanks to God for allowing you to be a part of His work. Ask Him to help you use your gifts and time on earth to glorify Him and lead others closer to Him.

YOUR TASK

Review yesterday's devotion before reading today's Scripture. Jesus restored Peter's ministry by asking him to teach God's people.

Now, read John 21:20–23 in your Bible.

> "If I want him to remain until I come," Jesus answered, "what is that to you? As for you, follow Me."—John 21:22

ANSWER THESE QUESTIONS:

- Why do you think Peter was curious about what would happen to the other disciple?
- Describe Jesus' response to Peter's question. Why is this important?
- Underline the phrase "As for you, follow Me" (v. 22). What does this statement indicate about where Jesus wanted Peter's focus? Explain.

RESPOND

God loves all of His followers, but His relationship with you is also unique. He wants you to focus on your relationship with Him and your responsibilities in His kingdom.

- God calls all believers to glorify Him in everything we do (1 Corinthians 10:31). Ask God to help you have the wisdom and courage to serve Him boldly this week.
- In your journal, use the following headings to examine specific things you can do to live out your faith this week.

  Love

  Forgive

  Serve

  Share Jesus

  Encourage

MY WITNESSES

Read John 20:19–23 in your Bible and complete the following:

- Summarize Jesus' words in verse 21.

- What did Jesus say when He breathed on His disciples? Why is this significant?

Now, read Acts 1:4–8 in your Bible.

> "But you will receive power when the Holy Spirit has come on you, and you will be My witnesses in Jerusalem, in all Judea and Samaria, and to the ends of the earth."
> —Acts 1:8

THINK THROUGH THE FOLLOWING:

- Reread verse 6 and describe the disciples' question in your own words.

- What would the Holy Spirit empower the disciples to do?

- Where would God send the disciples? What does this look like for believers today?

RESPOND

Jesus promised His disciples that the Holy Spirit would come. The Spirit didn't just come to bring peace or convict them of sins; the Holy Spirit was the presence of God on earth after Jesus' ascension. He came to bring power so that Jesus' followers could share their testimony of Him with the Jews (Jerusalem), the areas surrounding Jerusalem (Judea), areas far away (Samaria), and ultimately the ends of the earth. In your journal, record your answers to the following questions:

- Why do you need power to live a life that glorifies Christ?

- Do you sometimes try to live for Jesus through your own power?

- Where has Jesus sent you to share His message?

CRUCIAL

Read 1 Corinthians 15:12–19 in your Bible and think through the following.

And if Christ has not been raised, your faith is worthless; you are still in your sins.
—1 Corinthians 15:17

- Reread verses 14 and 15. List the issues with the Christian life Paul mentioned without the truth of Christ's resurrection.

- In verses 17–19, what three reasons did Paul give to explain why faith is worthless without the resurrection?

- Highlight verse 19. Rewrite the main idea of this verse in your own words.

RESPOND

The entire gospel message hinges on the truth of Christ's resurrection. Without the resurrection, our lives have no purpose.

- Remember what Paul said about the resurrection's importance to our faith. Does this affect the way you share the gospel?

- Take a minute to think through this question: If someone challenged my belief in the resurrection, could I respond confidently? Why or why not?

- Ask God to help you understand more about the resurrection. Pray that He will help you to know how to tell others about Him and how Christ's resurrection made it possible for them to have new life in Him.

GUARANTEED

Read 1 Corinthians 15:20–28 in your Bible.

> But now Christ has been raised from the dead, the firstfruits of those who have fallen asleep. . . . But each in his own order: Christ, the firstfruits; afterward, at His coming, those who belong to Christ.—1 Corinthians 15:20, 23

ASK YOURSELF:

- Circle the word *firstfruits* in verses 20 and 23. Now, describe the term in your own words.

- Highlight the phrase *those who belong to Christ* (v. 23). Why is it important to understand that believers belong to Him?

- Look closely at verses 24–27. List the things Jesus will abolish and rule over when He returns.

Because of Jesus' resurrection we can be sure that those of us who belong to Christ will also be resurrected when He returns.

RESPOND

Every human being is a part of Adam's family. Because we are in Adam's lineage, we can't avoid physical death. But spiritual death—that's another matter. At some point in life, each person can choose to become a part of God's family. And because Jesus defeated death, everyone who believes in Him will have eternal life.

- God put everything under Jesus' rule. In your journal, describe how knowing this gives you comfort.

- Prayerfully consider your own life. Do you know that you will be "made alive" (1 Corinthians 15:22) when Christ returns?

WINNING

As you read, underline any mention of words that refer to death and circle any words that refer to life.

Read 1 Corinthians 15:50–57 in your Bible.

> Listen! I am telling you a mystery: We will not all fall asleep, but we will all be changed, in a moment, in the blink of an eye, at the last trumpet. For the trumpet will sound, and the dead will be raised incorruptible, and we will be changed.—1 Corinthians 15:51–52

THINK THROUGH THESE QUESTIONS:

- According to verse 50, who can't inherit the kingdom of God? Why is this important?

- "We will not all fall asleep" (v. 51) means we won't all die before Christ's return. In the last part of this verse, what did Paul say would happen to all people? What does that mean?

- Look at verse 56. What is the sting of death? Explain.

Human rebellion has both physical and spiritual consequences. Thankfully, Jesus' redemption not only covers us spiritually, but also physically. Through Jesus' death and resurrection, we were forever freed from the reign and rule of our proud rebellion.

RESPOND

- Since death has been defeated, that means your disobedience has been dealt with. Since Jesus' resurrection, our victory is certain. Christ's life and obedience are counted as yours. How should these truths impact the way you live?

- In your journal, list 3–5 reasons you look forward to the events described in 1 Corinthians 15:51–52.

- Think on this: *Jesus' life and obedience are counted as mine.* Consider what this means for you. Thank God for sending Jesus to give you new life.

RESTORED

Walk into your backyard or your kitchen and find a seed. Tape it in your journal. Below that, draw a picture of a plant. Consider what must happen for the seed to become a plant. Keep these images in your mind as you examine today's Scripture.

Read 1 Corinthians 15:35–49 in your Bible.

> So it is written: The first man Adam became a living being; the last Adam became a life-giving Spirit. However, the spiritual is not first, but the natural, then the spiritual. The first man was from the earth and made of dust; the second man is from heaven.—1 Corinthians 15:45–47

ANSWER THESE QUESTIONS.

- Other than the seed in verse 37, what illustrations did Paul give for the resurrection body?

- Using verses 42–44 as a guide, what did Paul mean by *sown* in (earthly body) and *raised* in (resurrection body)?

Many Christians don't really think of the physical aspects of our eternal hope. Some tend to think of disembodied souls floating on clouds and strumming heavenly harps. Journal some characteristics of the resurrection body believers will receive (vv. 47–49).

RESPOND

Humans are a complex combination of material and immaterial aspects—of body, soul, and spirit. When Christ took on the fullness of human nature, minus the sinful aspects, He redeemed the fullness of human nature through His perfect life, death, and resurrection. Through Him, body, soul, and spirit will be perfectly restored.

- Of all the word pictures Paul used in this passage, which one makes the most sense to you? In your journal, sketch an image to represent that illustration.

- Is your future resurrection more about the destruction of the physical world and your body or the restoration of them? How does that give you hope?

HOPEFUL

Think about the word *source*. In your journal, list a few different types of sources. What do you think it means that Jesus is our source of hope?

Now, read 1 Peter 1:3–9 in your Bible.

> Praise the God and Father of our Lord Jesus Christ. According to His great mercy, He has given us a new birth into a living hope through the resurrection of Jesus Christ from the dead.—1 Peter 1:3

THINK THROUGH THE FOLLOWING:

- How did Peter encourage the believers in their suffering (vv. 3–6)? Explain.

- Highlight *new birth* (v. 3) and *salvation* (v. 5). Explain the significance of these terms in giving hope to believers.

- In your own words, describe the inheritance waiting for believers in heaven.

Trials are a part of life for every believer. (See John 16:33.) Peter's encouragement in these verses wasn't that believers won't have trials, but that those trials will refine us and make us more Christ-like.

RESPOND

- What trials or struggles are you facing right now? How does the resurrection change the way you think about those things? Journal your thoughts.

- Even believers sometimes struggle with fear about life after death—we're often afraid of the unknown. How could a person who is fearful become hopeful instead? Ask God to take away any fear you may feel about eternity and help you to feel hopeful and excited about spending eternity with Him.

- Journal a prayer of praise to God for the hope you have through Christ's resurrection.

REJOICE

What items or people bring you joy? List a few in your journal.

We can certainly enjoy those items or spending time with those people, but Jesus' resurrection should cause us to rejoice in a different way. Our joy comes from our salvation in Him.

Read Romans 5:10–11.

> For if, while we were enemies, we were reconciled to God through the death of His Son, then how much more, having been reconciled, will we be saved by His life! And not only that, but we also rejoice in God through our Lord Jesus Christ. We have now received this reconciliation through Him.—Romans 5:10–11

EXPLORE THE FOLLOWING:

- Highlight each instance of the words *reconciled* or *reconciliation*. Why is it so important that we are reconciled to God?

- What can believers look forward to because of Jesus' resurrection?

- Express the main idea of these verses in your own words.

RESPOND

Our sin caused a rift in our relationship with God and we needed to be reconciled to Him. Jesus' death and resurrection provided reconciliation—in other words, He brought peace to our relationship with God. But the good news didn't end there; Jesus' resurrection also gives us hope of eternal life with Him.

- Make this knowledge personal: *Jesus repaired the rift in my relationship with God through Jesus' death and resurrection.* Journal a prayer, thanking Jesus for reconciling you to God.

- Read Psalm 51. Even though salvation happens the moment you trust Jesus as Savior, sin can still harm your relationship with God. Confess to God any sin in your life using Psalm 51 as a model.

- In your journal, jot down two steps you will take this week to live more joyfully in light of your salvation.

GOSPEL MISSION

Read 1 Corinthians 15:58.

> Therefore, my dear brothers, be steadfast, immovable, always excelling in the Lord's work, knowing that your labor in the Lord is not in vain.—1 Corinthians 15:58

COMPLETE THE FOLLOWING:

- Circle the words *steadfast* and *immovable*. Define these terms in your own words.

- Why is it important to stand strong in your faith?

- According to Ecclesiastes 1:2–3, there is no gain for work that men do. The writer even called the work "futile" (Ecclesiastes 1:2). However, Paul said the work we do for the Lord is not without purpose. How should this encourage and motivate believers? Journal your thoughts.

Now, read 1 Corinthians 10:31 in your Bible.

> Therefore, whether you eat or drink, or whatever you do, do everything for God's glory.—1 Corinthians 10:31

Paul taught believers not to act in ways that caused others to struggle. How does the previous verse's admonition about "always excelling" (1 Corinthians 15:58) when doing God's work help you understand what Paul meant by instructing them to "do everything for God's glory" (1 Corinthians 10:31)?

The reality of the future, of eternity, shouldn't free us from our responsibility to be agents of change in the world—it should drive us to passionately proclaim the gospel message.

RESPOND

The gospel must be lived in the way we talk and act, but we must also share Christ's message verbally. An important part of our mission in this world is to see people repent and believe in the gospel of Jesus Christ.

- Do you believe that the way you speak and act today could affect eternity? How would your life look different this week if you really did believe that? Journal your thoughts.

- Sometimes Christians live like we don't believe in the spiritual and physical realties of heaven and hell. Pray, asking God to help you live with eternity in mind.

WAITING

Read 2 Peter 3:8–13 in your Bible.

Since all these things are to be destroyed in this way, it is clear what sort of people you should be in holy conduct and godliness as you wait for and earnestly desire the coming of the day of God. The heavens will be on fire and be dissolved because of it, and the elements will melt with the heat.—2 Peter 3:11–12

THINK THROUGH THE FOLLOWING:

- Reread verses 8–9. What reason does Peter give concerning Jesus' "delayed" promise? Explain.

- How does God's patience benefit people who don't know Him? Believers?

- Explain in your own words what it means to "earnestly desire" (v. 12) Christ's return.

- How should the certainty of His promise to return affect the way believers live?

- List a few ways believers can show compassion to those who don't know Jesus.

RESPOND

God's coming justice and His punishment of the ungodly should cause us to move with compassion toward those who presume on His patience. God, in His grace, gives us every breath we take. Since He is patient with those who continue to reject the gospel, we should be too.

- No one except the Father knows the day of Christ's return. (See Matthew 24:36.) However, God still wants to find us doing His work when His Son returns. In your journal, review some ways you can be working to share the gospel with others.

- How would your life look different if you lived every day as if you truly look forward to Christ's return? Journal your thoughts.

- In your journal, list the names of a few people you know who don't know Jesus. Commit to pray for those people this week.

HOLY, HOLY

When we say something is holy, it is usually connected to God or religion. It could also mean that the person you're referring to is of good religious or moral standing. In what ways do people often misuse the word *holy*? What do you think it means for believers to be holy?

Read 1 Peter 1:15–16 for more about being holy.

But as the One who called you is holy, you also are to be holy in all your conduct; for it is written, Be holy, because I am holy.—1 Peter 1:15–16

ASK YOURSELF:

- Summarize the command from these verses in your own words.

- Peter highlighted the holiness of God. Why should we honor this part of God's character?

- How can living a holy and pure life cause believers to stand out from the rest of the world?

RESPOND

- Living holy and pure is motivated by a desire to please God. Would you say your life is characterized by a desire to please God? Why or why not?

- You can make a choice right now to begin living a holy life. What steps will you take to be holy? Create a list in your journal.

SPIRIT OF CHANGE

Read Titus 3:4–7 in your Bible and answer the following questions.

> He saved us—not by works of righteousness that we had done, but according to His mercy, through the washing of regeneration and renewal by the Holy Spirit.—Titus 3:5

- What is the main focus of this passage?
- According to this passage, how are believers saved? Explain.
- Underline the words *regeneration* and *renewal*. Describe the Holy Spirit's role in salvation (v. 5).
- Examine the words *poured out* and *abundantly* in verse 6. What is the significance of these words in the lives of believers?

RESPOND

Good works don't transform us. Salvation in Christ turns our lives around—we move from standing with our backs turned on God to following Him instead. The Holy Spirit continually works out these changes in us.

- Think about your own life. How has the Holy Spirit changed you? Take a few minutes to praise God for the way He has made a difference in your life and how He continues working in you today.
- How would you explain the gospel to people who believe they aren't "good enough" for God? Record a script in your journal.

PRIORITY ONE

Read Philippians 2:5–11 in your Bible and answer the following.

> Make your own attitude that of Christ Jesus, who, existing in the form of God, did not consider equality with God as something to be used for His own advantage. Instead He emptied Himself by assuming the form of a slave, taking on the likeness of men.
> —Philippians 2:5–7

- Despite Christ's position in heaven, what sacrifice did He make in obedience to the Father?

- Paul said believers should take on the attitude of Christ. What does His attitude look like?

- Verse 7 says Christ voluntarily "emptied Himself." This doesn't mean that Jesus was any less God than when He was in heaven; it means that He chose not to take advantage of some of His divine rights while on earth. Should this "emptying" affect His status in our lives as believers? How should we prioritize Him?

- Reread verse 11. The word *every* does not suggest that everyone will be saved, but that everyone will acknowledge that Jesus is Lord. What is the importance of the fact that everyone will one day "confess that Jesus is Lord"?

RESPOND

- Think about Jesus' life, death, and resurrection. Pray, thanking God for the gift of His Son and the finished work of Christ on the cross—His forgiveness of our sins and our salvation.

- One day, all people will acknowledge Jesus as Lord. Have you placed faith in Christ as your Lord and Savior? If not, find a couple of trustworthy adults such as a parent, student pastor, or pastor and ask them to share their testimony with you.

- Remember that just because people call Jesus Savior doesn't mean that they have made Him the Lord of their lives. How does making Jesus Lord of your life make a difference? Journal your response.

REFOCUS

Think about your own life. Ask yourself: Where do I place my focus? What things are important to me? Where does my confidence lie?

It's easy to let our focus slip from Christ to the issues in our lives, things we want, or even the people around us. Journal about a specific time you removed your focus from Christ.

When we choose to follow Christ, our focus has to shift from the things of this world to pursuing a heavenly purpose. Read Philippians 3:4–11 in your Bible to see what Paul had to say about choosing Christ.

> More than that, I also consider everything to be a loss in view of the surpassing value of knowing Christ Jesus my Lord. Because of Him I have suffered the loss of all things and consider them filth, so that I may gain Christ and be found in Him, not having a righteousness of my own from the law, but one that is through faith in Christ—the righteousness from God based on faith.—Philippians 3:8–9

COMPLETE THE FOLLOWING:
- Should you brag about your accomplishments and good deeds? Why or why not?
- Paul said he considered "everything to be a loss" (v. 8) because of knowing Christ. What do you think he meant?
- According to this passage, where are true righteousness and confidence found? Explain.
- What do these verses teach you about a believer's outlook on life?

RESPOND
- How can you sometimes compromise your faith for things other than God? What can you do to guard against this? Journal your thoughts.
- Identify an area where you tend to be distracted from focusing on God. What step can you take this week to keep your focus on Him? Jot it down on a sticky note and place it where you can see it throughout this week.

UNWAVERING

Read Ephesians 5:6–21 in your Bible. Consider these questions:

> For you were once darkness, but now you are light in the Lord. Walk as children of light—for the fruit of the light results in all goodness, righteousness, and truth—discerning what is pleasing to the Lord. Don't participate in the fruitless works of darkness, but instead expose them.—Ephesians 5:8–11

- Circle phrases that speak of deception. What does it mean to be deceived?
- You can know the truth by knowing God, and avoid deception by following Him closely. What are some characteristics of people who follow God versus those who fall into deception?
- What do you think it means to walk in wisdom (v. 15)?
- Reread verses 15–21. List the ways Paul encouraged believers to walk as they pursue godly living.

RESPOND

God gives believers the wisdom they need to walk in His ways. The Bible is the ultimate source of truth and guides us as we navigate through a sinful world. Carefully following the ways of the Lord shows the change in our lives and allows us to be an example to the world. When He's the priority in our lives, we live differently.

- Think of some areas in which you tend to trust the world's opinion over God's Word. Ask God to help you trust in His Word and obey Him above all else.
- Consider this: What does it mean to truly follow God's will? Journal your response.

OUT OF THE DARKNESS

Consider God's calling on the lives of believers—we are to be different from the rest of the world, to stand out. What are some ways of living that the world finds useful that would not be useful to a believer? Explain.

In Ephesians 4 Paul described the ways of the world as futile, or having no useful result. Read Ephesians 4:17–19, 25–31 in your Bible to find out how God wants believers to live.

> Therefore, I say this and testify in the Lord: You should no longer walk as the Gentiles walk, in the futility of their thoughts.—Ephesians 4:17

EXPLORE THE FOLLOWING:

- Compare and contrast the "futility" (v. 17) and "darkened . . . understanding" (v. 18) of the Gentiles to the way Paul taught believers to live.

- Carefully reread verses 18 and 30. According to these verses, what do you think makes believers' lives different?

- List the points of guidance Paul gave to believers in verses 25–31.

RESPOND

- Consider your own life. In what ways are you tempted to live like the rest of the world? Confess those weaknesses to God and ask Him to help you stand strong in the face of temptation.

- Think back to the days before you knew Jesus. What did your words sound like? What did your actions look like? Are they different now that you know Him? Journal your response.

- Review your journal entry and prayerfully consider any areas of your life that you might need to adjust to live in a more Christ-like manner.

YOUNG AND BOLD

In the church, you'll frequently hear the word *testimony*. A testimony is a personal account of how something affected you. So, believers' testimonies would be the story of how they came to know Jesus as Savior and how He changed their lives.

· Take a minute to journal your own testimony.

For Christians, being young is not an excuse for living in ways that aren't pleasing to God. Instead, youth is a great opportunity to teach others about God's presence in the lives of believers. Look at the advice Paul gave in 1 Timothy 4:12.

> Let no one despise your youth; instead, you should be an example to the believers in speech, in conduct, in love, in faith, in purity.—1 Timothy 4:12

THINK THROUGH THE FOLLOWING:

- List the ways Paul advised Timothy to be an example.
- As a follower of Christ, why is it important to live as an example to other believers?
- Using the headings provided, examine the ways a believer might model purity to both other believers and non-believers.

RESPOND

- As a believer, your testimony is strengthened by having a good reputation. Does your reputation back up your claim of being a Christian? If not, ask God to guide you in living a life that points to Him.
- In your journal, jot down ways you can be an example to others in the following areas: Speech, Conduct, Love, Faith, Purity.

REFLECTING CHRIST

Read Philippians 2:12–15 in your Bible and consider the following questions.

> For it is God who is working in you, enabling you both to desire and to work out His good purpose.—Philippians 2:13

- Underline the phrase *work out* (v. 12). Here this phrase means to live out your salvation. Now, reread the verse and summarize the main theme in your own words.

- Why would believers need to live out their faith with "fear and trembling" (v. 12)? Explain.

- According to verse 13, why does God work in us?

- If believers allow God to have control of our lives, what did Paul say we could become (vv. 14–15)?

Working out your salvation is not something that can be done apart from Christ's power. It is His power alone, working to transform the heart of every believer that enables us to live out His message in our lives. The way we live speaks of the God we serve.

RESPOND

- List a few ways you can "work out your own salvation" (v. 12).

- In your journal, come up with a few ideas for stopping the grumbling and complaining in your life. Prayerfully commit to changing these habits this week.

- Consider this: Does my behavior and attitude point others to Christ? Ask God to help you live in such a way that others see His love through your words and actions.

RIGHTEOUS IN HIM

Have you ever taken credit for a success that wasn't yours to claim? Detail the situation in your journal.

People often try to take credit for God's work in their lives. This is a form of idolatry. Read Isaiah 46:6 for a further description of idolatry.

> Those who pour out their bags of gold and weigh out silver on scales—they hire a goldsmith and he makes it into a god. Then they kneel and bow down to it.—Isaiah 46:6

Though they may look different, our society also has idols too. What do people often worship in place of Christ?

Isaiah's words highlight the temptation to give credit to ourselves for our good works, but this thinking only leads to false worship. If you added all of your good works together, they would never come close to a perfect, holy God. However, God made a way for us to become righteous.

Now, read 2 Corinthians 5:21.

> He made the One who did not know sin to be sin for us, so that we might become the righteousness of God in Him.—2 Corinthians 5:21

CONSIDER THE FOLLOWING:

- Who was "the One who did not know sin" mentioned in this verse? How did He become sin? Explain.

- Why was He the only one qualified to accomplish righteousness for us?

- What do you think it means to "become the righteousness of God" through Jesus? Explain.

RESPOND

- We all sin, we all struggle, and we are all completely dependent upon Christ. Spend some time in prayer, asking the Holy Spirit to guide you as you examine your heart. In what ways does prideful thinking cause you to lose sight of your need for Jesus?

- If you haven't trusted Jesus as your Savior, find a couple of trustworthy adults such as a parent, student pastor, or pastor and ask them to share their testimony with you.

A NEW WAY

Read Philippians 2:12–15 in your Bible and consider the following questions.

> What should we say then? Should we continue in sin so that grace may multiply? Absolutely not! How can we who died to sin still live in it?—Romans 6:1–2

- Paul addressed a temptation believers may face—taking advantage of God's grace. But Paul reminded us (v. 2) that those who have trusted in Christ are dead to sin.

- Dying to sin doesn't necessarily mean we never want to do wrong things or never mess up. What do you think it means to die to sin?

- What spiritual act do new believers participate in that helps us identify with Christ's sacrifice by representing that we are dying to our old life and embracing new life? Explain.

- Reread this passage, focusing on the death and resurrection of Jesus. Christ died so you could truly live. List a few ways believers can fully embrace the new life given to us by Christ.

RESPOND

- While no person is without sin, belonging to Christ frees us from being slaves to sin. When we live in God's power, no sin can hold us. List a few areas you need to "die to the sin" in your life.

- Taking advantage of God's grace is tempting for many believers. When we choose to follow Him, we must die to our own desires and pursue Him above all else. Prayerfully consider if you have a tendency to take advantage of God's grace by continuing in sin.

- How can focusing on Christ's sacrifice help overcome your desire to sin? Journal your response.

MY IDENTITY

Name a few ways you might try to find your value in things other than God.

We all want to know that we have value, meaning, and purpose. But where do we find this value? Read Matthew 19:16–24 to see how Jesus answered this question for a rich young ruler.

"If you want to be perfect," Jesus said to him, "go, sell your belongings and give to the poor, and you will have treasure in heaven. Then come, follow Me."—Matthew 19:21

COMPLETE THE FOLLOWING:

- Highlight the question at the beginning of verse 17. Jesus' words indicate that the ruler wasn't focused on the right things. Knowing who you are as a follower of Christ requires asking the right question to the right person. You have to go straight to the Source of life and meaning—God.

- Jesus told the young ruler he must keep God's commandments in order to have eternal life. Write down the six commandments Jesus listed in verses 18–19.

- How did Jesus' answer teach the rich young ruler about the right way to live?

- Underline the phrase *Then come, Follow Me* (v. 21). What is the importance of this command?

- According to verse 22, where did the rich young ruler find his identity?

- In the young ruler's eyes, Jesus was asking a lot. But we know that He was offering much more. God is the only one who can give your life worth and meaning. And Jesus offered a way for us to have access to God when He sacrificed Himself for us on the cross.

RESPOND

- God wants you to follow His commands wholeheartedly. Ask the Holy Spirit to guide you as you examine your heart. Are you ever guilty of just going through the motions instead of pursuing God's way out of love for Him?

- Imagine you're like the rich young ruler. If Jesus asked you to give up all you had and follow Him, would you do it? Would it be a difficult decision? What do your answers reveal about your commitment to Christ and where you find your meaning and purpose? Journal your thoughts.

HE BEFORE ME

Review yesterday's devotion. Our value, purpose, and meaning come from God. Who we are is fully dependent upon Him, and He teaches us how to live as His people. Read John 3:30 to learn more about a believer's purpose in life.

> He must increase, but I must decrease.—John 3:30

Complete the following:

- Summarize this verse in your own words.

- We live to please God. Why is it important for us to please Him above all else?

Now, read 1 Thessalonians 4:1 in your Bible.

> Finally then, brothers, we ask and encourage you in the Lord Jesus, that as you have received from us how you must walk and please God—as you are doing—do so even more.—1 Thessalonians 4:1

ASK YOURSELF:

- According to this verse, what teaching did the Thessalonians receive?

- Do you think receiving this letter of encouragement would have increased their desire to please God? Why or why not?

RESPOND

Remember whom you're living for. You have a purpose much higher than your own desires and dreams.

- Think on this: *What will people say about me at the end of my life? What defines me?* Meditate on your answers for a minute. Then ask yourself: *What do I want them to know more than anything?*

- Living for God and pleasing Him should trump all other desires in our lives. Is it easier for you to live for God in certain environments, times, or situations? What consequences have you seen in your life when you walk your own way instead of following God? Journal your response.

- Think about your own journey with Christ. Do you currently have someone who encourages you to walk in a way that pleases the Lord? List the names of a few older believers you could ask to mentor you in this way.

SERVE IN LOVE

Read Matthew 22:37–39 and complete the following.

> He said to him, "Love the Lord your God with all your heart, with all your soul, and with all your mind. This is the greatest and most important command. The second is like it: Love your neighbor as yourself.—Matthew 22:37–39

- List the two commands given in these verses.
- Underline the three ways in which we are to love God (v. 37). What does it mean to love God with all that you are?

Loving God comes first. Through Him we learn to love others.

Now, read 1 John 4:10–12 in your Bible and think through the following.

- According to verse 10, why did God send His Son?
- Love involves sacrifice. In what ways might God call believers to sacrifice in order to love others better?

Finally, read John 13:3–5 in your Bible. Ask yourself:

- How did Jesus demonstrate a servant's heart in these verses?
- Jesus not only showed the disciples what it meant to have a servant's heart, but also what it meant to be humble in service. Explain how serving others helps them see God's love.

RESPOND

It can be difficult to love as God loved, but consider that God loves you even when you are at your worst. Jesus calls us to show our love through service. Think of times in your life when you served others with the love of Christ. Journal a few thoughts about the way those experiences impacted you.

LIVE BOLDLY

Read 1 Samuel 17:32–37, 40–47 and explore the following.

> David said to the Philistine: "You come against me with a dagger, spear, and sword, but I come against you in the name of Yahweh of Hosts, the God of Israel's armies—you have defied Him."—1 Samuel 17:45

- Using verses 34–37, describe the experiences David said prepared him for this confrontation with Goliath.

- David approached the Philistine with courage and confidence. Why do you think he was able to do this when the rest of the Israelite army remained in the camp?

- List the items David chose to use to defend Himself (v. 40). Why do you think he chose these instead of Saul's armor?

- Why do you think Goliath was insulted when he saw it was David who came to fight him (vv. 42–43)?

- Consider David's words to Goliath in verses 46–47. What was his motivation for standing up against Goliath?

RESPOND

- These passages served to highlight David's confidence in God. Because of God's past faithfulness to protect and defend him, David approached the Philistine with complete assurance that God would come through for him once again. Answer the following questions in your journal: Do you live your life with complete faith in God? Do you have solid confidence that God fights for you?

- In your journal, create two columns under the headings *God's Faithfulness* and *My Faith*. In the first column, jot down some different instances when God intervened on your behalf and proved Himself faithful. Under the next column, record the ways those experiences strengthened your faith.

THE GAIN IN GIVING UP

Read Luke 14:25–33 in your Bible and think through the following.

> Now great crowds were traveling with Him. So He turned and said to them: "If anyone comes to Me and does not hate his own father and mother, wife and children, brother and sisters—yes, and even his own life—he cannot be My disciple. Whoever does not bear his own cross and come after Me cannot be My disciple."—Luke 14:25–27

- The cost of following Jesus as His disciple comes with a great price. List what Jesus called us to be willing to give up in order to follow Him.

- It is not that you are to dishonor your family or neglect them but rather that your love for Jesus should be greater than the love we have for our family members. Following Jesus requires us to deny our own desires, and place following Him above all, even when we face persecution and painful situations. We are sometimes held captive by the items we own. No matter how much emphasis we place on our earthly possessions, they will not last. What does it mean to truly love Jesus more than anything or anyone else? What does this look like lived out? Explain.

Salvation happens only once: when you trust Jesus as your Savior. However, we must daily surrender ourselves to Christ, choosing Him above all else.

RESPOND

- Prayerfully consider your own life. Do you love Jesus above all? Are you willing to give up all your possessions or move away from your family and friends to follow Him?

- Surrendering your life to God can be scary. You don't know what He might ask you to give up or where He will ask you to go. What makes you anxious about complete surrender? Journal your thoughts.

IN JESUS' NAME

Review the definition of the word *disciple* from yesterday's devotion.

Read Matthew 28:16–20 to discover more about the importance of obediently following Jesus and learning from Him as His disciple.

> Then Jesus came near and said to them, "All authority has been given to Me in heaven and on earth. Go, therefore, and make disciples of all nations, baptizing them in the name of the Father and of the Son and of the Holy Spirit, teaching them to observe everything I have commanded you."—Matthew 28:18–20

COMPLETE THE FOLLOWING:

- Summarize Jesus' commands in verses 18–20.

- How did Jesus' final earthly teaching show us what discipleship looks like?

- Discipleship is not a one-time deal, but a lifestyle. Believers must follow Jesus' command to go and make disciples, but we don't do this in our own power. Underline the words *all authority* (v. 18) and *in the name of the Father and of the Son and of the Holy Spirit* (v. 19).

- Though Jesus empowers us to do as He commanded, what is the importance of obedience to this command?

RESPOND

- The call to go looks different for each believer. Think about your life right now. Where has God given you influence in your daily life?

- God calls us to make disciples "of all nations" (v. 19). This command includes your family and friends. Ask God to give you the courage and wisdom to share Jesus' message with them when the opportunity arises.

- In your journal, draw a line down the center of a new page. On the left side, write *Discipled Me* and above the right column *Called to Disciple*. Under the first heading, list the names of people who have helped you grow your faith and briefly describe the main way each one helped you. In the next column, list the names of anyone you know God is calling you to disciple.

CONFORMED OR TRANSFORMED

Read Romans 12:1–2 in your Bible and complete the following.

> Do not be conformed to this age, but be transformed by the renewing of your mind, so that you may discern what is the good, pleasing, and perfect will of God.—Romans 12:2

- Underline and write in your own words what the phrase *by the mercies of God* (v. 1) has to do with us presenting our bodies as holy and pleasing to Him.

- Responding to God's mercy requires completely dedicating our lives to Him. His mercy shouldn't encourage further sin, but holy living. We can't be completely committed to God while embracing the ways of the world. What do you think it means to present your body as a "living sacrifice" (v. 1)?

- How does our society determine what is holy and pleasing to God? How does that compare with what God determines to be holy and pleasing?

- Paul instructed believers to "be transformed" (v. 2). How did Paul instruct believers to go about this? Explain.

Ultimately, the Holy Spirit working through us makes this transformation in our lives. But we have to respond to His working and embrace the changes God calls us to make.

RESPOND

Note that you can't follow the ways of the world while being transformed into Christ-likeness. The ways of the world and God's ways don't co-exist.

- Ask the Holy Spirit to guide you as you examine your life. Are you living conformed or transformed?

- In your journal, honestly confess to God which word describes your life more: *conformed* or *transformed*.

SALT AND LIGHT

Read Matthew 5:13–16 in your Bible.

> "In the same way let your light shine before men, so that they may see your good works and give glory to your Father in heaven."—Matthew 5:16

- What two items did Jesus use to illustrate how believers' lives should look?
- Explain the purposes Jesus gave for each of those two items.
- Reread verse 16. What did Jesus say was the ultimate reason for being a light in the world?

God calls each believer to serve others, be an example to them, and live in a way that shows we know and follow Him. Now, read Philippians 2:1–5 in your Bible to find out how disciples can be united in sharing His gospel message.

ASK YOURSELF:
- According to these verses, how should believers treat one another as they pursue "one goal" (v. 2–4)?
- Jesus made Himself like us and then served us out of His love. Why is it important to have the same attitude as He did when it comes to serving others (vv. 5–11)?
- How do you think unity among believers and serving with the attitude of Christ will affect the world around you?

RESPOND
- What does it look like for you to be salt and light each day? Record your response in your journal.
- Prayerfully consider these questions: *Do the differences between me and other believers affect my decision to serve others? Should they? How can I guard against this in my life?*
- On a sticky note, list two ways you plan to improve how you work alongside other believers. Ask God to help you follow through with your plan.

WORKERS NEEDED

Read Matthew 9:35–38 in your Bible and complete the following.

> Then He said to His disciples, "The harvest is abundant, but the workers are few. Therefore, pray to the Lord of the harvest to send out workers into His harvest."
> —Matthew 9:37–38

- List Jesus' actions mentioned in verse 35.

- Describe the people mentioned in verse 36.

- What is the significance of Jesus' reaction to these people?

- Jesus' words in verse 37 provide hope by acknowledging that there is an abundant harvest: many people are still waiting to hear His good news. Why is the abundance of harvest and lack of laborers a problem? Explain.

- In your own words, record the command found in verse 38.

Jesus went to the people, He met their physical and spiritual needs, He was broken for them, and He prayed for others to join Him. We should follow His lead, in willingly serving and compassionately loving all people.

RESPOND

- Sometimes pain makes us uncomfortable. How can you reach out and help others instead of running when you see their needs or problems? In your journal, examine some issues that may keep you from seeing these people and reaching out to meet their needs.

- Compare and contrast your response and Jesus' response to others' needs.

- Ask God to continue to raise up believers willing to spread the gospel to all people. Pray that He would give us the compassion to love and serve others well.

UNCONDITIONAL

Have you heard someone make a promise and add the phrase *on one condition*? In this case, a condition is usually an amendment to or specification for an agreement. Knowing this, what do you think it means to do something unconditionally? Record your response in your journal.

Now, read Mark 1:16–20 in your Bible.

> "Follow me," Jesus told them, "and I will make you fish for people!" Immediately they left their nets and followed Him.—Mark 1:17–18

EXPLORE THE FOLLOWING:

- Simon and Andrew were fishing when Jesus approached them. Why was this important?

- How did the men respond? Why do you think they responded this way?

- Look back at verse 16 and underline the word *fishermen*. Fishing was their profession. Jesus called them to leave what they knew to follow Him.

- How was the response from Simon, Andrew, James, and John unconditional? Explain.

As soon as Jesus called these four men, they responded with an active yes. Jesus calls every person to serve Him, but we must be willing to answer, even if what He asks us to do seems scary.

RESPOND

Sometimes answering God's call, or even the thought of what He might ask us to do, causes us to feel anxious. We might ask: What if God asks me to leave everything and everyone I know? Sometimes He does. Take Simon, Andrew, James, and John for example—they "immediately" left everything they knew to step into the unknown of following Jesus.

- Consider your own relationship with Jesus. When you hear Jesus call, are you ready to abandon all to follow immediately? Take a minute to pray that the Lord will prepare your heart to follow with radical obedience.

- Journal a prayer to God, asking Him to fill you with unconditional love for Him and others. Ask God to help you obey Him immediately and serve Him out of love.

HEART UNDIVIDED

Read Luke 9:57–62 in your Bible.

> But Jesus said to him, "No one who puts his hand to the plow and looks back is fit for the kingdom of God."—Luke 9:62

CONSIDER THE FOLLOWING:

- Summarize Jesus' three responses to people's excuses for not following Him.

- Jesus made it abundantly clear that to follow Him as a disciple calls believers to be willing to give up our treasures on Earth and trust Him wholeheartedly knowing our treasure is in Him. Consider the phrase *count the cost*. How does this phrase relate to today's passage?

- What does it take to follow Christ 100 percent, no matter the personal cost?

- Underline the words *fit for the kingdom of God* (v. 62). What does this mean?

A believer's focus should be on God's kingdom and His purpose. This requires looking toward the future, while living out God's plan in the present. Your past will always be a part of your life, but it doesn't have to define your ministry and mission. Journal a few ways believers can keep their focus on God's kingdom.

RESPOND

- We're all about security—in money, education, relationships, and so forth. But Jesus' call on our lives asks us to be willing to loosen our grip on those things. This is what it means to "count the cost," to know what we may be asked to give up or pass by altogether.

- Prayerfully consider your life. What are some things or people in your life that may keep you from following Jesus 100 percent? Jot these down in your journal and ask the Lord for strength to give those areas completely to Him.

- Do you live in such a way that acknowledges the urgency of the gospel? Journal your thoughts.

NONE LIKE YOU

Holiness exists only in God, but can be reflected by those who follow Him. Consider the definition in your journal. List ways God's nature is different from our own.

Hannah prayed for a son, promising to dedicate him to the Lord for service. After God gave her a son, she kept her promise and took him to Eli at Shiloh. Once she gave Samuel over to Eli, she prayed again, praising God. Read 1 Samuel 2:2 to see how she recognized God's holiness.

> There is no one holy like the LORD. There is no one besides You! And there is no rock like our God.—1 Samuel 2:2

CONSIDER THE FOLLOWING:

- God's nature is above ours in every way. Think about what the world would be like if God were not different from us. Considering this, why is it important to note how much greater than us God is?

- Why is it necessary to acknowledge His holiness?

- According to 1 Thessalonians 4:7, God has called believers to live holy lives as well. How can believers look to God as the standard for holiness?

RESPOND

- God is entitled to set the standard for holiness because only He is truly holy. Imagine how you would describe this to a friend and jot down a script in your journal.

- Every day we face multiple decisions. Look at the week ahead and list a few decisions you might face.

- Prayerfully consider the following: *How can I reflect God's holiness in my decisions?*

A WORTHY PURSUIT

Review yesterday's devotion. Summarize why you think holiness is necessary.

Now, read Hebrews 12:14 in your Bible.

> Pursue peace with everyone, and holiness—without it no one will see the Lord.
> —Hebrews 12:14

COMPLETE THE FOLLOWING:

- • Underline the word *pursue*. Holiness is inherent in God, but it is something that believers are required to seek after. What should the pursuit of holiness look like?

- • Living a holy life is not simply a suggestion, but a requirement for Christian living. How does living in holiness affect different areas of believers' lives?

The phrase *without it no one will see the Lord* doesn't mean you can earn salvation through peace and holiness; instead it means because God is holy, and we must receive His holiness through salvation.

Now, read 1 Thessalonians 3:12–13 in your Bible and complete the following:

- • Underline the phrases *may the Lord cause* (v. 12) and *may He make* (v. 13). What do these phrases indicate about who initiates holiness in our lives? Explain.

- • For us to be holy, God must remove our record of sin. How did He do that? What does this mean for us?

RESPOND

Pursuing holiness means pursuing God Himself. Being distinctly holy and blameless is not something we can achieve on our own. It is the gift of God, manifested in our lives, as we draw near to Him and reflect more of His character.

- • What are some things you can do differently this week to draw near to God? Journal a few ideas.

- • List two ideas to help you make time to spend in the Word and in prayer this week.

- • Ask God to show you how you can reflect His holiness in the way you love others and respond to their needs.

HIS HOLINESS

Read Isaiah 64:6 in your Bible and summarize the verse.

Consider the way the Israelites saw themselves. When do you try to depend on righteous acts to make yourself holy?

We couldn't earn our holiness, and sin prevented us from being holy before God. We have no righteousness on our own and could never earn the right to call ourselves holy. Read 1 Peter 1:13–21 to see how Christ makes us holy.

> Therefore, with your minds ready for action, be serious and set your hope completely on the grace to be brought to you at the revelation of Jesus Christ.—1 Peter 1:13

Reread verses 13–17. List the action phrases that outline what we are called to do as we pursue holiness.

RESPOND

Only Jesus could conquer sin and give us a holy nature; we have no righteousness of our own. Instead, Jesus, as the only one who measured up to God's standard of holiness, sets us apart when we trust Him as Savior. While our holiness won't be fully achieved until we join Him in heaven, we are called to daily walk in His ways here on the earth.

- Think about specific areas in your life that may not reflect God's holiness. What needs to change so that you can "be holy in all your conduct" (1 Peter 1:15)? List a few ideas.

- Ask God to help you bring every area of your life into obedience and holiness.

A HOLY GUIDE

Read 1 Corinthians 2:10–12 in your Bible.

> Now we have not received the spirit of the world, but the Spirit who comes from God, so that we may understand what has been freely given to us by God.—1 Corinthians 2:12

ANSWER THE FOLLOWING QUESTIONS:

- Look back at verses 6–9. Summarize what was revealed by the Spirit.

- What role does the Spirit take in believers' lives?

- List two things Paul said the Spirit does that we can't do on our own.

Now, read Ephesians 1:13–14 in your Bible. According to these verses, what do you receive when you place your faith in Christ?

When you receive Christ, you are sealed by the Holy Spirit. Being sealed by the Spirit means His indwelling not only marks us as belonging to God, but also fills us with His presence—protecting and preserving us until Christ's return.

RESPOND

- The Holy Spirit lives in you as a follower of Christ. Meditate on the fact that God is with you wherever you go.

- Journal your thoughts on this: *How does this truth point me toward conviction of sin and the desire to live a holy life?*

SET APART

Read Ephesians 4:1–3 in your Bible and consider the following.

> Therefore I, the prisoner for the Lord, urge you to walk worthy of the calling you have received.—Ephesians 4:1

- What is the calling Paul said believers received?
- According to this passage, list the actions believers should display.
- Circle the word *diligently* (v. 3). What does this word indicate about believers' commitment to pursuing holiness?
- Record some actions that might detract from displaying characteristics of holiness in daily life and those that represent holiness.
- What did Paul say "binds" (v. 3) us as believers?

While we know that we are completely unworthy of the holiness granted to us through the gospel, we are called to live in a way that speaks of the gift we have received.

RESPOND

- Which of the actions listed in today's passage are most difficult for you? Why is this particular aspect of holy living a challenge? Journal your thoughts.
- Confess these challenges to God and ask Him to grow you in these areas. Be prepared— forging humility, gentleness, patience, love, and unity often occurs through difficulty.

A NEW CREATION

Read 2 Corinthians 5:17. As you read, underline the word *new* each time you see it.

> Therefore, if anyone is in Christ, he is a new creation; old things have passed away, and look, new things have come.—2 Corinthians 5:17

COMPLETE THE FOLLOWING:

- Summarize the promise made in this verse.
- What is the significance of the word *new*? Explain.
- In your own words, describe what the phrase *old things have passed away* means.
- List some ways Christ transforms our lives.
- What makes this transformation evident to others? Explain.

Now, read 1 Thessalonians 5:23 in your Bible.

Sanctification is the process of becoming more like Christ through being set apart in a pursuit of holiness. Looking at the definition above, why do you think God is the only one who can sanctify you completely?

RESPOND

- Sanctification is a process that begins at salvation and ends when we are ultimately glorified in heaven. List some actions you're taking to keep your soul, spirit, and body "sound and blameless" (1 Thessalonians 5:23) for Christ's return.
- What do you need to change in your life to make sure you are growing in holiness? Journal a few ideas.
- Consider the boundaries you have in place to protect your heart and mind. Quickly list them in your journal and prayerfully consider any items you may need to add.

IMITATORS OF GOD

In Ephesians 4:17–5:5 Paul named many temptations that believers must avoid. Carefully read the passage to see the characteristics Paul listed to describe the old and new self.

Highlight the characteristics as you read.

> Therefore, be imitators of God, as dearly loved children. And walk in love, as the Messiah also loved us and gave Himself for us, a sacrificial and fragrant offering to God. —Ephesians 5:1–2

CONSIDER THE FOLLOWING:

- Review the passage, paying specific attention to the concept of taking off the old self and putting on the new self. List some characteristics of each.

- In verses 22–24, how did Paul say this change occurred? Who would you say initiated the change?

- Closely examine verse 23. In your own words describe the process of "being renewed."

- Summarize what it means to be "imitators of God" (Ephesians 5:1).

RESPOND

- Ask yourself: *What steps am I taking to remove the old self? Are there habits, thoughts, or friendships I need to leave behind?*

- A key factor in sanctification is the process of discipleship. This means that you are renewing your mind by learning from God's Word as well as from others who are following Him. List some ways that God is teaching you now.

- For you to "put on the new self" (Ephesians 4:24) may require new habits, thoughts, or friendships. In your journal, record some changes you need to make to live more like Jesus.

FREE TO FOLLOW

Read Romans 7:25–8:11 in your Bible.

Therefore, no condemnation now exists for those in Christ Jesus, because the Spirit's law of life in Christ Jesus has set you free from the law of sin and of death.—Romans 8:1–2

- According to today's passage, people have two choices for how they want to live their lives. What are these two choices?

- Life in the flesh is our natural state without God. When we receive Christ and the Holy Spirit resides in us, we are able to live "in Christ" (v. 1) or life "according to the Spirit" (v. 4). Using verses 5–10, compare a life lived according to the Spirit and a life lived according to the flesh.

- After reading today's Scripture, what do you think sets the flesh and the Spirit at odds? Explain.

- In 1 Corinthians 6:19, Paul said a person's body is "a sanctuary of the Holy Spirit." How should this motivate us to live holy lives?

RESPOND
- The struggle in the flesh looks different for every person because we are all tempted in different ways. Take a minute and ask God to help you see some specific weaknesses of your flesh where you need to experience the power of the Spirit.

- Read Psalm 139:23–24 and consider how this prayer relates to the struggle between the flesh and the Spirit. Journal a prayer to God modeled after these verses.

SPEAKING HOLINESS

Consider the word *always*. Quickly list some themes and ideas that come to mind when you hear this word.

Now, read Psalm 34:1–3 in your Bible.

I will praise the Lord at all times; His praise will always be on my lips.—Psalm 34:1

ASK YOURSELF:
- What does it mean to say that "praise will always be on my lips" (v. 1)?
- Examine the words *proclaim* and *exalt* (v. 3). How do these words reflect God's presence in our lives?

Read Ephesians 5:18–21 and compare it to today's Scripture.

Now, read Romans 10:14–15 and summarize the point of these verses in your journal.

In these verses, we see an urgency to share the gospel. When we bless God with our words, we point others to Him. But we must also remember to directly share the gospel message. God's plan for the gospel requires those who belong to Him and live according to His will to verbally share His message. Highlight the phrase *How beautiful are the feet of those who announce the gospel of good things* (v. 15). What do you think this means?

RESPOND
- The whole world needs to hear God's amazing truth. Why do you think it is important to both live and speak the evidence of God's greatness? Why can't we just do one or the other? Journal your response.
- Think about your lifestyle, especially your words. How can you keep God's praise continually on your lips? List a few ideas on a note card and then share them with a friend who will hold you accountable to do those things.

SANCTIFIED THROUGH SCRIPTURE

List a few of your favorite books in your journal. Do any of these books define God? Do they define you? Why or why not?

Your favorite books may be good reads, but the Bible is more than that. The words within define God and redefine us as we learn them. Read 2 Timothy 3:16–17 to learn more about God's Word applied to believers' lives.

> All Scripture is inspired by God and is profitable for teaching, for rebuking, for correcting, for training in righteousness, so that the man of God may be complete, equipped for every good work.—2 Timothy 3:16–17

COMPLETE THE FOLLOWING:

- Explain the significance of the origin of Scripture.
- List the four purposes of Scripture given in these verses.
- In verse 17, why did Paul say these purposes were important?

RESPOND

- The truth of this passage cannot be overstated. Why is it important for believers to trust that Scripture is the actual Word of God? Journal your thoughts.
- In your journal, explain why it's dangerous for people to pick and choose which parts of Scripture they want to believe and follow.
- Examine your heart. Ask the Holy Spirit to guide you as you answer this question: *Do I live my life only following some of God's commands?*
- List two ways your life needs to change in order to live viewing God's Word as the ultimate authority.

GOD'S PEOPLE

What do you think of when you hear the word *church*? Sketch a picture in your journal.

Read Hebrews 8:10 in your Bible.

> But this is the covenant that I will make with the house of Israel after those days, says the Lord: I will put My laws into their minds and write them on their hearts. I will be their God, and they will be My people.—Hebrews 8:10

The old covenant was God's commitment to fulfill His promises to Abraham and required Israel to respond in obedience to His laws, pursuing holiness. The new covenant is the covenant of grace, and it is made between God and believers of all nations through the blood of Jesus Christ. All people who place their faith in Jesus are God's people.

ASK YOURSELF:

- What does the word *covenant* mean?
- Why is it important that God made a covenant with His people?
- Church is not just a building—the church consists of God's people, believers whose hearts and minds have been radically transformed by Christ. According to today's Scripture, who initiates the change in believers?
- What is significant about the fact that God writes His laws in believers' minds and hearts?

RESPOND

- Consider the following statements: *He is my God. I am part of His people.* Then, praise God for making a covenant with you through Jesus Christ.
- What do you need from God? What does He expect of you as one of His people? Journal your response.

HEAD OF THE HOUSEHOLD

Read Hebrews 3:1–6 in your Bible.

What does it mean to allow someone to rule over you? Journal your thoughts.

> But Christ was faithful as a Son over His household. And we are that household if we hold on to the courage and the confidence of our hope.—Hebrews 3:6

ASK YOURSELF:

- According to these verses, why does Jesus deserve more glory than Moses?

- Moses was a servant of God and witness for God. God entrusted Moses with "all [His] household" (Numbers 12:7). Jesus is the Son of God and therefore has a natural right to rule. His authority comes not from creation or adoption, but from His very nature. Journal some differences between a servant and a son.

The household simply means the entire house. We become part of God's household when we surrender our lives to Christ, calling upon Him for salvation and laying down our own selfish desires. Christ Himself is the head of this household, ruling over believers.

RESPOND

- Do you sometimes struggle with submitting to the authority of Christ? On an index card, list some ways that you can commit to following Christ and obeying His commands.

- Ask God to empower you to respect and submit to Christ as the head of your spiritual household.

- In your journal, list the ways your perspective of church changes when you view it as a spiritual household with Christ as the head.

CORNERSTONE

Read Ephesians 2:19–22 in your Bible.

> So then you are no longer foreigners and strangers, but fellow citizens with the saints, and members of God's household, built on the foundation of the apostles and prophets, with Christ Jesus Himself as the cornerstone.—Ephesians 2:19–20

THINK THROUGH THE FOLLOWING:

- The cornerstone is the principal stone placed first in the construction process of a masonry foundation. All other stones in a building are placed in reference to the cornerstone. List two groups of people named in this passage who are part of the foundation of the church.

- In your own words, explain what it means that Jesus is the Cornerstone.

- How should the knowledge of the importance of Christ as the foundation of the church change the way believers, as the church body, live?

- The church body is comprised of both Jews and Gentiles—a united household of believers, a dwelling place for God. We are still being built together to form this dwelling place for God, which should encourage believers when we see division, distrust, or disorder in the church. God isn't finished with us yet. What are some ways the church currently shows unity?

- What are some ways we can improve in our unity?

RESPOND

- Read aloud and meditate on Ephesians 2:19–20.

- Prayerfully consider this: *Have I tried to build my life using a cornerstone other than Jesus Christ?*

- Journal what it means to you personally to place Christ as the cornerstone of your life.

A HOUSE UNITED

Read 1 Corinthians 1:2.

> To God's church at Corinth, to those who are sanctified in Christ Jesus and called as saints, with all those in every place who call on the name of Jesus Christ our Lord— both their Lord and ours.—1 Corinthians 1:2

COMPLETE THE FOLLOWING:

- List the characteristics of the church mentioned in this verse.

- Underline the phrase *with all those in every place . . . both their Lord and ours.* What does this indicate about Christ's role in unity within the church? Explain.

Now, read Ephesians 4:4–6 in your Bible. Consider these questions:

- Circle the word *one* each time it appears in these verses. Now, highlight each occurrence of the word *all.* What does this tell you about the importance of oneness within the church?

- Jesus loves the church so much that He gave His life for us. His desire is that the church be completely united. What are some ways that the church shows a lack of unity? How does this damage the purpose Christ has given us?

The gospel calls believers to break free of our self-centeredness and embrace the grand purpose of the life Christ has called us to. The church exists to declare the good news that Jesus has risen and has the power to unite our divided world. In what ways can the gospel message unite different kinds of people? Explain.

RESPOND

- Think about your own life: Do your attitude, actions, or words keep you from being united with other believers? Confess any struggles to God and ask Him to remove barriers in your life to unity with the believers around you.

- On a sticky note, list some ways you can work to create unity with other believers this week.

A SHEPHERD LEADER

Journal some of the main duties of a shepherd.

Paul used shepherding language to describe the responsibilities of leadership in the church. Shepherds lovingly care for their flock and protect them from danger. They guide, provide, and care for their sheep.

Read Acts 20:28 in your Bible and pay attention to the way church leaders are called to shepherd God's people.

> Be on guard for yourselves and for all the flock that the Holy Spirit has appointed you to as overseers, to shepherd the church of God, which He purchased with His own blood.—Acts 20:28

COMPLETE THE FOLLOWING:

- What do you think it means for church leaders to be "on guard" for themselves?
- Examine the word *overseers*. Describe this term in your own words.
- How was the church purchased? Why is this important?

Church leaders hold positions of authority within the church. The church has a responsibility to submit to and obey their leadership as they lead us into closer relationship with God.

Read John 10:14–16. Underline the *I am* statement Jesus made in these verses. How is Jesus the ultimate example of leadership?

RESPOND

- In your journal, list the names of your church leaders. Under each name, record specific ways you can pray for that person throughout the week.
- Glance over your list of leaders. Pray for them each day this week, asking God to give them wisdom as they lead and to be their source of strength.
- Take a few minutes to jot down a note to a leader who has played a significant role in your spiritual development. Use this as an opportunity to encourage this leader.

DEVOTED TO GOD, TOGETHER

Read Acts 2:37–47 in your Bible and consider the following.

> Every day they devoted themselves to meeting together in the temple complex, and broke bread from house to house. They ate their food with a joyful and humble attitude, praising God and having favor with all the people. And every day the Lord added to them those who were being saved.—Acts 2:46–47

- List actions the early believers took together as a group (vv. 44–46).

- What do these actions tell us about the attitude of the early church? About their priorities?

- Describe the message and the purpose of this church as a body of believers.

- How should this help us as we examine and organize our priorities?

The believers in Acts 2 experienced true community in Christ. They were light in a dark world, and provided a source of refuge and hope in the midst of chaos. They reached beyond their group, taking to heart Christ's command to go and make disciples (Matthew 28:19–20).

RESPOND

We don't have to wait for heaven to experience true community as believers—if we make His Word our foundation and choose to obey His commands to share the gospel and His love, we can be confident God will use us to be light and truth as well.

- How are you serving and sharing the gospel with others? In your journal, list some ways that you can increase your commitment to the work of the church.

- Ask yourself: *How can I help other believers see the importance of being devoted to God, serving together, and sharing the gospel?*

ROYAL PRIESTHOOD

Think back to our earlier devotion on the cornerstone. Read 1 Peter 2:1–10 in your Bible, to see how Peter portrayed the church as a living temple, with each believer as a stone used in the building process.

> But you are a chosen race, a royal priesthood, a holy nation, a people for His possession, so that you may proclaim the praises of the One who called you out of darkness into His marvelous light.—1 Peter 2:9

ASK YOURSELF:

- What does this passage tell you about the importance of interdependence among Christians?

- How can our efforts be multiplied when we work together with other believers?

- What does it mean to be called out of darkness and into light? Why is this important?

- How do we communicate the importance of unity and living in the light to other believers?

- Highlight the phrase *Once you were not a people* (v. 10). What is the significance of now being God's people? How should this affect the church and the way individual believers live within the church?

RESPOND

- Ask God today to reveal people in your life who need to hear the truth of the gospel. Record those names in your Bible beside today's Scripture.

- Review your list of names. Pray that those people would come to know Jesus' saving power through the gospel message. Pray that God would give you the courage and opportunity to tell them about Him.

ALL ARE BLESSED

Read Genesis 12:1–3 in your Bible. Summarize God's promises to Abraham in this passage. What significance did these promises have for future generations?

Now, to see how God fulfilled these promises, read Galatians 3:6–9, 27–29 in your Bible.

> For as many of you as have been baptized into Christ have put on Christ like a garment. There is no Jew or Greek, slave or free, male or female; for you are all one in Christ Jesus. And if you belong to Christ, then you are Abraham's seed, heirs according to the promise.—Galatians 3:27–29

ASK YOURSELF:

- What made Abraham righteous? Explain.

- What makes people children of Abraham and "heirs according to the promise"?

- How did God fulfill His promise to Abraham that all nations would be blessed through him?

- Why is it important that there are no distinctions between Jews and Gentiles in the church?

RESPOND

- What does it mean to you personally to be a part of the family of God? What are the implications for how we should treat our brothers and sisters in Christ? Journal your thoughts.

- How can you share God's message of redemption—telling people about what Christ did for you and how they can become a part of God's family? List a few ideas on a note card and carry it with you this week. Whenever you see the card, pray for all the people you'll have a chance to share with this week.

ALL FOR HIM

Read Colossians 3:1–4 in your Bible.

> So if you have been raised with the Messiah, seek what is above, where the Messiah is, seated at the right hand of God. Set your minds on what is above, not on what is on the earth.—Colossians 3:1–2

THINK THROUGH THESE QUESTIONS:

- What does Christ's position at the right hand of God teach us about Him?
- How should we view life considering Christ's sovereignty over all things?
- When Paul said "seek what is above" (v. 1), what did he mean?
- Record characteristics of things "above" and "on the earth" (v. 2).
- What does it mean that believers' lives should be hidden in Christ (v. 3)? What does this look like lived out?

RESPOND

It's easy to be preoccupied by chores, homework, relationships, activities, and family dynamics. The way we live makes it easy for us to get stressed out, worked up, and burned out. So how do we seek God and His plans for our lives above all else?

- How would setting your mind on things above help you respond to Christ's call on your life? In your journal, list some practical ways you can remind yourself to think about heavenly things.
- Ask God to help you stay focused on Him and pursuing His plan for your life.

A NEW TEMPLE

Consider the word *holy*. Jot down the definition in your own words.

Now, read 1 Corinthians 3:9, 16–17 in your Bible.

> Don't you yourselves know that you are God's sanctuary and that the Spirit of God lives in you? If anyone destroys God's sanctuary, God will destroy him; for God's sanctuary is holy, and that is what you are.—1 Corinthians 3:16–17

COMPLETE THE FOLLOWING:
- List the three descriptions given for believers in verse 9.
- What do you think it means that we are "God's coworkers" (v. 9)?
- In what ways do you see God using believers to accomplish His purpose in the world?
- According to this passage, what is God's sanctuary?
- What did Paul mean when He said that "the Spirit of God lives in you"?

RESPOND
- In your journal, record some ways you can respect your body as a temple of the living God.
- How should your life change knowing that God's presence, the Holy Spirit, dwells within you? Ask God to give you the wisdom, strength, and courage to make changes in your life that will allow you to live more in line with His will.
- Christ made us holy through His perfect sacrifice. Reflect on the significance of this transaction. Journal your thoughts.

AT THE CENTER

Consider the words *contrary* and *dissension*. Both words imply something that goes against the norm, or diverts from the original purpose. How might these two concepts be harmful to the church? Journal your response.

Now, read Romans 16:16–18 in your Bible.

> Now I urge you, brothers, to watch out for those who cause dissensions and obstacles contrary to the doctrine you have learned.—Romans 16:17

COMPLETE THE FOLLOWING:

- Summarize verse 16 in your own words. What was the significance of Paul's greeting?

- Underline the word *avoid* (v. 17). Why do you think Paul used such a strong word here?

- What did Paul mean by the phrase *the doctrine you have learned* (v. 17)?

- In verse 18, underline *smooth talk and flattering words*. Explain this phrase in your own words.

- Why do you think it's important to watch out for people who "deceive the hearts of the unsuspecting" (v. 18)?

RESPOND

God gave us His Word to help us know Him and how to live for Him. His Word is truth, and we can't stay grounded in His truth if we don't know His Word. Knowing our beliefs and standing firm in His truth is central to maintaining a healthy church body.

- What kinds of people try to deceive believers today? What types of things do they say? Record your response in your journal.

- Choose a verse from today's devotion and commit to memorizing it this month. Repeat the verse aloud each day to remind you of the importance of knowing and standing on the truth of God's Word.

ONE HEART, ONE CHURCH

Read Colossians 3:12–17 in your Bible.

> Above all, put on love—the perfect bond of unity. And let the peace of the Messiah, to which you were also called in one body, control your hearts. Be thankful.—Colossians 3:14–15

- According to Paul, love perfectly unifies believers. Why is it important to "put on" (v. 14) this characteristic?

- Jot down the five actions Paul commanded believers to take in verses 12–16.

- In verse 15, what did Paul mean when he instructed believers to "control your hearts"?

- Underline the phrases *above all* (v. 14) and *whatever you do* (v. 17). Why are these two qualifiers so important in believers' lives?

As God's chosen people and His representatives here on earth, believers must love one another as Christ loves us. A strong bond among believers requires both love and forgiveness. In essence, we must learn to love each other unconditionally and forgive no matter the offense.

RESPOND

Journal your response to the following questions:

- Why do you think living holy and godly lives is such an important part of our testimony?

- Why do you think we have such a hard time living in the perfect bond of unity and loving each other unconditionally?

- How can allowing Christ's peace to rule in your life help you be a good representative of His love?

- Consider this: *Do I reflect Christ as I serve others? What does my attitude look like? What about my words? Do I reflect Christ in my interactions with other believers?*

BUILD UP TO BUILD

Read Hebrews 10:24–25.

> And let us be concerned about one another in order to promote love and good works, not staying away from our worship meetings, as some habitually do, but encouraging each other, and all the more as you see the day drawing near.—Hebrews 10:24–25

- List the three instructions given by the writer of Hebrews in these verses.
- Why do you think it is important to worship with other believers?
- What does it mean to "be concerned" (v. 24) about each other?
- Underline the word *promote* (v. 24). What does it mean to "promote love and good works"?
- Examine the phrases *all the more* and *drawing near* in verse 25. What does this indicate about the importance of loving and encouraging fellow believers?

RESPOND

It is impossible for one Christian to accomplish the work of God without being connected to the church as a whole. Being present within the church benefits the individual and the corporate church. We are a community, living out the gospel and working together to help others see the truth of God's Word. Every day we come nearer to Christ's return. As that day approaches, we have an ever-increasing obligation to be more committed to living out God's design for love and good works.

- In your journal, list the names of five believers you know. Under each name, jot down a few ways you could encourage those people this week.
- Ask God to help you be an encouragement to other believers and an example to those who don't yet know Him. Pray that He would give you many opportunities to share His love this week.

LIVE RESPONSIBLY

Read Romans 12:9–21 in your Bible. A hypocrite is someone who claims to believe in something, but fails to live in ways that line up with those beliefs.

> If possible, on your part, live at peace with everyone.—Romans 12:18

ASK YOURSELF:

- What did Paul mean when he told the Roman believers to love "without hypocrisy" (v. 9)?

- Highlight the phrases *detest evil* and *cling to what is good* (v. 9). Note characteristics of someone who obeys these commands.

- Christians have a responsibility to treat others well. Believers are brothers and sisters in Christ. Knowing this, how can you show "family affection" and "brotherly love" (v. 10) to those around you?

- This passage is full of commands for godly living. List five commands that deal more with your inner state. Now, list five commands that are more directed at others.

- Consider what it means to "live at peace with everyone" (v. 18). How might believers accomplish this in a world so filled with unrest?

RESPOND

- Ask God to help you live peaceably with all people, loving them as He loved and walking in humility and honor. Pray that He will give you the strength and courage to live this way.

- What's one practical way that you can follow through with one of the commands that Paul gave in these verses? Journal your response.

THE HEAD

The head of the body gives direction to its members—your brain keeps your heart beating and your lungs breathing. In the same way, the church couldn't function without Christ.

Now, read Colossians 1:18.

> He is also the head of the body, the church; He is the beginning, the firstborn from the dead, so that He might come to have first place in everything.—Colossians 1:18

Paul said that Christ functions like the head of the body, the church. List the three titles given to Jesus in this passage.

Now, read Ephesians 4:15.

> But speaking the truth in love, let us grow in every way into Him who is the head—Christ.—Ephesians 4:15

ASK YOURSELF:

- What did Paul mean when he said Christ is the head of the church? Explain.
- Underline the appropriate response from believers to Christ as the head. What does this tell us about Jesus' identity, purpose, and plan?
- Note the phrase *in every way.* Why is this significant?

RESPOND

As you've read this month, the church is more than a building. The church is made up of all believers, everywhere. Although each physical church has a leader, Christ is the leader of the church body as a whole. He was in charge in the beginning and will be in charge until the end. Believers need Him.

- In your journal, reflect on what you've learned about Christ as the head of the church body. Then, list a few ways you can better honor Him with your life.
- Ask God to help you view Christ as the authority in your life, and to help you respond to Him appropriately.

A SANCTUARY

In the Bible, the word *sanctuary* often referred to a place—like the most holy place in the temple. Sanctuary also often referred to a spiritual state of peace, freedom from hostility and harm. However, in 2 Corinthians 6:16, Paul offered a different definition of sanctuary.

> And what agreement does God's sanctuary have with idols? For we are the sanctuary of the living God, as God said: I will dwell among them and walk among them, and I will be their God, and they will be My people.—2 Corinthians 6:16

ASK YOURSELF:

- In this verse, what does *sanctuary* mean?
- What does it mean to be "the sanctuary of the living God"?
- Explain the significance of God walking among us and believers being His people.
- Underline the word *idols*. In this passage, what do you think Paul was talking about?

RESPOND

- Journal your response to being "the sanctuary of the living God." Considering this, describe how you might need to live differently. Also, note ways that the church may need to live differently.
- In your journal, list some idols that might distract the church body, or God's dwelling place, from being holy. Review how placing other things or people before God might go against the grain of being God's people/sanctuary.
- Praise God for being your God and dwelling with you. Thank Him for the privilege and honor of being His people. Ask Him to help the church be a holy sanctuary for Him.

BRIDE OF CHRIST

Read 2 Corinthians 11:2 in your Bible. Paul reminded the Corinthian church of their commitment to follow Christ and only Christ. How important do you think it is that believers live fully devoted to God?

Now, read Ephesians 5:22–33 in your Bible.

> This mystery is profound, but I am talking about Christ and the church.—Ephesians 5:32

EXPLORE THE FOLLOWING:

- Examine the word *submit* (v. 22). In the Bible, submission is not forced, rather it is the voluntary act of placing oneself under the authority and care of another. With this definition in mind, why should the church, as the Bride of Christ, submit to His leadership?

- According to Paul, wives should submit to (v. 22) and respect (v. 33) their husbands. In what ways can the church show their respect to Christ?

- Knowing that the church is called the Bride of Christ, what does this passage teach you about the way Jesus loves us? About the way we should respond to Him?

- Believers become united with Christ through salvation. What does it mean to be united with Christ?

RESPOND

Christ's love makes the church whole. His words evoke her beauty. Everything He does and says is designed to bring out the best in her. In turn, the Bride of Christ should be fully devoted to Him.

- Consider this: *Have I failed to be fully devoted to Him in certain areas of my life?* Journal your response.

- Honestly confess to God any struggles you may have with being fully devoted to Him. Ask Him to give you the strength to stay completely committed to Him.

- In your journal, record your thoughts about being part of the Bride of Christ. What was your initial reaction to this metaphor? How does this language affect the way you see Jesus' love for you? In what ways does your life need to change as you prepare for His return?

322

BODY OF CHRIST

Consider your own family, church, or school—each person has a specific role to play. What would happen if one person failed to play the correct role? Journal your response.

Now read 1 Corinthians 12:15–23, 27–30 in your Bible.

> But now God has placed each one of the parts in one body just as He wanted.
> —1 Corinthians 12:18

Paul emphasized the value of every part of the body. In the same way, every member of the church has a unique role to play—and the whole body hurts if one person shirks his responsibility. Despite the fact that roles within the body have varying degrees of responsibility, no one has a greater purpose than the other.

CONSIDER THE FOLLOWING:
- Why is it necessary for the body of Christ to have different roles?
- What do you think would happen if each believer failed to align with God and His plan?
- Reread verses 17–19, 23, 27–30. Using these verses to support your answer, give reasons for not complaining about our place in the church body.
- Why is it important to be content with the role He gives us?

RESPOND
- Think about your own life: In what ways do you believe God has called you to serve Him? What would your role be in the body of Christ? Journal your response.
- Do you ever become jealous because of the way someone else gets to serve God? Ask God to help you see the value of your own role in His kingdom. Pray that God would help you to love others in the body of Christ and appreciate the work they do for Him.

A UNIFIED BODY

Read 1 Corinthians 12. Then, review yesterday's devotion by answering these questions in your journal.

- What does the phrase *body of Christ* mean?
- Who is a part of the body of Christ? Does each person have a specific role? Explain.
- What is my role in the body of Christ?

In the body of Christ, no one believer is more important than another. Continue reading Paul's explanation in 1 Corinthians 12:12–14.

> For as the body is one and has many parts, and all the parts of that body, though many, are one body—so also is Christ.—1 Corinthians 12:12

COMPLETE THE FOLLOWING:

- Circle the word *one* each time it appears in these verses. Consider Paul's emphasis of the fact that the church is one in Christ. Why is this important?
- How does understanding that you are a part of something bigger help you maintain a healthy perspective about church?
- Do you think differences among believers make it more or less difficult to work together? Why or why not?
- List some ways believers can work together despite our differences.

God created the church with a diversity of gifts. But our differences should not create problems in the church; they should strengthen it. Our differences should complement each other and provide opportunities for church members to grow together.

RESPOND

- Consider this: The church as a body means that believers are a part of something bigger than themselves.
- Believers need other believers to teach, encourage, support, and confront them as they grow in their walk with God. In your journal, list the names of some other believers you can meet with regularly who will help you grow your relationship with God.
- Below the list of names in your journal, jot down some ideas for ways you can be better about working alongside other believers to share the gospel instead of competing with them.

A CARING BODY

People have a tendency to be self-centered. We focus on our own needs and our own desires. When we focus on self, showing true compassion to others is hard. Why do you think it is so difficult for us to set our attention on others? Journal your response.

Now, read 1 Corinthians 12:24–26 in your Bible.

> So if one member suffers, all the members suffer with it; if one member is honored, all the members rejoice with it.—1 Corinthians 12:26

PONDER THE FOLLOWING QUESTIONS:

- Consider the words *honor* and *honorable* in verse 24. If God gives honor, then how should we treat other believers, no matter their role in the body of Christ?

- What did Paul mean when he said believers should "have concern" for one another (v. 25)? Explain.

- What does it mean to suffer with others? What is the impact on the body if one member is hurt or missing?

- What does it mean to rejoice with others? What is the impact on the body when one member is honored in some way?

- Every person, every part of the body of Christ is both needed and important. How should believers interact with each other?

RESPOND

A self-centered response to the suffering of others is apathy. A self-centered response to another receiving honor is jealousy. But Scripture calls us to care for other believers.

- What are some ways self-centeredness may affect the body of Christ? How can you refrain from becoming self-centered? Journal your response.

- In your journal, create two columns with the headings *Suffering* and *Successful*. In the appropriate column, jot down the names of a few people you know who are suffering and others who are experiencing success. What would it mean to suffer or rejoice with each of these people?

MARRIAGE OF THE LAMB

You've probably attended a few weddings or at least seen one in a movie. Journal about a scene that comes to mind. The marriage of Christ to the church is one of the great word pictures in the Book of Revelation. Read about the wedding in Revelation 19:7–8.

Let us be glad, rejoice, and give Him glory, because the marriage of the Lamb has come, and His wife has prepared herself.—Revelation 19:7

ASK YOURSELF:

- What do you think John meant when he wrote that the wife had "prepared herself"?

- Just like a marriage is a celebration of two people joining their lives, the marriage of the Lamb consists of believers joining their lives fully with Christ. According to this verse, what three actions are we to take in celebration of this "marriage"?

Read Revelation 21:9–11 in your Bible and consider the following:

- Underline the phrase *the wife of the Lamb* (v. 9). Who is the Lamb? Who is the wife of the Lamb? Explain.

- Describe the significance of the fact that the new Jerusalem came down from God.

- What do you think it means that the bride was "arrayed with God's glory" (v. 11)?

RESPOND

A marriage is often something that we long for and anticipate. In this marriage, God's people are a bride-to-be, the wife of the Lamb. The bride includes those who believe Christ loved them first and who have responded to Him in love.

- What things do you look forward to concerning heaven? Journal your response.

- Glance through the news headlines and consider the state of our world today. How do these headlines show you a need for Christ's return? What tragedies do you read about today that you can rejoice will no longer occur when Christ returns? Journal your response.

COMPLETE CONTROL

Think about your own life. Do people ever treat you poorly because of what you believe? As Peter and John began to spread the gospel and help grow the early church, they faced opposition and were even arrested for teaching the resurrection. Read Acts 4:23–28 in your Bible to see how the early believers responded to this persecution.

> For, in fact, in this city both Herod and Pontius Pilate, with the Gentiles and the people of Israel, assembled together against Your holy Servant Jesus, whom You anointed, to do whatever Your hand and Your plan had predestined to take place.—Acts 4:27–28

THINK THROUGH THE FOLLOWING:

- Do you think the people were surprised that Peter and John were persecuted? How did they respond to the news?
- Jot down any words in their prayer that stood out to you.
- How did their prayer indicate their complete trust in God? Explain.

Before the believers requested anything from God, they acknowledged God's power and plan. Despite their seemingly dismal circumstances, they knew God's power extended much further than that of the religious elite.

RESPOND

- When you face difficult situations, do you typically seek the Lord in prayer as a first response or last resort? Do you acknowledge God's power and plan regardless of the outlook? Journal your thoughts.
- In your journal, make a time line of the last five years, noting all the ways you've seen God at work in your life. Do His plans and your plans align? How have you responded to His plan for you?
- Look over your time line and praise God for His work in your life. Thank Him for always having the best plan.

SERVING CHRIST

Read 1 Peter 4:7–11 in your Bible.

If anyone speaks, it should be as one who speaks God's words; if anyone serves, it should be from the strength God provides, so that God may be glorified through Jesus Christ in everything. To Him belong the glory and the power forever and ever. Amen.—1 Peter 4:11

COMPLETE THE FOLLOWING:

- Highlight the actions Peter instructed believers to take.

- What does it mean to love each other with "an intense love" (v. 8)? How should this affect our service?

- What has God given every believer (v. 10)? How should this be used?

- God gives His _____ and _____ to His people as they serve (v. 11). What does this tell you about the root of believers' service? Why is this important?

God's love is the root of our love. Only through Him can we love others the way He calls us to. (See John 13:34.) When you speak His Words and serve in His power, He is the one who will be glorified.

RESPOND

- If you aren't sure about your spiritual gifts or how to use them, seek out your youth pastor or another trusted leader in your church. Ask them to pray with you to help you discover how God has gifted you to serve others.

- Set aside time today to pray for your local church. Pray that God will be glorified in your church and that He will use your church to draw unbelievers to salvation.

SET FREE

Read Galatians 5:1–15 in your Bible.

> For you were called to be free, brothers; only don't use this freedom as an opportunity for the flesh, but serve one another through love.—Galatians 5:13

- According to this passage, how are believers justified? Explain.

- Why is trying to be justified by the law incompatible with the gospel? Explain.

- Does having freedom in Christ mean believers can do whatever they want? Why or why not?

- How does loving your neighbor as yourself fulfill the law?

- What do you think happens when churches focus on issues that divide rather than loving and serving others?

RESPOND

Believers are called to freedom in Christ and His grace. Though the law guides our behaviors, we are no longer condemned by it. As a believer, you can glorify God by living according to His standards and lovingly serving other people.

- How do you view your freedom in Christ? Is it a license to sin or freedom to live apart from the bondage of sin? Journal your thoughts.

- The law should guide your behavior as a believer, but it should never be seen as a list of rules for you or anyone else to keep in order to be saved. If you find yourself thinking of your faith as driven by rules or checklists, repent and ask the Lord to help you remember that salvation is by faith in Christ alone.

FILLED WITH THE SPIRIT

Earlier this week, you studied the first church—how they prayed and trusted in God's plan even though they were being persecuted for their beliefs. Review Acts 4:23–38 before you read today's devotion. Now, read Acts 4:31 to see how God empowered these believers to do His work.

> When they had prayed, the place where they were assembled was shaken, and they were all filled with the Holy Spirit and began to speak God's message with boldness.
> —Acts 4:31

ASK YOURSELF:

- What do you think it means that these believers were filled with the Holy Spirit? What was the result?

- If the church as a whole modeled the church in Acts 4, how would this make a difference in our world?

Read Matthew 18:19–20 in your Bible and think through the following.

- Summarize these verses in your own words.

- Journal how this passage connects with Acts 4:31.

RESPOND

- What is the difference between living a life led by the Holy Spirit and trying to go at it alone? In your journal, use the following headings to record some specific examples of each: *Spirit-led* and *Self-led*.

- Look back over the chart and circle the items that characterize your life right now. Ask the Lord to help you live a life filled with the Holy Spirit so you can become bold in sharing your faith with others.

- Prayerfully consider the people in your life who don't know Jesus as Savior. Jot down their names beneath the list in your journal and pray for them to come to know Him. Ask God to help you see how you might share specifically with those people.

HE GIVES CONFIDENCE

In your own words, describe the church's job.

Now, read Ephesians 3:10–13 in your Bible.

> In Him we have boldness and confident access through faith in Him.—Ephesians 3:12

THINK THROUGH THE FOLLOWING:

- According to this passage, how is God's wisdom revealed?
- With whom can the church share God's wisdom? What are some ways believers can go accomplish this?
- What eternal purpose did Jesus fulfill? How should believers respond to this?
- Look closely at verse 12. List what believers have in Christ.
- What does this mean? How does this change the way you live? Explain.

RESPOND

- Consider the fact that you have direct access to God through Jesus. You can talk to Him at any time or place. What is one thing you need to boldly approach Him about today?
- Earlier in the week you recorded the names of people who don't know Jesus as Savior. Review those names and commit to pray for these people, asking God to give you the confidence needed to share the gospel with them.

UNIFIED CHURCH

Read Philippians 2:1–5 in your Bible.

> If then there is any encouragement in Christ, if any consolation of love, if any fellowship with the Spirit, if any affection and mercy, fulfill my joy by thinking the same way, having the same love, sharing the same feelings, focusing on one goal.—Philippians 2:1–2

EXPLORE THE FOLLOWING:

- In verse 1, underline the phrases *in Christ* and *with the Spirit*. How does the Holy Spirit help believers remain unified in love and sharing the gospel?

- What is the "one goal" Paul referred to in this passage? Do you think the church's mission is the same today?

- How do rivalry and conceit hurt the church? Have you seen this happen? Explain.

- In what ways might this rivalry negatively affect Christ's mission for the church?

- Circle the words *in humility* (v. 3). How does considering others as more important than yourself help the church? Explain.

RESPOND

- If all believers would adopt "knowing Jesus and making Him known" as their mission, would this change the face of the church? How? Would it change believers as individuals? Journal your thoughts.

- In your journal, list three steps you can take to promote unity in your church.

- Ask God to help you and other believers follow Him completely, seek unity, and love and encourage each other as you share His gospel message with the rest of the world.

BOLD PRAYERS

What images come to mind when you hear the word *bold*? Bold colors? Bold move? Bold text? Considering these things, create a definition of the word *bold*.

Earlier this week, you read about how Peter and John were arrested for speaking the truth of the gospel. After their arrest, they gathered with other believers and began praying. They started by acknowledging God's greatness, sovereignty, and power. In Acts 4:29–30, they made a request for spiritual boldness.

> And now, Lord, consider their threats, and grant that Your slaves may speak Your message with complete boldness, while You stretch out Your hand for healing, signs, and wonders to be performed through the name of your holy Servant Jesus.—Acts 4:29–30

THINK THROUGH THE FOLLOWING:

- Circle all the requests Peter and John made. Summarize what they asked from the Lord.

- Where was their focus—on themselves or on God? Explain.

- How did Peter and John pray for their oppressors? What stands out about their prayer?

- How did this prayer set an example for all believers? Explain.

RESPOND

- Go back to the time line you created in your journal earlier this week. As you review it, make a note of all the times you've seen God answer prayer. How does this encourage you? Keep this time line as a reminder of God's work in your life.

- Who in your life needs you to pray boldly on their behalf? List a few names in your journal and commit to pray for them.

PRAYING FOR OTHERS

Read Ephesians 3:14–21 in your Bible.

> I pray that He may grant you, according to the riches of His glory, to be strengthened with power in the inner man through His Spirit, and that the Messiah may dwell in your hearts through faith.—Ephesians 3:16–17

CONSIDER THE FOLLOWING:

- List Paul's prayer requests in this passage.

- What do his requests tell you about his love for the church at Ephesus?

- From Paul's example, what can you learn about God's character and love for us?

- How does Paul's prayer model how believers should pray for others? Do you think it is important for believers to live out these things as well? Explain.

RESPOND

- List the names of a few of other believers. Then, use these verses as a model to pray for them. Let them know you prayed for them by writing them a note or sending a text message.

- Meeting regularly with another believer is a great way to make sure you are spending time in God's Word and in prayer. Do you have people in your life who hold you accountable in your walk with the Lord? If so, take some time now to thank God for these people. If not, pray now for God to send someone to help you remain accountable.

COMMISSIONED

Read Matthew 28:19–20 in your Bible.

"Go, therefore, and make disciples of all nations, baptizing them in the name of the Father and of the Son and of the Holy Spirit."—Matthew 28:19

- In your own words, describe the mission that Jesus gave to His disciples.
- What three specific commands did Jesus give in this passage? Explain.
- Is this mission still the same for believers today? Why or why not?
- Who gave Jesus His authority? Explain.
- What promise did Jesus make at the end of the passage?
- How would the mission be different without these two things? Explain.

RESPOND

- Spending the majority of your time with other believers can be much easier than going out into the world. Think about how you spend your days. Do you need to break out of your "Christian bubble" and build relationships with lost people? In your journal, list some ways you can get more involved in your school or community.

- Sharing your faith is not always easy, but with the help of the Holy Spirit, you can do it. Pray that you would have the courage and opportunity to share the gospel with people who don't know Jesus.

THE SON OF MAN

Read Daniel 7:9–14 in your Bible.

> I continued watching in the night visions, and I saw One like a son of man coming with the clouds of heaven. He approached the Ancient of Days and was escorted before Him.—Daniel 7:13

- Underline the name *Ancient of Days* (v. 9). This name highlights God as eternal.

- Focus on verses 9–10. Sketch a picture of the scene described here.

- Summarize the main point from verses 13–14. How do you think these words would have encouraged the Israelites while they were in captivity?

- Read Daniel 8:17 in your Bible and jot down the point of the verse in your own words. Why is this significant?

Read Daniel 12:2–3 in your Bible. Consider the following: What do these two verses show you about the final reality for all people in eternity?

RESPOND

Whenever we have an encounter with God, we have an opportunity to respond. As you see more of who God is, you can never stay the same. In your journal, list some areas of your life in which God may desire to see you make some changes.

ALL THINGS RESTORED

Read Acts 3:21–26 in your Bible.

> Heaven must welcome Him until the times of the restoration of all things, which God spoke about by the mouth of His holy prophets from the beginning.—Acts 3:21

Think through the following: Peter was addressing a large group of Jews about how the Old Testament prophets pointed to the Messiah who would restore all things. This passage clearly points out that Jesus' coming was not a new concept, but was indicated in the Scriptures since the very beginning. Why is this important?

The prophets, including Moses, spoke God's message to the people. Jesus was a different kind of prophet—God in human form, speaking God's words. He was more than the messenger; Christ Himself was the message.

ASK YOURSELF:

- In verse 23, what did Moses say would happen to those who did not listen to the Prophet (Jesus) who was sent?

- Another role of the prophet was to call people to repentance. In the same way, we are also called to take God's message of repentance to those who don't know Him. In what way does proclaiming the gospel help with Jesus' plan to restore all things to God?

- According to verse 26, why did God send Jesus? Why is this important?

RESPOND

God has begun the process of restoring all things and making them new. The process began when Jesus came for the first time and will be complete when Jesus comes for the second time. Journal your response to the following:

- What are some ways you see evidence of God's restoring you? Of being a work in progress?

- How does it give you hope to know that God will ultimately restore all things?

TEMPORARY DEPARTURE

Read John 14:1–3 in your Bible.

If I go away and prepare a place for you, I will come back and receive you to Myself, so that where I am you may be also.—John 14:3

THINK THROUGH THE FOLLOWING:

- Reread verse 1. Jesus encouraged His disciples not to be worried, but to believe in Him. Why is it important to trust that Jesus will do what He promised?

- In what ways can believers draw comfort from Jesus' words in verse 2? Explain.

- What does this passage show you that Jesus is doing now?

Read Acts 1:11 in your Bible. Answer the following questions:

- What does this passage tell us about Jesus' second coming?

- In both of these passages, note the disciples' reaction to Jesus going away. Why do you think the disciples reacted that way? What encouragement was offered to them in both passages?

RESPOND

You can probably identify with the disciples' sadness if one of your close friends has moved away. However, Jesus promised to return and that we will be with Him forever.

- Ask God to give you strength for life's challenges as you wait for Jesus to return.

- Consider this: Jesus is specifically creating a place for you to be with Him forever.

SALVATION IS COMING

And just as it is appointed for people to die once—and after this, judgment—so also the Messiah, having been offered once to bear the sins of many, will appear a second time, not to bear sin, but to bring salvation to those who are waiting for Him.
—Hebrews 9:27–28

Read Hebrews 9:27–28 again in your Bible.

- What was the purpose of Jesus coming the first time?

- What will be the purpose of Jesus coming the second time?

- What do you think it means that "it is appointed for" all people to die and face judgment (v. 27)? How does this differ from what you imagine will happen after death? Explain.

No one can escape the reality of death and judgment; however, salvation is secure for believers. We will not be condemned, because Jesus lived God's law perfectly in our place and we are covered by His righteousness when we step before God's throne of judgment. For us, judgment is the final entryway to our inheritance as co-heirs with Christ.

RESPOND

When Jesus first came to earth, He lived a perfect life and defeated sin. When He returns for us, He will complete our salvation by taking believers to the place He has prepared for us.

- Journal your story of how you experienced Jesus' salvation. Include your life before Jesus, how you met Jesus, and how your life has changed since then.

- If you haven't trusted Jesus as your Savior, find a couple of trustworthy adults such as a parent, student pastor, or pastor and ask them to share their testimony with you.

- On a sticky note, jot down the names of some people who don't know Jesus. Commit to sharing the gospel with these people this week.

BE READY

Read Luke 21:29–36 in your Bible. Consider the following: Jesus taught His disciples that there would be signs to help us recognize His return. We're to watch for these so that we're always prepared for Jesus' second coming.

"Heaven and earth will pass away, but My words will never pass away."—Luke 21:33

COMPLETE THE FOLLOWING:

- Summarize the promise Jesus made about the certainty of these events in verse 32.
- What did Jesus say would pass away? Never pass away? What does this mean?
- List the things that Jesus said could cause His followers to not be ready for His return (vv. 34–35).
- Jesus promised that the day of His return would affect everyone. No one is exempt, and everyone is called to be ready. In verse 36, what did Jesus say His followers should do while waiting for His return?

RESPOND

It's possible for Jesus to return at any time, and He said that the day would "come on you unexpectedly" (v. 34). This means we need to live lives that are always alert and ready for His return.

- Think about the fact that Jesus could return at any time. Take a minute to consider your life: *Am I living the life He called me to? How can I live in a way that would be considered alert and ready?*
- If Jesus returned today, would your life be honoring to Him? Why or why not? Journal your response.

A TASK TO COMPLETE

Read Matthew 25:14–30 in your Bible.

"His master said to him, 'Well done, good and faithful slave! You were faithful over a few things; I will put you in charge of many things. Share your master's joy!'"
—Matthew 25:21

- According to verse 15, what did the master give to each of his slaves? Explain.
- Compare and contrast the reactions of the slaves who were faithful over what they were given to the one who did nothing with his talent.
- In your own words, jot down the message from the master to the slaves who did well.
- Why was the master not pleased with the servant for at least keeping the one talent he had been given?
- God has entrusted you with gifts, abilities, and, most importantly, the good news about new life in Jesus. The gospel is a gift, but God didn't mean for us to keep this gift to ourselves. What important truths about sharing the gospel can believers learn from this Scripture?

RESPOND

God has given you a mission to accomplish until Jesus returns. In what ways are you sometimes tempted to stray from that mission? How might you better focus on and live out that mission? Journal your thoughts.

WITH THE FATHER

Read John 14:27. Jesus' encouragement to the disciples in this verse indicates that the disciples were probably a little anxious about Him leaving. Now, read John 14:28–31 in your Bible to see how He encouraged them further.

> "You have heard Me tell you, 'I am going away and I am coming to you.' If you loved Me, you would have rejoiced that I am going to the Father, because the Father is greater than I."—John 14:28

CONSIDER THE FOLLOWING:

- Reread verse 28. What had Jesus promised the disciples? Why is this important? Explain.

- Jesus gave the qualifier *if you loved me* and the reason *because the Father is greater than I* (v. 28) for rejoicing over His promise. Why did Jesus say the disciples should rejoice? How could this apply to believers today?

- Explain the reason Jesus gave for giving this information to His disciples in advance.

- What comfort can believers take from the fact that the Devil has no power over Jesus (v. 30)?

RESPOND

- What are some ways you sometimes struggle with trusting God? How are you tempted to give in to fear? When do you struggle to have peace? Where do you struggle with trusting God? Journal your response.

- On a note card, jot down some promises of God from the Bible. Flip the card over, and describe how you can trust in those promises.

A CALL TO GATHER

Read Matthew 24:27–31 in your Bible.

And they will see the Son of Man coming on the clouds of heaven with power and great glory.—Matthew 24:30

THINK THROUGH THESE QUESTIONS:

- How will Jesus' return be different from His birth?

- Jesus is certainly our friend, but in what other ways did Matthew describe Him in these verses?

- In verse 29, Jesus stated four events that would occur to signify His coming. What are these events? How do they illustrate God's power?

- Describe the events that Jesus foretold in verses 30–31.

- In light of eternity, why is it important for believers to know information about Jesus' return now? Why is it important to have a sense of urgency when spreading the gospel? Explain.

RESPOND

- Consider what your response would be right now if you saw Jesus coming on the clouds. What does that say about your relationship with Him? How can you improve your relationship with Him?

- How would you explain to a friend that Jesus is both the gentle, sacrificial Lamb as well as the powerful God who will return in power and glory? Journal your response.

UNEXPECTED ARRIVAL

Read Matthew 24:39–44 in your Bible.

> "This is why you also must be ready, because the Son of Man is coming at an hour you do not expect."—Matthew 24:44

- Reread verses 39–41. What do these verses tell you about the nature of Christ's return?
- Circle the word *therefore* in verse 42. The word *therefore* indicates a reason for an action previously noted. Knowing this, why is it important to be watchful of the Lord's coming?
- Jesus gave the warning about His unexpected return to believers (v. 42). Many Christians believe their preparation is complete when they trust in Jesus as Savior. In what other ways should believers be preparing for His return?
- Explain the main theme of verses 43–44.

RESPOND

Respond to the following prompts in your journal.

- In these verses, believers and unbelievers are working side by side. Which unbelievers work, study, or play beside you?
- What will you do this week to help them be prepared for Christ's unexpected coming?
- What will you do today to be better prepared for His unannounced return?
- What advice would you give to someone who gets caught up in daily tasks and forgets to focus on being prepared for Christ's return?

SEEN BY ALL

Read Revelation 1:7–8 in your Bible.

> Look! He is coming with the clouds, and every eye will see Him, including those who pierced Him.—Revelation 1:7

THINK THROUGH THE FOLLOWING:

- Underline the phrase *Look! He is coming with the clouds, and every eye will see Him.* Why do you think it's important that every person will see Him, in glory and majesty?

- List differences between Christ's first and second comings.

- Although some believe the mourning in verse 7 represents repentance, it is more likely the realization that people's rejection of Jesus earned them eternal punishment. What can believers do today to help friends and loved ones avoid this mourning?

- In what ways might the words *This is certain. Amen* in verse 7 affect believers? Non-believers?

- Why is it important that Jesus is the beginning and the end and that people see Him as such?

RESPOND

- Ask God to give you peace and help you to trust Him no matter what situation you face.

- Meditate on Revelation 1:8. Every time you are tempted to be overwhelmed by a person or circumstance, repeat this verse.

- Journal your response to these verses. In what ways do they encourage you? How do they move you to action in regards to sharing the gospel?

COMPLETED

Read Luke 21:27–28 in your Bible.

"Then they will see the Son of Man coming in a cloud with power and great glory."
—Luke 21:27

CONSIDER THE FOLLOWING:

- Underline the words *power* and *great glory* (v. 27). Why is it significant that Jesus will return in this way?

- The way Jesus returns will likely strike fear into the hearts of the people who don't know Him. Why should believers' reactions be different?

- Reread verse 28. What were Jesus' instructions for believers' responses to His return? What do you think He meant when He said, "your redemption is near" (v. 28)?

- What does Jesus' instruction for believers to "lift up your heads" (v. 28) indicate about the way He will return?

Part of the believer's response is to acknowledge that we will no longer be living by faith alone, we will get to see Jesus. All the bad things in life that Jesus promised would end—death, crying, fear, and pain—will be no more. Our Lord, our Redeemer, will come to fulfill His promises to judge and rule on the earth.

RESPOND

Glorifying Jesus isn't only reserved for the majesty and power of His return—we are called to glorify, honor, and praise Him even now.

- Contemplate verse 28. Consider what will be different for you when Christ returns in power and great glory and completes your salvation. Thank Him for the work He is doing in you to prepare you for that day.

- Consider what God wants you to learn right now. Ask Him to help you continue growing in Him, in preparation for that great day.

CHANGED

Read 1 Corinthians 15:45–53 in your Bible.

> Listen! I am telling you a mystery: We will not all fall asleep, but we will all be changed, in a moment, in the blink of an eye, at the last trumpet. For the trumpet will sound, and the dead will be raised incorruptible, and we will be changed.—1 Corinthians 15:51–52

THINK THROUGH THESE QUESTIONS:

- Compare the first and second man mentioned in verse 47.

- Look at verse 50. What characteristics from the first man can keep us out of God's kingdom? How did Christ's sacrifice remedy this?

- In verse 51, underline the phrase *we will all be changed*. For the believer, death doesn't mean the end to life; death means transformation. Describe what will take place when the trumpet sounds (v. 52).

- Summarize the change that will take place when the dead are raised (v. 53).

RESPOND

Only Christ, because He took on the fullness of human nature, has the power to restore humanity in body, soul, and spirit, while securing our freedom permanently.

- Consider the word *restoration*. Turn to a clean page in your journal, and label it *Restoration*. Under this heading, jot down things around you in the world, your culture, your family, and your own life that need to be restored. Thank God that, as His child, you will be restored physically and spiritually.

- Pray for others you know who need restoration, whether physical, spiritual, mental, or all three. Ask God to help them have faith and patience as they wait for restoration.

REUNITED

Read 1 Thessalonians 4:13–18 in your Bible.

Since we believe that Jesus died and rose again, in the same way God will bring with Him those who have fallen asleep through Jesus.—1 Thessalonians 4:14

CONSIDER THESE QUESTIONS:

- What do you think Paul meant when he wrote that believers were "asleep"?
- What is the difference between grieving with hope and grieving without hope? Why can believers grieve with hope?
- What did Paul say would happen to believers who died before Christ's return? What about those still living when He returns?
- What encouraging promises did Paul make in verse 17?
- How might you use these verses to encourage a believer who has lost a loved one?

RESPOND

- Think about your life: Are you living mostly for the here and now or living a life that looks forward to Christ's return? How might your life need to change to be prepared for His return?
- Jot down a few names of people who have recently lost loved ones. Pray for each one individually and consider writing a note of encouragement to them.

WORTH FIGHTING FOR

Read 1 Timothy 6:12–16 in your Bible.

I charge you to keep the command without fault or failure until the appearing of our Lord Jesus Christ.—1 Timothy 6:13–14

THINK THROUGH THESE QUESTIONS:

- What do you think Paul meant when he said "fight the good fight" (v. 12)? Explain.
- List some ways Paul challenged Christians to live out their faith in verse 12. What actions might go against or keep a believer from living in these ways?
- What are some things Christians have to fight against?
- If someone is already saved, why should he or she make such an effort to live a certain way?
- How does active anticipation of Christ's return motivate believers to live in a way that honors God?
- When encouraging ourselves or others to continue to fight for our faith, how could verses 15–16 be helpful? Why?

RESPOND

Christians are defined by a higher purpose—to love God, serve Him, and make Him known. Living this way isn't easy. Believers do have to fight and choose to live for God each day.

- Prayerfully consider how God wants you to live differently in anticipation of His coming.
- In your journal, jot down some ways you can fight the good fight for the faith. How might this look lived out? Below that, write out a prayer to God for strength to be victorious in your battles.

NO DELAY

Some people say that to be on time is to be late. Are you typically late, early, or on time? How do you think your perception of time differs from others?

As you read 2 Peter 3:8–9 in your Bible, note how God sees time differently.

> Dear friends, don't let this one thing escape you: With the Lord one day is like a thousand years, and a thousand years like one day. The Lord does not delay His promise, as some understand delay, but is patient with you, not wanting any to perish but all to come to repentance.—2 Peter 3:8–9

CONSIDER THE FOLLOWING:

- Circle the phrase *come to repentance* (v. 9). Explain this concept in your own words.

- Why do you think God is patient with us, wanting many people to come to know Him? How does this affect believers' mission? Explain.

- Summarize these verses. What does this message mean for those who already know Jesus as Savior?

- God's perspective on time is completely different from ours. What thoughts does this bring to mind?

RESPOND

God's actions are not random and He doesn't leave things to chance. He is a God of order and purpose.

- Think of a few people you know who need to know Jesus as Savior. Ask God to give you the strength and courage to share the gospel with them.

- In your journal, jot down some ways you can make the most of the time you've been given. Ask yourself questions like: *How can this motivate me to share the gospel? How does this affect my outlook on God and Christ's return, knowing that He is patient? In what ways could I share this news with others?*

GOD'S CARE

Read Isaiah 51:12–13 in your Bible. Complete the following:

- Jot down some of the characteristics of God and humanity listed in these verses.

- Summarize the main reason Isaiah gave for fearing the Lord above men.

Now, read Matthew 10:28–31 in your Bible.

"Don't fear those who kill the body but are not able to kill the soul; rather, fear Him who is able to destroy both soul and body in hell."—Matthew 10:28

ASK YOURSELF:

- Why do you think it's important to fear the One who can destroy both body and soul? Why is it particularly important to fear Him above people?

- A healthy fear of God encourages His people to live in obedience to His Word. But He doesn't ask us to give more than He's already given. In fact, He continues to give in the way He cares for us. Reread verses 30–31. What do these verse tell us about our worth to God? How He takes care of us? Explain.

- For the believer, even death can be faced with peace and hope. Describe how these verses support that fact.

RESPOND

- Find a Scripture that you can return to when you need a reminder that God is in control.

- Jot down your Scripture on a note card. Place the card where you can look over it often.

- In your journal, write a letter to God, thanking Him for the way He cares for you. Thank Him for specific instances in which He has protected you and provided for you. Commit to following Him no matter what may come.

SHEEP AND GOATS

Read Matthew 25:31–40 in your Bible.

"Then the King will say to those on His right, 'Come, you who are blessed by My Father, inherit the kingdom prepared for you from the foundation of the world.'"—Matthew 25:34

ASK YOURSELF:

- When Jesus returns, what will He do? How will He separate people?

- What are the different outcomes for the people on the right or the left? Explain.

- According to verses 35–36 and 40, what actions did the righteous take to serve the Lord?

- Summarize the main point of this parable.

- Review the difference between serving the Lord out of fear of the coming judgment and serving Him out of love. What should believers do?

Through Jesus, God will judge the world—both the righteous and the unrighteous. Even though the sheep were commended for serving the Lord, their works didn't save them. The only way we can receive salvation is by faith alone, in Christ alone.

RESPOND

The consequences in this passage may seem harsh, but death is the payment for sin. The good news is that for those who trust in Jesus as Savior, that debt of death has already been paid through Christ's sacrifice on the cross.

- Reread verse 34. Examine the verse in depth and consider how this relates to you. Journal a prayer of thankfulness and rejoicing.

- In what ways can you show Jesus love by showing love to others? Create a list on a plain piece of paper and tape it to the back of your door. Commit to taking one action from your list each day this week.

SO LOVED

Read John 3:16–18 in your Bible.

"Anyone who believes in Him is not condemned, but anyone who does not believe is already condemned, because he has not believed in the name of the One and Only Son of God."—John 3:18

- Underline the word *so* in verse 16. The word *so* here doesn't mean because; instead it demonstrates how God loves His people. In what way did God show His love?

- Jesus is God's "_____ and _____ Son" (v. 16). Though believers are adopted into His spiritual family, Jesus shares unique qualities and attributes with God.

- Verse 16 indicates that eternal life begins at the time one believes in Christ. We have this opportunity to spend eternity with God because of what Christ did for us on the cross. In summary, this is the gospel. After reading these verses, record what stands out to you about God and Jesus. List characteristics, actions, and so on.

- In your own words, describe why Jesus came to earth (v. 17).

- According to these verses, who is condemned? Why? Explain.

RESPOND

- What are some ways you can reach out to those who are condemned, or lost? Jot down two ways in your journal. Commit to doing at least one this week.

- Think on this: *What does it mean to me that I am free? I have salvation in Christ and that was secured the moment I chose to trust in Him. What can I do to reach those who don't trust in Him?*

LISTEN UP

Now, read Acts 3:22–23 in your Bible.

> And everyone who will not listen to that Prophet will be completely cut off from the people.—Acts 3:23

THINK THROUGH THE FOLLOWING:

- In verse 22, why do you think Peter brought attention to Moses' prophecy about a greater Prophet? Explain.

- Circle the word *everything* in verse 22. Why is it important to listen to everything Jesus says? How do believers' reactions to His words vary from that of non-believers? Explain.

- Underline the word *everyone* in verse 23. No one gets a free pass. If we want to know Jesus, to trust in Him for salvation, we have to listen to what He says. No matter what Jesus said or how He said it, His oneness with God meant that when Jesus spoke, God spoke.

- Believers have the Holy Spirit living within us. He empowers us to do God's work. In what ways are we like the prophets, taking His message to the world?

- What are some things that might make it difficult for believers to share God's gospel message today? Explain.

RESPOND

In your journal, record a prayer to God about the following:

- Ask God to help you to better know and listen for His voice.

- Pray that God would help you to see the needs of those around you and give you a heart to respond.

- Ask God to grant you the wisdom and courage to call others to repent and trust in Jesus.

HIS RETURN

Have you ever been late for something? Maybe you were late for class, basketball practice, dress rehearsal, or church. What did you learn from this experience? How did this affect your timeliness in the future? Journal your thoughts.

Now, read Matthew 25:1–13 in your Bible.

> "When they had gone to buy some, the groom arrived. Then those who were ready went in with him to the wedding banquet, and the door was shut."—Matthew 25:10

EXPLORE THE FOLLOWING:

- According to these verses, why were some of the virgins considered sensible and some foolish? Record the characteristics of each.

- What words would you use to describe the sensible virgins' refusal to share their oil? Why?

- Although the women knew a general time for the groom's arrival, they didn't know specifics. The wise were prepared and the foolish were not, though both had expressed a desire to be at the wedding with him. What does this parable tell you about being prepared for Jesus' return? How can believers prepare?

RESPOND

We prepare by placing our faith in Jesus as Savior; only those who are prepared for Jesus' return will enter the kingdom of God.

- Consider this: All people have been invited to be a part of God's kingdom. You have been invited to be a part of God's kingdom. Write out a prayer of praise to God for inviting you to be a part of His kingdom.

- What does it mean to prepare for Jesus' return? How can you remind yourself to stay focused on being ready? Journal your thoughts.

THE ONLY ONES

What comes to mind when you hear the word *judgment*?

Maybe you've heard someone say, "They're so judgmental" or "Don't judge me." Phrases like these might lend to misunderstanding what God's judgment is and why it's significant that judgment comes for both the righteous and the unrighteous. In 1 Peter 4:17–19, Peter presented judgment as God's decision about the outcome for both the godly and ungodly.

> For the time has come for judgment to begin with God's household, and if it begins with us, what will the outcome be for those who disobey the gospel of God?—1 Peter 4:17

ANSWER THE FOLLOWING:
- When Christ returns, whom did Peter say would be judged? Why is this significant?
- Before Jesus returns, the righteous will suffer. What did Peter say the righteous would do? What did he indicate about those who persecute God's people?
- Highlight the words *entrust themselves to a faithful Creator* (v. 19). What do you think it means to completely entrust yourself to God?
- Circle the phrase *while doing what is good* (v. 19). What does this phrase suggest believers should do even while being persecuted and entrusting themselves to God?

RESPOND
- Think about the outcome of eternal separation from God that will be the reality for those who do not obey the gospel while on earth. Ask God to use your life—all that you say and do—to point the lost toward Him.
- How does this passage help you trust God? How can you help others see their need for Him and turn from ungodliness? Journal your response.

JOY RESTORED

In the beginning Adam and Eve knew the joy of living with God, but that all changed when they sinned and were removed from the garden where they had enjoyed His continuous presence (Genesis 3). Sin changed the relationship between God and man. The first time Jesus came, He began the process of restoring that relationship; and when He returns restoration will be complete and our joy will be full.

Read Isaiah 65:17–19 in your Bible and answer these questions.

> "I will rejoice in Jerusalem and be glad in My people. The sound of weeping and crying will no longer be heard in her."—Isaiah 65:19

- God promised that He would create a new heaven and a new earth. Using these verses, describe what that will be like.

- God promised that "the past events will not be remembered" (v. 17), and that the "sound of weeping and crying will no longer be heard" (v. 19). What thoughts come to mind when you read these promises?

- How do these promises relate to God's command to "be glad and rejoice forever" (v. 18)?

- Not only will you be rejoicing but God also promised that He would rejoice over you. How does this affect you?

RESPOND

- The joy of God's presence was not only for Adam and Eve, but through Jesus, you can also experience His presence. In your journal, describe how God's presence has brought you joy.

- In your journal, make a list of all the reasons you have to rejoice in God and then thank Him for each one.

NEW HEAVEN AND EARTH

Read Revelation 21:1–2 in your Bible.

> Then I saw a new heaven and a new earth, for the first heaven and the first earth had passed away, and the sea no longer existed. I also saw the Holy City, new Jerusalem, coming down out of heaven from God, prepared like a bride adorned for her husband.—Revelation 21:1

- In this vision, the new heaven and earth immediately followed the great judgment where God had demolished the old heaven and earth (Revelation 16–20). How do you think this new vision would bring John hope?
- How could it bring hope to believers in light of our present circumstances?
- The sea often represented darkness or evil. Why do you think it's significant that the new heaven and new earth will not have the sea? Explain.
- The new Jerusalem that John saw coming down from heaven represented all of God's people. How did John describe them?
- The analogy of a bride was commonly used to refer to God's believers, and a wedding the ultimate union between God and His people. The bride would be prepared, just as Jesus went away to prepare a place for His followers (John 14:1–2). What can believers do to be prepared? Explain.

RESPOND

God promised that the world as you know it now would one day be completely transformed. This means that all the evil, pain, and sorrow will be gone forever.

- Take a moment and think about what that will be like. Journal a prayer thanking God for this hope.
- Just as a bride prepares for her wedding, so must God's people prepare for Christ's return and being restored to Him. In your journal, list a few ideas about what it would mean for you to prepare for His return.

ALL THINGS NEW

Read Revelation 21:5–6 in your Bible:

And He said to me, "It is done! I am the Alpha and the Omega, the Beginning and the End. I will give water as a gift to the thirsty from the spring of life."—Revelation 21:6

- What do you think Jesus meant when he said, "I am making everything new" (v. 5)? Explain.

- In verse 5, Jesus said these words are "faithful and true." Jesus wants you to know that His Word is completely trustworthy; that what He promises, He will do. Why is it important to trust Him when it comes to Him making all things new?

- How should the truth of this promise affect the way believers live today? How could it affect the way non-believers view the current evil in the world and the future?

Jesus called Himself "the Beginning and the End." It was by His power that all things were created in the beginning and it will be by His power that all things will be made new. However, it is also important to remember that His believers were made new by grace through faith in Him (2 Corinthians 5:17). He promised that we would live with Him in a perfect relationship.

ASK YOURSELF:
- What comes to mind when you think of living intimately with Christ without the barrier of sin?

- How does sin keep us from fully experiencing relationship with Christ?

RESPOND
- Consider how our lives will change when we live with Christ without the barrier of sin. What do you think your relationships with others will be like? What will worship be like?

- The book of Revelation is full of symbolism. In your journal, sketch a symbol that represents how grateful you are for the hope that you have in Christ.

JESUS, THE NEW TEMPLE

Review yesterday's devotion. Today's Scripture is a continuation of the beautiful vision that John had of the new Jerusalem, the holy city.

Look outside. You probably see either the sun or moon in the sky. Consider the light that each one brings. Now, think about the way and place you go to worship. Read Revelation 21:22–27 in your Bible to see how all of this will change in the new heaven and earth.

> I did not see a sanctuary in it, because the Lord God the Almighty and the Lamb are its sanctuary . . . Nothing profane will ever enter it: no one who does what is vile or false, but only those written in the Lamb's book of life.—Revelation 21:22, 27

ASK YOURSELF:

- The Holy City will be filled with the presence of God—worship will be everywhere. How does this relate to the way believers worship today?

- God's glory and the light of Jesus Christ will illuminate the whole city, dispelling all darkness. The biblical picture of light versus dark is often symbolic of the contrast between righteous living and sinful lifestyles. With this in mind, how do you think life will be different in the new Jerusalem?

- Underline the phrase "the kings of the earth will bring their glory into it" (v. 24) and consider verse 26. The Greek word for *glory* in both of these verses can also mean praise, honor, or worship. Why is this significant?

RESPOND

Only those who have trusted Jesus as their Savior and whose names are written in His book of life will be allowed to enter the holy city, the new Jerusalem. Journal about your journey to knowing Jesus and trusting Him as your Savior. When did you realize you needed to trust in Jesus? What made you come to this realization? Were you tempted to continue on in your current way of life?

NO MORE TEARS

Before you dig into God's Word, reread Revelation 21:1–3 in your Bible and review the past devotions. Reflect on what the new heaven and earth will be like. Take a minute to journal about what you've learned.

Now, read Revelation 21:4.

> He will wipe away every tear from their eyes. Death will no longer exist; grief, crying, and pain will exist no longer, because the previous things have passed away.
> —Revelation 21:4

THINK THROUGH THE FOLLOWING:

- The new heaven and earth will be saturated with the presence of God and life will be completely different than it is now. According to verse 4, what will no longer exist?

- Why do you think it's important to note that these are "previous things" that "have passed away"?

- Why do you think it would be impossible for these things to coexist in the presence of God?

- God promises that He will personally wipe away all of your tears. In light of the pain that you have experienced in your lifetime, how does this promise give you hope?

RESPOND

Life is often difficult and we often experience painful situations. During those difficult times, the future promises found in Revelation 21:4 seem of little comfort in the here and now. However, God promises that He is with you and will comfort you now. In your journal, jot down one word that represents something painful in your life. Below that word, list ways that you can seek God's presence and comfort daily. Plan to do one each day.

RIGHTEOUSNESS WINS

You can't watch the news or scroll through your social media without coming across a story about an atrocity committed against humanity. Jot down a quick list of injustices that are prevalent today.

In light of these things, why do you think people sometimes think God is indifferent or distant?

Read 2 Peter 3:11–13 in your Bible.

> But based on His promise, we wait for the new heavens and a new earth, where righteousness will dwell.—2 Peter 3:13

ANSWER THE FOLLOWING:

- What did God promise would happen when Christ returns? (vv. 11, 13)
- How do these verses dispel the lie that God is indifferent or distant?
- One day all evil will be destroyed and only righteousness will dwell on earth, but until then what kind of life should believers live?
- How can choosing to live a godly life affect the unrighteousness around you?

RESPOND

- Spend time in prayer asking God to reveal anything in your life that isn't pleasing to Him. Confess your struggles to God and ask Him to help you live a life of holiness.
- On a sticky note, jot down the words *holy conduct* and place the note where you will see it daily. Let these words serve as a reminder of how God has called you to live.

ETERNALLY WITH HIM

When you hear the word *worship*, what thoughts come to mind? Most people relate worship to something done on Sunday mornings. How does worship extend beyond the church service?

Now, read Isaiah 66:22–23 in your Bible.

> "For just as the new heavens and the new earth, which I will make, will endure before Me"—this is the Lord's declaration—"so your offspring and your name will endure. All mankind will come to worship Me from one New Moon to another and from one Sabbath to another," says the Lord.—Isaiah 66:22–23

THINK THROUGH THE FOLLOWING:

- List the promises God made in these two verses.

- Circle the word *endure* (v. 22). Describe any thoughts you have about the fact that God and God's people will endure forever.

- According to verse 23, what is our role as believers on the new earth?

- The time frame of "one New Moon to another and from one Sabbath to another" goes to show that we will always be engaged in worship. Who will be worshiping? Why is this significant?

RESPOND

Jesus already provided a way for you to have a relationship with God, however; because of the fallen world we live in, our fellowship and worship can be hindered. Unforgiveness or conflict between believers can definitely affect worship. Take a few minutes to confess to God any areas of unforgiveness in your life. Ask God to give you the courage to repair any broken relationships.

SERVE GOD

Read Hebrews 12:25–29 in your Bible.

> Therefore, since we are receiving a kingdom that cannot be shaken, let us hold on to grace. By it, we may serve God acceptably, with reverence and awe, for our God is a consuming fire.—Hebrews 12:28–29

- Identify God's warning, His actions, and the believer's expected response.
- Israel had experienced the wrath of God because they chose to reject His message. He warned that the same would happen to those who reject the message of Jesus' salvation. What thoughts come to mind when you consider the wrath of God? Can anyone escape His wrath? If so, how?
- The shaking of the earth in judgment involves the destruction of all created things, and all that will be left is the greater spiritual reality—your relationship with Christ. How does the security of your position in Christ give you an incentive to endure in faithfulness?

Your security in Christ should cause you to serve Him in thankfulness, reverence, and awe—being thankful for His grace, having reverence for His greatness, and being in awe of His mighty power.

RESPOND

- In your journal, record the names of people you know who do not know Christ and are in danger of experiencing God's wrath. Pray for God to open their hearts to the gospel and to give you the opportunity to share His message with them.
- Praise God for sending Jesus to take on His wrath in our place. Thank Him for the gift of salvation.

LIVING WITH GOD

Read Revelation 21:3, 7 in your Bible.

Glance through this week's devotions and jot down what life will be like after Christ's return.

"The victor will inherit these things, and I will be his God, and he will be My son."
—Revelation 21:7

- Summarize what John heard in verse 3.

- God's desire to dwell with man began before creation. After Adam and Eve sinned, God could no longer dwell with man. His presence dwelled within a tent or a temple. Yet He still longed to be among His people. His permanent remedy to the sin separation became evident when He sent His Son to take on flesh and made His dwelling among us. (See John 1:14.) Through salvation believers have the presence of God dwelling within them. How do you think their relationship will change when He dwells among them on the new earth?

- According to verse 7, how intimate will your relationship with God be? Explain.

RESPOND

God will fulfill His promise to forever restore fellowship between Himself and His people. Though there are times when it seems like God is far away, He will draw near to us as we draw near to Him. One day, He will again dwell among us.

- Journal about a time when God seemed distant. How did it affect your faith? How does it bring you hope to know that one day your fellowship with God will be completely unhindered?

- Examine your life. Ask God to help you to be encouraged by the inheritance He promised to you.

TO REIGN FOREVER

The final scene of John's vision vividly depicts the glory of eternal life. Read Revelation 22:1–5 in your Bible and briefly summarize each verse in your journal.

> Night will no longer exist, and people will not need lamplight or sunlight, because the Lord God will give them light. And they will reign forever and ever.—Revelation 22:5

ASK YOURSELF:

- When Christ comes to rule, the curse of sin, disease, and death will be abolished, and all believers will eat freely from the tree of life for eternity (Revelation 2:7). In what ways has the curse affected life here? How should believers live, knowing that one day we will be free from the curse?

- Believers will live in the presence of God, will see Him face-to-face, and He will write His Name on their foreheads. What does this tell you about the way believers' relationship with God will be different in the new Jerusalem?

- According to the end of verse 5, what will believers be doing for eternity? Explain.

RESPOND

- In your journal, sketch a picture of the Tree of Life and inside it record the names of Unengaged Unreached People Groups (UUPGs) or names of countries that need to know Jesus, the Giver of Life. (Hint: You can find a list of unengaged people groups at imb.org/globalresearch.)

- Review your sketch and the names of Unengaged Unreached People Groups and countries. Commit to praying for a different group each day this week.